Lecture Notes in Computer Science 16135

Founding Editors

Gerhard Goos
Juris Hartmanis

Editorial Board Members

Elisa Bertino, *Purdue University, West Lafayette, IN, USA*
Wen Gao, *Peking University, Beijing, China*
Bernhard Steffen, *TU Dortmund University, Dortmund, Germany*
Moti Yung, *Columbia University, New York, NY, USA*

Ghada Zamzmi · Annika Reinke · Ravi Samala ·
Meirui Jiang · Xiaoxiao Li · Holger Roth ·
Mariia Sidulova · Thijs Kooi · Shadi Albarqouni ·
Spyridon Bakas · Nicola Rieke
Editors

Bridging Regulatory Science and Medical Imaging Evaluation; and Distributed, Collaborative, and Federated Learning

First International Workshop, BRIDGE 2025
and 6th International Workshop, DeCaF 2025
Held in Conjunction with MICCAI 2025
Daejeon, South Korea, September 23 and September 27, 2025
Proceedings

Editors
Ghada Zamzmi
HeartFlow
Mountain View, CA, USA

Ravi Samala
United States Food and Drug Administration
Silver Spring, NH, USA

Xiaoxiao Li
University of British Columbia
Vancouver, BC, Canada

Mariia Sidulova
Medtronic
Minneapolis, MN, USA

Shadi Albarqouni
University Hospital Bonn
Bonn, Germany

Nicola Rieke
Nvidia GmbH
Munich, Germany

Annika Reinke
German Cancer Research Center
Heidelberg, Germany

Meirui Jiang
Chinese University of Hong Kong
Hong Kong, Hong Kong

Holger Roth
Nvidia
Washington, WA, USA

Thijs Kooi
Lunit
Seoul, Korea (Republic of)

Spyridon Bakas
Indiana University
Bloomington, IN, USA

ISSN 0302-9743   ISSN 1611-3349 (electronic)
Lecture Notes in Computer Science
ISBN 978-3-032-05662-7   ISBN 978-3-032-05663-4 (eBook)
https://doi.org/10.1007/978-3-032-05663-4

This Springer imprint is published by the registered company Springer Nature Switzerland AG
The registered company address is: Gewerbestrasse 11, 6330 Cham, Switzerland

If disposing of this product, please recycle the paper.

Contents

Proceedings of the MICCAI Workshop on Bridging Regulatory Science and Medical AI (BRIDGE 2025)

BRIDGE Preface

The BRIDGE Workshop (Bridging Regulatory Science and Medical AI) is dedicated to fostering collaboration and dialogue—building a bridge!—across artificial intelligence, medical imaging, computer-assisted intervention, and regulatory science. As AI technologies such as generative models, AI agents, autonomous systems, surgical robotics, and digital humans continue to evolve at an unprecedented pace, the gap between technological innovation and our ability to properly evaluate, safely deploy, and effectively regulate these systems continues to widen. Robust evaluation serves as the cornerstone of effective regulation as without the ability to rigorously assess a technology's performance and understand its risk profiles, we cannot regulate it effectively.

To address these mounting challenges in AI evaluation, deployment, and regulation, direct collaboration between those developing medical AI technologies and experts in regulatory science is essential. The BRIDGE workshop facilitates these critical collaborations by bringing together researchers, developers, clinicians, and regulatory experts from academia, industry, and regulatory bodies to tackle the pressing issues facing the field. It introduces regulatory science to the MICCAI community as an essential—yet often overlooked—pillar for translating medical AI research into safe, effective, and deployable solutions.

The BRIDGE program comprised three sessions. The first featured keynote presentations: a U.S. Food and Drug Administration speaker (Nicholas Petrick) addressed regulatory science and AI challenges; a computer-assisted intervention expert (Danail Stoyanov) examined surgical AI deployment issues; and a medical image computing researcher (Lena Maier-Hein) discussed imaging AI validation challenges and future directions. The second session showcased accepted papers through poster presentations, enabling attendees to engage directly with authors and explore evaluation frameworks, deployment, and regulatory science challenges. The workshop concluded with a panel discussion featuring leading experts Ben Glocker (Imperial College London), Nicholas Petrick (FDA), Federica Zanca (European Innovation Council), Suhyeong Park (Lunit), and Oliver Eidel (OpenRegulatory), who addressed current deployment challenges and shared actionable strategies for safe, effective AI integration into clinical practice, while emphasizing the need for stronger cross-sector collaboration.

All submissions underwent rigorous double-blind peer review through Open-Review. Each paper was evaluated by three independent reviewers from academia, industry, and regulatory science, ensuring balanced multidisciplinary perspectives. Papers were assessed on relevance, clarity, structure, and alignment with the workshop's focus. Seven of 17 submitted papers were accepted for publication and poster presentations. One paper was withdrawn after acceptance. We extend our sincere thanks to the authors, reviewers, and attendees who made BRIDGE 2025 a success, and to the organizing, program, and advisory committees for their invaluable contributions.

October 2025

Ghada Zamzmi
Ravi Samala
Annika Reinke
Mariia Sidulova
Thijs Kooi
Xiaoxiao Li

BRIDGE Organization

Workshop Chairs

Ghada Zamzmi	Heartflow, USA
Ravi Samala	U.S. Food and Drug Administration, USA
Annika Reinke	German Cancer Research Center, Germany
Mariia Sidulova	Medtronic, USA
Thijs Kooi	Lunit Inc, South Korea
Xiaoxiao Li	University of British Columbia, Canada

Program Committee

Yee Lam Elim Thompson	U.S. Food and Drug Administration, USA
Adarsh Subbaswamy	University of Maryland, USA
Shakith Fernando	Philips, Netherlands
Mu Zhou	Stanford University, USA
Paul Yi	St. Jude Children's Research Hospital, USA
Rucha Deshpande	Washington University in St. Louis, USA
Sameer Antani	National Institutes of Health, USA
Miguel Lago	U.S. Food and Drug Administration, USA
Sema Candemir	Eskisehir Technical University, Turkey
Thibaud Coroller	Novartis, Switzerland
Seyed Kahaki	U.S. Food and Drug Administration, USA
Siva Rajaraman	National Institutes of Health, USA
Suhyoung Bahk	Lunit Inc, South Korea
Theodore Papamarkou	PolyShape, UK

Advisory Board

Aldo Badano	U.S. Food and Drug Administration, USA
Amir Khan	General Electric Healthcare, USA
Ehsan Adeli	Stanford University, USA
Federica Zanca	European Innovation Council and SMEs Executive Agency, Belgium
Jana Delfino	U.S. Food and Drug Administration, USA
Lena Maier-Hein	Heidelberg University, Germany
Marzyeh Ghassemi	Massachusetts Institute of Technology, USA

Evaluation of Deformable Image Registration Under Alignment-Regularity Trade-Off

Vasiliki Sideri-Lampretsa[1]([✉]), Daniel Rueckert[1,2,3], and Huaqi Qiu[1]

[1] Chair for AI in Healthcare and Medicine, Technical University of Munich (TUM),
TUM University Hospital, Munich, Germany
`vasiliki.sideri-lampretsa@tum.de`
[2] Munich Center for Machine Learning (MCML), Munich, Germany
[3] Department of Computing, Imperial College London, London, UK

Abstract. Evaluating deformable image registration (DIR) is challenging due to the inherent trade-off between achieving high alignment accuracy and maintaining deformation regularity. However, most existing DIR works either address this trade-off inadequately or overlook it altogether. In this paper, we highlight the issues with existing practices and propose an evaluation scheme that captures the trade-off continuously to holistically evaluate DIR methods. We first introduce the alignment-regularity characteristic (ARC) curves, which describe the performance of a given registration method as a spectrum under various degrees of regularity. We demonstrate that the ARC curves reveal unique insights that are not evident from existing evaluation practices, using experiments on representative deep learning DIR methods with various network architectures and transformation models. We further adopt a HyperNetwork-based approach that learns to continuously interpolate across the full regularization range, accelerating the construction and improving the sample density of ARC curves. Finally, we provide general guidelines for a nuanced model evaluation and selection using our evaluation scheme for both practitioners and registration researchers (Code is available at: https://anonymous.4open.science/r/arc-3F80).

Keywords: Image registration · Deformable Registration · Evaluation

1 Introduction

Image registration is one of the most fundamental tasks in medical imaging and analysis. The core aim of image registration is to find spatial transformations that align anatomical structures or functional elements across two or multiple images. This is often achieved by automatically adjusting a transformation model to optimize the *alignment* according to a predefined dissimilarity measure. In deformable image registration, the transformation model is allowed high

© The Author(s), under exclusive license to Springer Nature Switzerland AG 2026
G. Zamzmi et al. (Eds.): MICCAI 2025, LNCS 16135, pp. 5–14, 2026.
https://doi.org/10.1007/978-3-032-05663-4_1

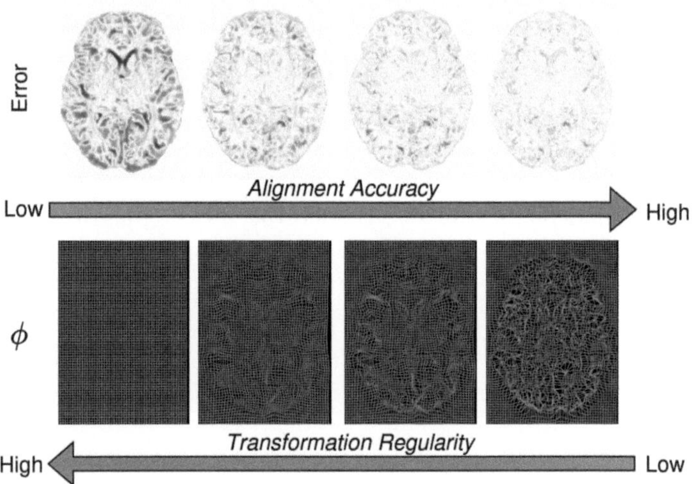

Fig. 1. Illustration of the balance between *alignment* accuracy and transformation *regularity* during inter-subject brain registration

degrees of freedom, which warrants additional regularization to enforce desirable properties, or *regularity*, and constrains the solution space for more efficient optimization. Concretely, many deformable image registration algorithms, including iterative optimization registration and modern learning-based registration methods, solve the following energy optimization problem to register a pair of images [17,19]:

$$\tilde{\phi} = \arg \min_{\phi}[\mathcal{D}(T(I_m, \phi), I_f) + \lambda \mathcal{R}(\phi)] \tag{1}$$

Here the dissimilarity term $\mathcal{D}$ quantifies the alignment between the *moving* image I_m transformed by T using the transformation ϕ (*moved*), and the reference image I_f. The transformation is constrained by the regularization term $\mathcal{R}$, which is usually derived to enforce desirable properties on the transformation, such as smoothness or topology-preservation. This governs the regularity of the transformation. The weighting hyperparameter λ in Eq. (1) influences the balance between the two energy terms. The resulting dynamic is a trade-off between the accuracy of the alignment and the regularity of the transformation. A visual illustration of this trade-off is shown in Fig. 1. Formally, we term this trade-off as the alignment-regularity characteristic (ARC) of a given registration algorithm, inspired by the use of receiver operating characteristic (ROC) curves [3] in evaluating classification methods under the precision-recall trade-off.

Issues with Current Practices: Evaluating DIR algorithms in the context of ARC is not trivial. We observe that many registration works do not consider the ARC trade-off when evaluating and comparing results. For example, many methods only tune λ to maximize alignment accuracy. We argue that this is problematic in a few ways: *1) Lack of controlled comparison:* Performance between methods is often compared without controlling for alignment or regularity. For example, many works in learning-based deformable image registration

(LDIR) regard the optimal hyperparameter λ value to be the one that maximizes anatomical alignment (e.g., Dice score) [2,4,13]. Therefore, alignment results are often reported with non-comparable regularity of the transformation. As we demonstrate later, this can lead to misleading or ambiguous conclusions since it is unclear whether a higher degree of alignment at the expense of regularity is preferable. *2) Discrete-points bias:* Most existing DIR works in the literature report and compare results at discrete points on the alignment-regularity trade-off spectrum [5,8] (with the only limited exception found in [10]). However, we found that LDIR methods often exhibit different relative performances at different levels of the regularity. This renders comparison on discrete points incomplete even if alignment or regularity are controlled to be comparable, since different conclusions can be drawn at different points of the spectrum. Moreover, finding comparable discrete points for evaluation can be challenging. The parameters and configurations of the algorithms usually do not control the metric values precisely and continuously due to the stochastic nature of the optimization process. As demonstrated later, adopting a more continuous comparison scheme could help mitigate this issue. *3) Ignoring application-dependent preferences:* An incomplete evaluation of the alignment and regularity trade-off omits crucial information since the desired registration algorithm properties are often application-dependent. For example, atlas-based segmentation may tolerate topological changes to improve structural matching and label propagation, while applications such as multi-modal fusion or respiratory motion tracking expect the transformation to be well-behaved and topology-preserving. Providing performance evaluation in a wider range of settings provides the users with more information enabling them to select the optimal algorithm for their applications.

Contributions: To address the issues mentioned above, we introduce an evaluation scheme that examines the alignment-regularity characteristic of DIR algorithms holistically to better inform model evaluation and selection. We focus on deep learning methods that utilize the optimization objective in Eq. 1, although our evaluation scheme is not limited to learning-based methods. Our contributions are summarized as follows:

1. We propose the construction of ARC curves based on alignment accuracy and deformation regularity metrics, demonstrating that these curves provide valuable and unique insights for method evaluation and comparison.
2. We employ a HyperNetwork-based approach that learns a continuous functional mapping between the regularization hyperparameters to the registration networks parameters, as a model-agnostic solution to accelerate ARC curve construction.
3. We demonstrate our evaluation scheme on representative methods and two widely-used datasets from the Learn2Reg challenge, namely the MRI brain dataset OASIS and the CT lung dataset NLST.

2   Alignment-Regularity Characteristics Curve

Method: To construct the alignment-regularity characteristic (ARC) curve for a given registration algorithm and dataset, we perform registration using varying levels of regularization by varying the weighting λ in Eq. 1. The ARC curve is then generated by aggregating the metric measurements across the test dataset and plotting the accuracy metric against the regularity metric. Crucially, we use the regularity metric instead of the regularization weight to normalize across the variation of loss formulation and implementation between methods. Examples of these curves are shown in Fig. 2. In the following sections, we show empirically that valuable insights and comprehensive performance evaluation can be obtained by comparatively analyzing different methods using ARC curves.

Experimental Settings: We acquire registration results and construct ARC curves using a range of different registration methods and two distinctive datasets.

- *Network Architectures:* We trained and evaluated several well-studied and state-of-the-art methods that demonstrate different architectural characteristics. We include VoxelMorph [2] and TransMorph [4], which are single-resolution models learning non-parametric dense deformations using a U-Net [16] and a Swin-Transformer [11]-based architecture, respectively. We also include two representative methods that focus on multi-resolution (LapIRN [13]) or multi-cascade (RCN [21]) refinement through composition.
- *Transformation models:* To study the effect of transformation models on ARC, we include MIDIR [15] which learns a parametric transformation model based on control points (free-form deformation or FFD [18]), as well as variants of all the aforementioned architectures that predict the stationary velocity field (SVF) [1] for diffeomorphic large deformation. We set the number of Scaling-and-Squaring integration steps to 7 for all SVF models. Non-parametric displacement field methods are denoted by "Disp".
- *Training strategy:* To obtain the ARC spectrum, we trained each method with a set of regularization weights $\lambda = (0.0, 0.001, 0.005, 0.1, 0.2, 0.5, 1.0)$ for 300 epochs each, using the ADAM [9] optimizer with a learning rate of 10^{-4} and a batch size of 2. We use negative normalized cross-correlation (NCC) as the dissimilarity term $(\mathcal{D})$ and the diffusion regularizer [7] $(\mathcal{R})$.
- *Datasets:* We perform our experiments on two widely-benchmarked datasets from the Learn2Reg challenge [5]. With the OASIS [12] dataset, we construct inter-subject registration pairs out of the T1-weighted brain MR images and 4-label segmentations[1] of 394 subjects for training/validation, and 20 subjects for testing. From the NLST [20] dataset, we use 150 pairs of inhale-exhale CT scans with lung masks and automatically detected landmarks for intra-subject registration, with a 90%-10% train/val-test split.
- *Evaluation metrics:* Due to the lack of ground truth transformation, evaluations of alignment accuracy in DIR are usually measured with surrogate metrics. For OASIS, we evaluate the *alignment* by measuring the overlap between

---

[1] https://github.com/adalca/medical-datasets/blob/master/neurite-oasis.md

the segmentation labels of the fixed scan and the warped moving scan via Dice score. For NLST, we utilize the available anatomical landmarks and evaluate the Target Registration Error (TRE), which measures the Euclidean distance between registered landmarks. The transformation *regularity* is evaluated by both the percentage of grid points with a negative Jacobian determinant (folding ratio), which is a proxy metric for topological changes, and the standard deviation of the logarithm of the Jacobian determinant (stdLogJ) [5], which indicates deformation smoothness.

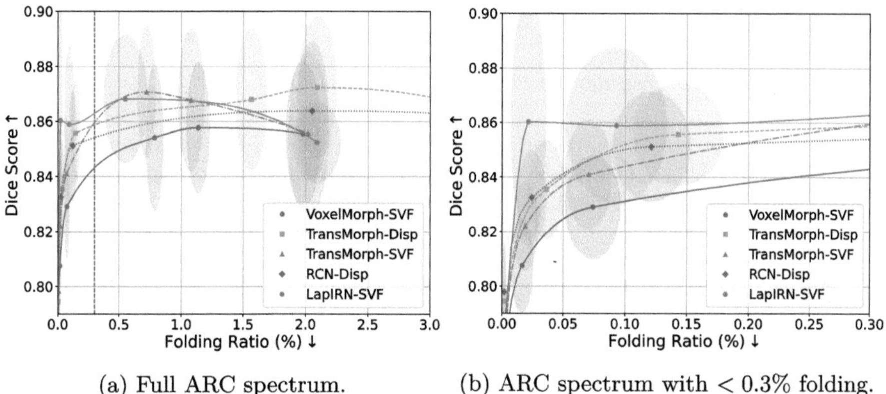

(a) Full ARC spectrum.   (b) ARC spectrum with < 0.3% folding.

Fig. 2. Full spectrum (a) and low folding ratio regime of the same spectrum (b) of the ARC curves for representative methods for inter-subject brain registration on OASIS dataset. The red dashed line on (a) indicates a 0.3% folding ratio. The shaded ellipse around each data point indicates the standard deviation of the metrics across the test pairs (Color figure online)

Insight 1. Holistic Model Comparison Using ARC Curves: Existing learning based deformable image registration methods often tune the regularization level to optimize an alignment accuracy metric, such as the Dice score, without considering whether or not the transformation regularity at these operating points is comparable with competing methods [2,13]. The issue with this approach is exposed when we compare a few methods using the proposed ARC evaluation, as we empirically demonstrate with ARC curves constructed from a range of methods using the OASIS dataset shown in Fig. 2.

Firstly, we can see that different methods exhibit optimal Dice scores with distinctively different folding ratios. This means simply comparing the maximum Dice score omits the differences in regularity and their consequences in different applications. For example, we can see from Fig. 2a that the TransMorph-SVF, TransMorph-Dips, and RCN-Disp all outperform LapIRN-SVF in terms of maximal Dice score, but at the cost of much higher ($\sim 6\times$) folding ratio. Therefore, one cannot conclude that LapIRN-SVF performs inferior compared to the other two methods without considering if this higher deformation irregularity is acceptable in their specific application. For applications that require well-regularized

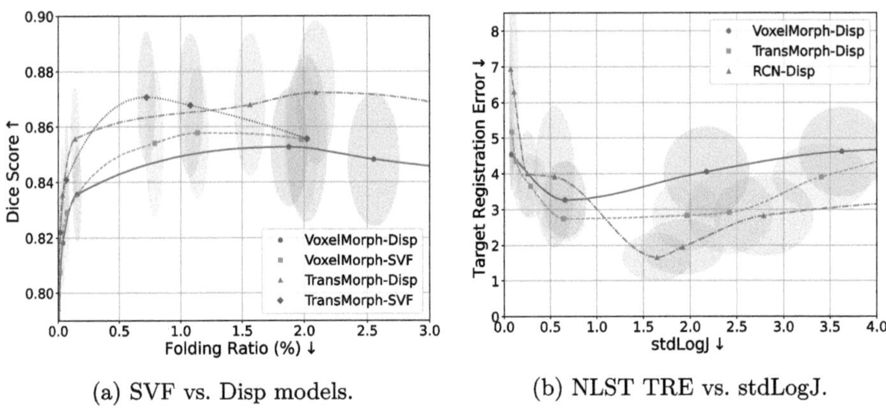

(a) SVF vs. Disp models.   (b) NLST TRE vs. stdLogJ.

Fig. 3. ARC curves demonstrating (a) the effect of the SVF vs Disp transformation models on the performance under varying levels of regularization and (b) different metrics using the NLST dataset

transformations (i.e. lower folding), the LapIRN-SVF model should be preferred. We highlight this by focusing on the low-folding regime of the ARC curves shown in Fig. 2b. *Secondly*, while existing works report relative performances with comparable but discrete points of alignment accuracy and regularity (numbers in tables), the effectiveness of such comparisons is hindered by the choice of where the values are compared on the spectrum. Different conclusions can be drawn from "slicing" at different points on the ARC spectrum, as made evident by comparing Fig. 2a with Fig. 2b. Therefore, a continuous representation of performances is necessary to compare models comprehensively across the entire regularity spectrum. Similar conclusions can be reached when examining ARC curves with landmark-based TRE as alignment accuracy and Jacobian variation as regularity on the NLST dataset, as shown in Fig. 3b.

Insight 2. Influence of Transformation Models: In this section, we examine the effect of the SVF model on the performance of LDIR methods using ARC curves. SVF is a diffeomorphic transformation model with good theoretical regularity while capable of modeling large deformations. We noticed that recent SVF-based models reported in registration literature often under-perform models using simple displacement fields with the same network architecture [4,13]. However, from our experiments shown in Fig. 3a, we observe that SVF methods are only less accurate than displacement methods in the extreme low-folding regime. Both SVF models show higher accuracy than their displacement counterparts when allowed a slightly higher folding ratio (e.g. around 1%, which is still significantly lower than the displacement models at optimal Dice). We hypothesize that researchers often apply higher regularization on the velocity fields to enforce zero folding since SVF models are expected to be diffeomorphic, resulting in lower accuracy and narrowly missing the optimal operating points. In addition, we found that the SVF models are more robust to lower regularization weights, especially in the lower folding ratio zone. These insights are valuable to model selection and are only revealed through the ARC curves.

3   Amortized Alignment-Regularity Characteristic

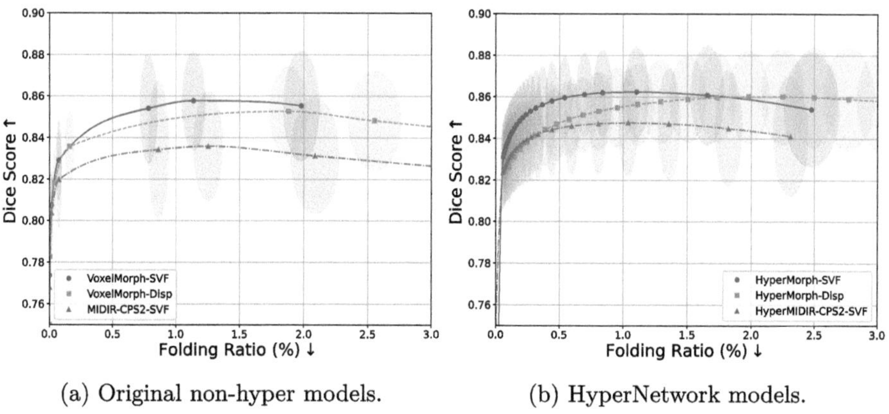

(a) Original non-hyper models.   (b) HyperNetwork models.

Fig. 4. ARC curves demonstrating the ARC spectrum of the (a) original versus the (b) HyperNetwork SVF and Disp models

Despite showing promise in improving evaluation, ARC curves constructed using the method introduced in Sect. 2 have two main drawbacks. First, acquiring the curves is computationally expensive as each point on an ARC curve is a training-testing instance of a LDIR model using a specific regularization weight. This contributes to the second limitation, which is the sparsity of the data points. This necessitates post-hoc interpolation to approximate a smooth spectrum, which hinders the completeness of ARC curve-based evaluation as data points usually do not cover the whole spectrum evenly, as exemplified by Fig. 4a.

To address these problems, we leverage the hyperparameter amortization framework from HyperMorph [6] to enable fast and dense sampling of ARC data points without having to train a model for each regularization weighting λ. This is facilitated by using HyperNetwork, which is a network that learns a continuous functional mapping between regularization weights to the parameters of the registration networks. Consequently, we can sample the model regularity at arbitrary points on the spectrum at test time significantly more densely than conventional hyperparameter tuning without additional training. We favor HyperMoprh over the conceptually similar conditional LapIRN [14] framework as the former theoretically supports any network architecture. To meaningfully utilize this system for our ARC evaluation scheme, we experiment with using this framework to capture the regularization characteristics of different network architectures and transformation models. Specifically, we trained HyperNets to amortize λ for VoxelMorph but with a different transformation model (SVF) and MIDIR [15], which has a different network architecture adapted for FFD.

The results of these experiments are presented in Fig. 4b, where the Hyper-Networks are shown to be capable of capturing relative performances between different network architectures and transformation models. More advantageously, these hyper-models are able to sample the regularization weight λ in a more continuous manner across the entire ARC spectrum without incurring additional training time. This provides more detailed information for model evaluation and selection in a computationally efficient way at test time.

4   Conclusion and Discussion

General Guideline for Model Evaluation and Selection: *For researchers* working on DIR algorithms, we advocate for reporting ARC curves of any proposed methods and baseline methods to enable a fairer assessment of the contribution and provide a performance profile for downstream users. This could also clarify research directions for the registration community. *For practitioners* applying registration algorithms, we recommend constructing ARC curves for candidate algorithms with various configurations using a small subset of the data. The application-dependent optimal range of regularity can be identified by qualitatively examining the deformation field and deformed images at varying levels of regularity. Then, the best algorithm can be chosen according to the performances and trends in the optimal/acceptable regularity range on the ARC curve. The sensitivity of the competing algorithms to the regularization hyperparameters can also be assessed via ARC curves, which can be critical in selecting the optimal solution. In both cases, the amortized ARC system (Sect. 3) can also be utilized to accelerate the evaluation process if the additional computational cost can be afforded.

Limitations: The studies in this work should be expanded to more datasets, algorithms, and evaluation metrics such as intensity-based metrics for alignment and non-Jacobian-based metrics for regularity. A single-value metric, such as area under the ARC curves (AUC-ARC) similar to AUC-ROC, can provide a simpler solution to the evaluation problem. However, the exact formulation of AUC-ARC is not trivial since the theoretical bounds are empirically difficult to achieve. We are actively working on a solution and will present the results in a future work.

Conclusion: This work highlights the issues in current evaluation practices of deformable image registration under the alignment-regularity trade-off, and proposes an evaluation scheme using alignment-regularity characteristic curves to address these issues. We demonstrated the utility of such an evaluation system through several unique and valuable insights gained from applying the system, along with accelerated HyperNetwork-based variants. Finally, we provide general guidelines for researchers and practitioners on using the ARC scheme to evaluate and select deformable image registration methods.

Acknowledgements. This research was supported by the ERC (Deep4MI - 884622).

Disclosure of Interests. The authors have no competing interests to declare that are relevant to the content of this article

References

1. Ashburner, J.: A fast diffeomorphic image registration algorithm. Neuroimage **38**(1), 95–113 (2007)
2. Balakrishnan, G., Zhao, A., Sabuncu, M.R., Guttag, J., Dalca, A.V.: Voxelmorph: a learning framework for deformable medical image registration. IEEE Trans. Med. Imaging **38**(8), 1788–1800 (2019)
3. Bradley, A.: The use of the area under the roc curve in the evaluation of machine learning algorithms. Pattern Recognit. **30**(7), 1145–1159 (1997)
4. Chen, J., Frey, E.C., He, Y., Segars, W.P., Li, Y., Du, Y.: Transmorph: transformer for unsupervised medical image registration. Med. Image Anal. **82**, 102615 (2022)
5. Hering, A., et al.: Learn2reg: comprehensive multi-task medical image registration challenge, dataset and evaluation in the era of deep learning. IEEE Trans. Med. Imaging (2022)
6. Hoopes, A., Hoffmann, M., Greve, D.N., F., B., Guttag, J., Dalca, A.: Learning the effect of registration hyperparameters with hypermorph. J. Mach. Learn. Biomed. Imaging **1**, 003 (2022)
7. Horn, B., Schunck, B.G.: Determining optical flow. Artif. Intell. **17**(1–3), 185–203 (1981)
8. Jena, R., Sethi, D., Chaudhari, P., Gee, J.: Deep learning in medical image registration: magic or mirage? Adv. Neural. Inf. Process. Syst **37**, 108331–108353 (2025)
9. Kingma, D., Ba, J.: Adam: a method for stochastic optimization. CoRR (2015)
10. Kuang, D., Schmah, T.: FAIM – a convnet method for unsupervised 3D medical image registration. In: Suk, H.-I., Liu, M., Yan, P., Lian, C. (eds.) MLMI 2019. LNCS, vol. 11861, pp. 646–654. Springer, Cham (2019). https://doi.org/10.1007/978-3-030-32692-0_74
11. Liu, Z., et al.: Swin transformer: hierarchical vision transformer using shifted windows. In: Proceedings of the IEEE/CVF International Conference on Computer Vision (ICCV), pp. 10012–10022 (2021)
12. Marcus, D.S., Wang, T.H., Parker, J., Csernansky, J.G., Morris, J.C., Buckner, R.L.: Open access series of imaging studies (OASIS): cross-sectional MRI data in young, middle aged, nondemented, and demented older adults. J. Cogn. Neurosci. **19**, 1498–1507 (2007)
13. Mok, T.C.W., Chung, A.C.S.: Large deformation diffeomorphic image registration with laplacian pyramid networks. In: Martel, A.L., et al. (eds.) MICCAI 2020. LNCS, vol. 12263, pp. 211–221. Springer, Cham (2020). https://doi.org/10.1007/978-3-030-59716-0_21
14. Mok, T.C.W., Chung, A.C.S.: Conditional deformable image registration with convolutional neural network. In: de Bruijne, M., et al. (eds.) MICCAI 2021. LNCS, vol. 12904, pp. 35–45. Springer, Cham (2021). https://doi.org/10.1007/978-3-030-87202-1_4
15. Qiu, H., Qin, C., Schuh, A., Hammernik, K., Rueckert, D.: Learning diffeomorphic and modality-invariant registration using b-splines. In: International Conference on Medical Imaging with Deep Learning (2021)

16. Ronneberger, O., Fischer, P., Brox, T.: U-net: convolutional networks for biomedical image segmentation. In: Navab, N., Hornegger, J., Wells, W.M., Frangi, A.F. (eds.) MICCAI 2015. LNCS, vol. 9351, pp. 234–241. Springer, Cham (2015). https://doi.org/10.1007/978-3-319-24574-4_28
17. Rueckert, D., Schnabel, J.: Medical image registration. In: Biomedical Image Processing, pp. 131–154. Springer (2010)
18. Rueckert, D., Sonoda, L.I., Hayes, C., Hill, D.L.G., Leach, M.O., Hawkes, D.J.: Nonrigid registration using free-form deformations: application to breast MR images. IEEE Trans. Med. Imaging **18**, 712–721 (1999)
19. Sotiras, A., Davatzikos, C., Paragios, N.: Deformable medical image registration: a survey. IEEE Trans. Med. Imaging **32**, 1153–1190 (2013)
20. team, N.: The national lung screening trial: overview and study design. Radiology **258**(1), 243–253 (2011)
21. Zhao, S., Dong, Y., Chang, E.I., Xu, Y., et al.: Recursive cascaded networks for unsupervised medical image registration. In: Proceedings of the IEEE/CVF International Conference on Computer Vision, pp. 10600–10610 (2019)

Some Hidden Traps of Confidence Intervals in Medical Image Segmentation: Coverage Issues

Pascaline André[1]([✉]), Charles Heitz[1], Evangelia Christodoulou[2,5,6], Annika Reinke[2,4], Carole H. Sudre[3,7,8], Michela Antonelli[7,8], M. Jorge Cardoso[7], Antoine Gilson[1], Sophie Tezenas du Montcel[1], Gaël Varoquaux[9], Lena Maier-Hein[2,4,5,10,11], and Olivier Colliot[1]

[1] Sorbonne Université, Institut du Cerveau - Paris Brain Institute - ICM, CNRS, Inria, Inserm, AP-HP, Hôpital de la Pitié-Salpêtrière, Paris, France
`pascaline.a0307@gmail.com`
[2] Intelligent Medical Systems, German Cancer Research Center (DKFZ), Heidelberg, Germany
[3] Unit for Lifelong Health and Ageing at UCL, Department of Population Science and Experimental Medicine and Hawkes Institute Centre for Medical Image Computing, Department of Computer Science, University College London, London, UK
[4] DKFZ Heidelberg, Helmholtz Imaging, Heidelberg, Germany
[5] National Center for Tumor Diseases (NCT), NCT Heidelberg, a partnership between DKFZ and Heidelberg University Hospital, Heidelberg, Germany
[6] AI Health Innovation Cluster, Heidelberg, Germany
[7] School of Biomedical Engineering and Imaging Science, King's College London, London, UK
[8] Hawkes Institute, Department of Computer Science, University College London, London, UK
[9] SODA project team, INRIA Saclay-Île de France, Palaiseau, France
[10] Faculty of Mathematics and Computer Science, Heidelberg University, Heidelberg, Germany
[11] Medical Faculty, Heidelberg University, Heidelberg, Germany

Abstract. Medical imaging AI models are usually assessed by reporting an empirical summary statistic of the performance metric, most commonly the mean or median. Recent work has shown that most studies overlook the uncertainty of these estimates, potentially leading to misleading conclusions and hampering clinical translation of medical imaging AI models. To address this issue, systematic reporting of confidence intervals (CIs) has been recommended, but numerous different CI methods exist, and there is very little literature on their behavior in medical imaging. A fundamental property of a CI method is its coverage. This paper contributes towards filling this literature gap in the context of medical image segmentation, studying the coverage of five CI methods for the two arguably most common summary statistics, the mean and

P. André and C. Heitz—Shared first authors.

G. Varoquaux, L. Maier-Hein and O. Colliot—Shared last authors.

G. Zamzmi et al. (Eds.): MICCAI 2025, LNCS 16135, pp. 15–24, 2026.
https://doi.org/10.1007/978-3-032-05663-4_2

the median. To that purpose, we perform a large-scale analysis of CI coverage using non-parametric simulations based on benchmarks instances representing diverse real-world distributions of two common segmentation metrics (Dice similarity coefficient and normalized surface distance). For the mean, all CI methods have decent coverage for most instances when sample sizes exceed 50, even though there are exceptions. For CIs of the median, we unveil major pitfalls: two common bootstrap CI methods have a catastrophic behavior on average whereas another only fails on very degenerate distributions. We believe these pitfalls are important to communicate to the community and that these findings will contribute to future efforts to provide standardized guidelines on confidence interval reporting in medical imaging AI.

Keywords: Medical imaging · Validation · Confidence intervals · Segmentation

1 Introduction

The new FDA guidelines for AI devices [11] require to report not only a summary statistic of the performance but also a measure of uncertainty. Current practice in medical imaging AI is to only report an empirical summary statistic of the performance (most often the mean, sometimes the median), without assessing how precise this estimate is. For example, a recent study found that the majority of segmentation papers from MICCAI 2023 did not assess performance variability at all, while only a single paper reported confidence intervals (CI) [6]. They further showed that such practices can sometimes be highly misleading and lead to spurious conclusions. These practices may also contribute to little industrial and clinical translation of academic research. Overall, reporting CIs is thus highly recommended.

However, different methods exist for computing CIs. The most popular methods can broadly be divided into parametric and non-parametric methods. Parametric methods rely on assumptions on the distribution of the data. Non-parametric methods are mainly different types of bootstrap.

We are not aware of any study that compares the adequateness of different CIs methods in medical imaging AI, a situation which is different from other research fields such as psychology [18] or economics [5] for instance. In generalist AI, a major company just released guidelines on reporting variability [15]. The formula they provide assumes that the test set is large and is only applicable when the summary statistic is the mean. In medical imaging AI, sample sizes often range from small to moderate. Furthermore, there are cases where the mean is not the most suited summary statistic, for instance in the presence of outliers or skewness, and other statistics, such as the median, need to be reported.

Different properties guide the choice of a given CI method, including coverage and width. The first property to assess is coverage. In particular, CI methods with low coverage lead to overconfidence in the precision of performance estimates. Then, among CI methods with adequate coverage, one can look at other properties such as width.

This work aims at studying the coverage of different CI methods for the arguably two most common summary statistics: the mean and the median.

Specifically, we perform a large-scale analysis of 228 benchmarking instances, covering 12 segmentation tasks and 19 algorithms, for two performance metrics, the Dice Similarity Coefficient (DSC) and the Normalized Surface Difference (NSD). For each instance, we analyze the behavior of CIs using non-parametric simulations that adequately represent real-life scenarii. We unveil pitfalls which are of practical importance for the community.

2   Methods

2.1   Confidence Interval Methods

A CI is a way to provide information about the precision of a summary statistic. A X% CI method for a statistic is a procedure which generates intervals such that, when multiple sets are drawn from the same distribution and one computes an interval for each set, X% of the intervals will contain the true value of the statistic. For instance, considering a 95% CI method to estimate the mean (resp. median) of a distribution, if we take 100 sets from this distribution, 95 intervals should contain the true mean (resp. median). The proportion of CIs that should contain the true value of the statistic is called theoretical coverage, whereas the observed proportion is called empirical coverage.

CI methods can be broadly divided into two categories: parametric and non-parametric methods. Parametric methods provide theoretical fixed-sample guarantees about the empirical coverage using assumptions on the distribution of the data. The most common non-parametric methods are arguably variations of the bootstrap. They give less guarantees about empirical coverage than the parametric methods, but require no assumption on the distribution of the data [8].

In this paper, we studied five CI methods, which we perceive to be particularly frequently used: two parametric methods using normality assumptions, and the three bootstrap methods implemented in SciPy [19], considering that our community is mostly Python-based [9]. A detailed description of each method can be found in [8], but we will briefly recall them here. The two parametric methods are "parametric t" and "parametric z". They are both based on normality assumptions. "Parametric z" supposes the true variance is known (in practice this is reasonable when the sample size is large), whereas "parametric t" makes a correction for variance estimation ("parametric t" tends to "parametric z" when sample size goes to infinity). The studied bootstrap methods are "percentile", "basic" (also known as reverse percentile) and "BCa" (bias-corrected and accelerated). "Percentile" works by computing bootstrap sets and the statistic of interest for each set, then taking the quantiles of the bootstrap distribution to form a CI. "Basic" aims at reducing the bias of the bootstrap distribution. One computes the bootstrap distribution of the difference to the estimated statistic and a CI is given by mean ± quantiles of the difference. "BCa" aims to correct for bias and skewness in bootstrap distributions. It is based on a bias coefficient and an acceleration coefficient which uses a jackknife estimate of the statistic of interest to correct for skewness. "BCa" is the default method in SciPy.

Note that, beyond making no assumptions about the metric's distribution, bootstrap methods offer the advantage of being applicable to a wide range of summary statistics, unlike "parametric t" or "parametric z".

2.2   Dataset

In this study, we used the Medical Segmentation Decathlon (MSD) [3] challenge which features a wide range of 17 diverse tasks across 10 different organs along with model performance for a large set of 19 models. Details about tasks and models can be found in the MSD paper [3]. To ensure statistical robustness, we selected only the 12 subtasks with test sets containing more than 50 3D images. Test set sizes vary between 59 and 263 (median $= 139$). During the challenge, 19 different models were submitted, and tested on each subtask independently, amounting to 12 tasks $\times$ 19 models $= 228$ different benchmarking instances. For each instance, we analyzed the values of the Dice Similarity Coefficient (DSC) and the Normalized Surface Distance (NSD) across all test set 3D images.

2.3   Assessing Confidence Interval Methods

The purpose of our analysis was to investigate the following research question: do the different CI methods have adequate coverage? For a CI method to be adequate, its empirical coverage needs to be close to its theoretical coverage. If the coverage is too low, the user is misled to believe that the estimates are more precise than they actually are.

However, empirical coverage computation requires simulating from a distribution because the ground truth value of the statistic must be known. In our case, the distribution would be that of the segmentation metric for a given benchmarking instance. We thus first need to fit a distribution to each of the benchmarking instances. We then perform simulations by sampling from the fitted distribution, for each instance. It is essential that these simulations reflect the reality of the data. Across the literature, these simulations are most often performed under parametric assumption (e.g. [13,14,16]). However, it is unknown if segmentation metrics follow a parametric distribution. We assessed this by performing Kolmogorov-Smirnov tests to see if our distributions matched any of a wide variety of common parametric distributions, including Normal, SkewNormal, 1-LogNormal, 1-Exponential, Beta and Logistic distributions. As shown in the results, none of these parametric distributions was an adequate fit for DSC nor NSD. Therefore, parametric simulations would not correspond to the reality of these segmentation metrics and non-parametric simulations need to be used instead. To achieve this, for each of the 228 instances and for the two metrics (DSC and NSD), we first estimated the underlying metric distribution using kernel density estimation (KDE) with the Epanechnikov (parabolic) kernel. This peculiar kernel choice was made following [20]. It provides a concentrated and smooth interpolation around data points, thus keeping the interpolated distribution close to the original data. To tackle the problem of our bounded metric, we used an adaptive bandwidth to keep all the mass inside the domain. From each of the 2×228 KDE distributions, we drew 10000 sets (i.e. random realizations of the distribution) of varying size n, thus resulting in 2×228 experiments. We call "instance" the actual metric distribution, and "experiment" the analysis and simulations performed on each instance. For each set, we computed the corresponding CI for each method. Across the 10000 sets, we computed the proportion of CIs containing the true value of the statistic (mean or median), i.e. the empirical coverage.

We repeated this process for $n = 10$, 25, 50, 75, 100, 125, 150, 200, 250, to place ourselves in regimes close to those present in the MICCAI papers. Indeed, we meta-analyzed the segmentation papers published at MICCAI 2023 and found that the median test set size was 62 (IQR: 25–223).

3   Results

We first briefly describe the results on parametric fits before moving to our main results on CI, which correspond to the core research question of this paper. DSC and NSD are in general non-normal: the Gaussian distribution was rejected in 78% (181/228) of cases for DSC and in 86% for NSD (198/228). Other distributions were rejected between 27% and 86% of cases. A realistic simulation had therefore to be non-parametric.

The behavior of CIs is presented in Figs. 1 (CIs of the mean) and 2 (CIs of the median). Behaviors were similar for both DSC and NSD.

For CIs of the mean, all methods behave decently across the majority of experiments when the test set size is larger than 50. However, there are exceptions: a few instances have low coverage for all methods. For sets smaller than 25, "parametric t" and "BCa" exhibit better coverage. "Basic" performs systematically worse than others, even though the difference is minimal when n is large.

For CIs of the median, we unveiled that "basic" bootstrap performs catastrophically for a large number of experiments. "BCa" bootstrap degrades as n increases, and exhibits huge undercoverage for a rather large number of instances. On the other hand, the "percentile" bootstrap behaves correctly across almost all 2×228 experiments and across all test set sizes. Note that all outliers with very high coverage actually correspond to distributions containing a Dirac weighing more than half the total distribution mass. In such cases, overcoverage is a normal behavior.

4   Discussion

To our knowledge, this work presents the first systematic comparison of CI methods for medical image segmentation metrics. To that purpose, we performed an extensive analysis across 228 experiments covering a variety of tasks and segmentation methods.

Reporting CIs is crucial, both for proper validation of methods and to align with clinical and regulatory guidelines [7] which is key for translation. However, there are yet no guidelines on how to compute CIs in practice in medical imaging AI. In this preliminary study, we focused on coverage properties and two common performance metrics for image segmentation. We unveiled some major pitfalls.

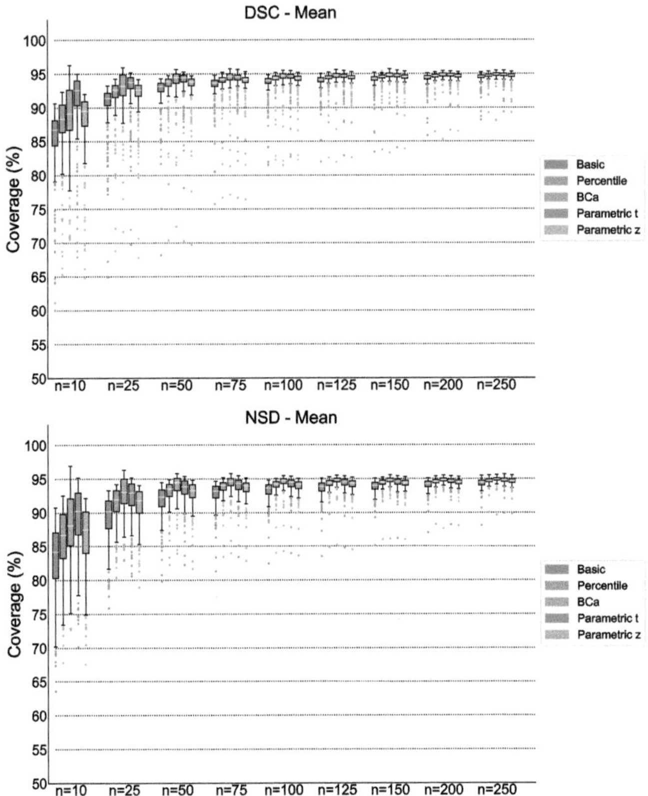

Fig. 1. Coverage of CIs of the mean. All studied methods have adequate coverage for the majority of instances when n is larger than 50. But there are exceptions with some instances exhibiting low coverage. For smaller values of n, "parametric t" and "BCa" have better coverage. For both the DSC (top) and the NSD (bottom), coverage is shown for each of the tested methods, as a function of the test set size. The boxplots represent the distribution of coverage across experiments. Boxes correspond to median and inter-quartile range (IQR) while whiskers correspond to 2.5 and 97.5 percentiles. Points represent outliers

Critically, the choice of the CI method depends upon the summary statistic: mean vs median (or any other order-based statistic).

The most striking results are for CIs of the median, where "basic" and "BCa" bootstrap led to some catastrophic failures while "percentile" was adequate across all experiments. We believe that these results are important. Median is a common robust statistic for central tendency. Many users can be tempted to blindly rely on "BCa" or "basic" because they are often recommended over "percentile" and because "BCa" is the default in some bootstrap implementations. For CIs of the mean, the results are less surprising, but there are still some interesting lessons. All methods behave decently when n is large enough but "BCa" and "parametric

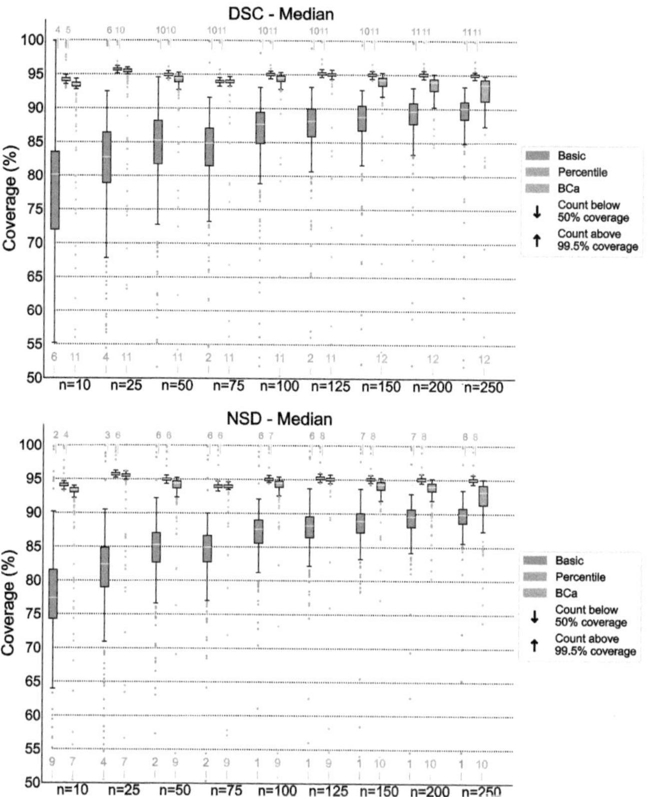

Fig. 2. Coverage of CIs of the median. Percentile bootstrap is adequate across all n and all experiments. Basic fails dramatically. BCa degrades as n increases, and produces catastrophic failures. For both the DSC (top) and the NSD (bottom) coverage is shown for each of the tested methods, as a function of the test set size. The boxplots represent the distribution of coverage across experiments. Boxes correspond to median and inter-quartile range (IQR) while whiskers correspond to 2.5 and 97.5 percentiles. Points represent outliers

t" offer a substantial advantage when n is small. Perhaps more surprising is that some experiments exhibit poor coverage across all methods, even for relatively large n. We inspected the metric distributions corresponding to these benchmarking instances and found that they either have major outliers or concentrate large mass in a single point. Thus, in such cases, the mean alone can be misleading and adequate CIs can require a large sample size.

The failures of "BCa" when used for CIs of the median can be explained by the way the so-called acceleration factor corrects for skewness using a jackknife estimate. Indeed, the denominator of this factor is the variance of leave-one-out estimates of the statistic which can easily become zero or very small for the median (or for any order statistic). The jackknife failure for non-continuous summary statistics is thus natural when one looks at the formula and has indeed been described [1], but we believe it is not common knowledge. The curious reader may have noticed that "BCa" is worse when n is even than when n is odd. Again, this can be explained from the acceleration formula: the leave-one-out estimates of the median are more likely to be equal when n is even. The "basic" bootstrap has been debated, with some arguing that it provides some bias correction while others say that it is "asymmetric in the wrong direction for skewed data" [12]. Indeed, our results show that for segmentation metrics, where skewness is highly common, "basic" is the worst method both for mean and median.

Availability in software packages is likely a driving factor underlying researchers' choices, and the AI community is almost entirely Python-based. It is extremely useful that the function bootstrap is available in SciPy [19], because it "democratizes" the use of this statistical methodology. The function implements the three most common versions which are "basic", "percentile" and "BCa", the default method being "BCa". Our results show that there is no "one-size-fits-all" method. We thus invite the medical imaging community to carefully consider the available options when using the function: going beyond the default is easily overlooked.

There is very little work on CIs for validation metrics in medical imaging. Typical values of CI width have been reported [10] but without assessing coverage which is fundamental to know whether a CI method is adequate. Other studies provide insights about image-derived quantities [4,17,21], but not for validation metrics. This lack of literature in medical imaging is in sharp contrast with other fields including psychology [13], neuroscience [18], social sciences [14] and generalist AI [2,15]. In general, these works do not come to the same conclusions as we do which can be explained by major differences: some other works rely on parametric simulations which are inadequate for segmentation metrics, some look only at the mean, some deal with cases where n is very large. We thus believe that medical imaging requires specific studies on the behavior of CIs.

This work has the following limitations. So far, we have only studied the case of segmentation and two metrics, and future work will need to tackle other tasks and other relevant metrics. In particular, the case of metrics with discrete or unbounded support is important and is left for future work. Moreover, due to space constraints, we focused on CI coverage. CI width is another important property that guides selection of a CI method among those which provide adequate coverage.

Even though preliminary, our results have immediate consequences on how to compute CIs for medical image segmentation. Indeed, we unveiled cases where some CI methods behave catastrophically which should have immediate impact on researchers reporting practices. Our work contributes towards the creation of standardized guidelines on CI reporting in medical imaging AI.

Acknowledgments. The authors are grateful to Reuben Dorent for stimulating discussions. The research leading to these results has received funding from the French government under management of Agence Nationale de la Recherche as part of the

"France 2030" program (reference ANR-23-IACL-0008, project PRAIRIE-PSAI), as part of the "Investissements d'avenir" program (reference ANR-19-P3IA-0001, project PRAIRIE 3IA Institute and reference ANR-10-IAIHU-06, project Agence Nationale de la Recherche-10-IA Institut Hospitalo-Universitaire-6) and from the European Union's Horizon Europe Framework Programme (grant number 101136607, project CLARA). This publication received funding from the European Research Council (ERC) under the European Union's Horizon 2020 research and innovation program (grant agreement no. 101002198, NEURAL SPICING). Part of this work was also funded by Helmholtz Imaging (HI), a platform of the Helmholtz Incubator on Information and Data Science. Moreover, this project has received funding from the National Center for Tumor Diseases (NCT) Heidelberg's Surgical Oncology Program.

Disclosure of Interests. The authors have no competing interests to declare that are relevant to the content of this article.

References

1. Abdi, H., Williams, L.: Jackknife. In: Salkind, N. (ed.) Encyclopedia of Research Design. Sage Publishing (2010)
2. Agarwal, R., Schwarzer, M., Castro, P.S., Courville, A.C., Bellemare, M.: Deep reinforcement learning at the edge of the statistical precipice. Adv. Neural. Inf. Process. Syst. **34**, 29304–29320 (2021)
3. Antonelli, M., Reinke, A., Bakas, S., et al.: The medical segmentation decathlon. Nat. Commun. (2022)
4. Bansal, R., et al.: Calculation of the confidence intervals for transformation parameters in the registration of medical images. Med. Image Anal. **13**(2), 215–233 (2009)
5. Chang, P., Liu, R., Hou, T., Yan, X., Shan, G.: Continuity corrected score confidence interval for the difference in proportions in paired data. J. Appl. Stat. **51**(1), 139–152 (2024)
6. Christodoulou, E., et al.: Confidence intervals uncovered: are we ready for real-world medical imaging AI? In: International Conference on Medical Image Computing and Computer-Assisted Intervention, pp. 124–132. Springer (2024)
7. Collins, G.S., Reitsma, J.B., Altman, D.G., Moons, K.G.: Transparent reporting of a multivariable prediction model for individual prognosis or diagnosis (tripod) the tripod statement. Circulation **131**(2), 211–219 (2015)
8. Davison, A.C., Hinkley, D.V.: Bootstrap methods and their application. No. 1 in Cambridge Series in Statistical and Probabilistic Mathematics. Cambridge University Press (1997)
9. Eisenmann, M., et al.: Biomedical image analysis competitions: the state of current participation practice. arXiv preprint arXiv:2212.08568 (2022)
10. Jurdi, R., Varoquaux, G., Colliot, O.: Confidence intervals for performance estimates in brain mri segmentation. Med. Image Anal. **103**, 103565 (2025)
11. FDA: FDA-2024-D-4488: Artificial intelligence-enabled device software functions: Lifecycle management and marketing submission recommendations. https://www.fda.gov/regulatory-information/search-fda-guidance-documents/artificial-intelligence-enabled-device-software-functions-lifecycle-management-and-marketing. Accessed 27 Feb 2024
12. Hesterberg, T.C.: What teachers should know about the bootstrap: resampling in the undergraduate statistics curriculum. Am. Stat. **69**(4), 371–386 (2015)

13. Kelley, K.: The effects of nonnormal distributions on confidence intervals around the standardized mean difference: bootstrap and parametric confidence intervals. Educ. Psychol. Measur. **65**(1), 51–69 (2005)
14. Luo, H.: Generation of non-normal data: a study of Fleishman's power method. Department of Statistics, Uppsala University (2011)
15. Miller, E.: Adding error bars to evals: a statistical approach to language model evaluations. arXiv preprint arXiv:2411.00640 (2024)
16. Newcombe, R.G.: Confidence intervals for proportions and related measures of effect size. CRC Press (2012)
17. Obuchowski, N.A., Bullen, J.: Quantitative imaging biomarkers: effect of sample size and bias on confidence interval coverage. Stat. Methods Med. Res. **27**(10), 3139–3150 (2018)
18. Rousselet, G., Pernet, C.R., Wilcox, R.R.: An introduction to the bootstrap: a versatile method to make inferences by using data-driven simulations. Meta-Psychol. **7** (2023)
19. Virtanen, P., et al.: Scipy 1.0: fundamental algorithms for scientific computing in python. Nat. Methods **17**(3), 261–272 (2020)
20. Wilcox, R.R.: Introduction to robust estimation and hypothesis testing. Academic Press (2022)
21. Wunderlich, A., Noo, F., Gallas, B.D., Heilbrun, M.E.: Exact confidence intervals for channelized hotelling observer performance in image quality studies. IEEE Trans. Med. Imaging **34**(2), 453–464 (2014)

Enabling PSO-Secure Synthetic Data Sharing Using Diversity-Aware Diffusion Models

Mischa Dombrowski[1(✉)] and Bernhard Kainz[1,2]

[1] Friedrich–Alexander University Erlangen–Nürnberg, Erlangen, Germany
`mischa.dombrowski@fau.de`
[2] Department of Computing, Imperial College London, London, UK

Abstract. Synthetic data has recently reached a level of visual fidelity that makes it nearly indistinguishable from real data, offering great promise for privacy-preserving data sharing in medical imaging. However, fully synthetic datasets still suffer from significant limitations: First and foremost, the legal aspect of sharing synthetic data is often neglected and data regulations, such as the GDPR, are largley ignored. Secondly, synthetic models fall short of matching the performance of real data, even for in-domain downstream applications. Recent methods for image generation have focused on maximising image diversity instead of fidelity solely to improve the mode coverage and therefore the downstream performance of synthetic data. In this work, we shift perspective and highlight how maximizing diversity can also be interpreted as protecting natural persons from being singled out, which leads to predicate singling-out (PSO) secure synthetic datasets. Specifically, we propose a generalisable framework for training diffusion models on personal data which leads to unpersonal synthetic datasets achieving performance within one percentage point of real-data models while significantly outperforming state-of-the-art methods that do not ensure privacy. Our code is available at https://github.com/MischaD/Trichotomy.

Keywords: Privacy · Data-sharing · Conditional Image Generation · Diffusion Models

1 Introduction

Generative models have recently gained significant attention for their ability to produce highly realistic images, sometimes even deceiving trained clinicians [34]. This opens the possibility of generating synthetic datasets that can be openly shared without the legal constraints of real medical data [33]. However, this potential raises important legal and practical questions. Primarily, these concern (1) the privacy of patients whose data were used during training and (2) the performance of synthetic datasets on downstream tasks.

To address privacy, we consider the General Data Protection Regulation (GDPR), one of the most comprehensive legal frameworks for data protection worldwide. Its central goal is "to protect the fundamental rights and freedoms

G. Zamzmi et al. (Eds.): MICCAI 2025, LNCS 16135, pp. 25–35, 2026.
https://doi.org/10.1007/978-3-032-05663-4_3

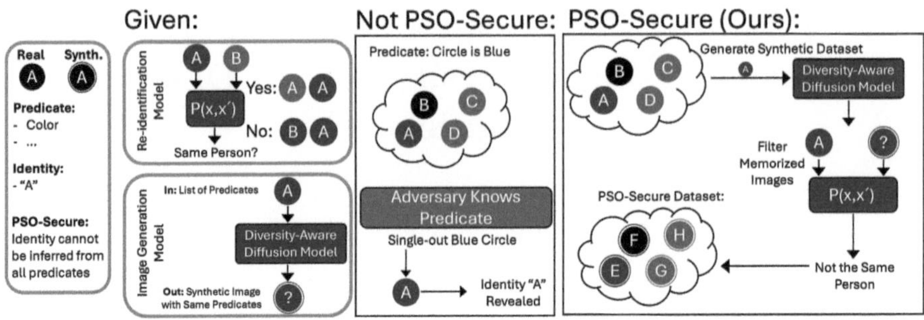

Fig. 1. Illustration of PSO-secure dataset generation. A diffusion model, guided by pre-computed features, generates synthetic images that preserve specific predicates (*e.g.*, color) while altering identity. A re-identification model ensures that identities are not retained. As a result, the synthetic dataset maintains relevant attributes of the real data without revealing personal information, making it non-personal under GDPR and suitable for sharing

of natural persons, and in particular their right to privacy, with regard to the processing of personal data" [2]. Importantly, the GDPR applies only if the data in question are considered personal data. The regulation intentionally leaves key terms, including personal, broadly defined to allow case-by-case interpretation. This flexibility enables courts and regulators to balance individual privacy against legitimate public interests [1].

Recital 26 of the GDPR specifies that "the principles of data protection should not apply to anonymous information", meaning data that do not relate to an identified or identifiable person [3]. Therefore, a central legal question becomes whether a given dataset can be considered anonymous. Recital 26 further clarifies that identifiability should be assessed in terms of all means reasonably likely to be used" for identification, including the possibility of singling out an individual [3]. This notion of singling out refers to the use of a combination of observable predicates to uniquely identify a person. Such predicates might include attributes like gender, medical conditions, height, or more context-specific features, for example, the presence of a ring in a radiograph [8].

To formalize this legal concept, Cohen et al. [6] propose a mathematical definition of singling out. They introduce the notion of Predicate Singling-Out security (PSO-security) to describe datasets where such identification is impossible. This framework defines a practical threshold for when synthetic data can be considered legally anonymous under the GDPR. However, identifying all relevant predicates a priori is infeasible in practice, making PSO-secure generation a technically and legally challenging problem.

Even if privacy were fully assured, another fundamental issue remains: the performance of synthetic data. Despite recent advances, generative models have not yet been shown to match real data in downstream tasks. Their primary applications remain in augmentation, imputation, and balancing of real datasets [5,7,12,26,27,29,34,36,37,39–41]. If synthetic images were truly equivalent to real ones, we would not require real data for model training. However, attempts to fully replace real datasets with synthetic counterparts have consistently resulted in performance degradation [9,10,13,14,17,19,28,31,33].

Recent research has therefore focused on evaluating synthetic data quality using metrics beyond image fidelity. Some studies use re-identification models to evaluate temporal consistency in videos [10]. Others emphasize sample diversity as a core metric for synthetic dataset quality [10,11,17]. Despite its relevance, diversity remains under-optimized in current generative approaches.

Contribution: We present a framework for generating synthetic datasets that are both PSO-secure and competitive with real data in downstream tasks. Our approach extracts learned predicates from training data and conditions generation on these predicates. By explicitly ensuring that the generated images do not preserve the identity of training samples, we produce synthetic counterparts that share predicates but differ in identity. As a result, singling out is no longer possible, rendering the synthetic data PSO-secure under the GDPR framework. We empirically demonstrate that our method outperforms the current state-of-the-art in downstream performance. Furthermore, we show that models trained exclusively on our synthetic data generalize better than those trained on real data alone. The full pipeline is illustrated in Fig. 1.

2   Related Work

Privacy-Preserving Techniques: Privacy preservation remains a critical challenge in image generation and has been addressed in several studies. Although generative models are designed to avoid the direct replication of real samples, recent work has shown that diffusion models may memorize and inadvertently leak private information if not trained with care [33]. This raises serious concerns for medical data sharing, where regulations such as HIPAA and GDPR mandate strict privacy safeguards. A potential mitigation strategy involves using re-identification models trained to determine whether two samples originate from the same individual [30]. Such models leverage subject labels in the training data to perform re-identification, as demonstrated in [10,33]. While these methods address the technical aspect of privacy and incorporate filtering mechanisms to enforce it, they do not account for the associated legal considerations.

Image Generation: Diffusion models have become the leading approach for image generation following their reintroduction with improved noise schedules and architectural enhancements [15]. A major breakthrough was the development of latent diffusion models, which significantly reduced training and sampling times, enabling large-scale commercialization [35]. Subsequent work further optimized schedules and architectures to improve training stability [23,25]. The guidance network is an auxiliary denoising model and has been shown to play a key role in tuning and enhancing generation quality [16]. State-of-the-art methods now employ a less-trained version of the same model to balance efficiency and performance [24]. Despite these advances, class-conditional diffusion models often suffer from limited diversity [11]. To address this, [11] introduced DiADM, a diversity-aware diffusion model guided by precomputed pseudo-conditional features from a pre-trained network. Using an Inception network as a feature extractor, DiADM separates image quality from diversity, aiming to generate realistic yet varied datasets. However, their evaluation does not consider downstream task performance or privacy implications.

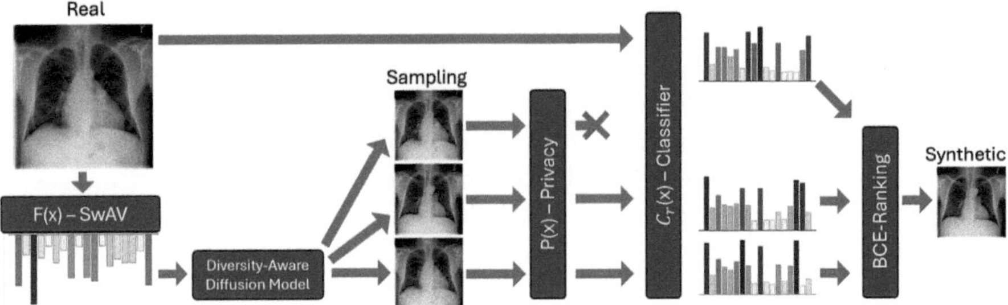

Fig. 2. Method illustration: We adapt recently established diversity aware diffusion models (DiADM) [11] to generate multiple images that share the same predicates according to the SwAV feature encoder. A privacy filter ensures that the identity is not preserved. Finally, the images are ranked according to how well they preserve the predicates

3   Methods

Formally, we aim to generate a synthetic dataset $\mathcal{D}'$ of the same size and the same label distribution as the real dataset $\mathcal{D}$ that achieves comparable performance on a downstream task of predicting c_d, while at the same time staying PSO-secure. The labels shall only be used for downstream evaluation, but not for conditioning, to remain generalizable to cases where no data is present. To compare real and synthetic performance, we assume that sharing classifiers is always possible, regardless of their train set. Classification models trained in real data are called $\mathcal{C}_r(x)$, and those trained in synthetic data are called $\mathcal{C}_s(x)$. In practice, hospitals often rely on locally trained models, limiting their ability to benefit from external datasets. Our approach mimics the case, where PSO-secure datasets can be shared across institutions. Therefore, we train a model $\mathcal{C}_s(x)$ on the combined synthetic datasets to demonstrate the potential of using synthetic datasets for the purpose of data sharing. To ensure privacy, we use a re-identification filter which removes privacy violating samples following [10,33].

Image Generation: For image generation, we introduce a novel sampling strategy, unique to DiADM-based models. DiADM leverages a knowledge database to improve generative performance by conditioning on pre-trained feature vectors. Inspired by this concept, we adopt a similar approach and observe that the method proposed by [11] applies the same principle to enhance sample diversity through pseudo-conditional features, denoted as c_s. Unlike [11], we use features extracted by a pre-trained SwAV model [4], as our preliminary experiments showed that these visual features align better with the reconstruction loss of the diffusion model.

Our approach allows us to take the pseudo-label c_s of a real image x which was used to generate the corresponding synthetic image x' and assess memorization by evaluating the prediction of $\mathcal{P}(x, x')$, which is a binary classification model trained on re-identification following [30]. For each $x \in \mathcal{D}$, we extract c_s and generate a batch of synthetic images $\mathcal{D}'_x$ of size $b = 32$. We then apply a privacy filter to identify and remove any synthetic images that exhibit excessive similarity to real training samples, ensuring that memorization is mitigated. Finally, we select the most suitable synthetic sample by computing the alignment between the real and generated images. This alignment ensures that the predicates of the real image are equal to the predicates of the synthetic image. Specifically, we choose the synthetic image that minimizes the binary cross-entropy (BCE) loss between the predictions of $\mathcal{C}_r(x)$ on the real image x and the synthetic candidate x'. Formally, this selection process is defined as:

$$x' = \arg \min_{x' \in \mathcal{D}_x^-} \mathrm{BCE}(\mathcal{C}_r(x), \mathcal{C}_r(x')) \quad \text{for} \quad \mathcal{D}_x^- := \{x' | \mathcal{P}(x, x') = 0\} \qquad (1)$$

where $\mathcal{P}(x, x') = 0$ ensures that knowing predicates c_s does not imply knowledge of the identity. In rare cases where all generated samples are flagged as privacy risks, we reduce the classifier guidance strength by 0.1 and re-sample. The entire sampling process is also visualised in Fig. 2.

4   Experiments

Dataset: We use MIMIC-CXR (CXR) [22], CheXpert (CXP) [20], and ChestX-ray8 (NIH) [38] focussing on the eight shared disease classes. We use a train, validation, test split of (70, 10, 20). For training and validation, we filter out images with multiple pathology labels to enable a comparison with SOTA approaches like EDM-2 and EDM-2-AG.

Metrics: To assess the quality of image generation we use the Fréchet Inception distance (FID) that compares features extracted from a pre-trained Inception model between real and synthetic data. To assess diversity we use image retrieval score (IRS), a recently proposed method, that treats image generation as an image retrieval problem and measures how many images of the real dataset can be retrieved using synthetic samples [11]. Finally, to assess utilization, we train a downstream model for multi-class classification and report the AUCROC score on real data, selecting the best model using a validation set. Specifically, we use DenseNet-121 [18], following the approach suggested by [32]. We train models on real data $\mathcal{C}_r(x)$ and compare them to models trained on synthetic data

$C_s(x)$. All models are trained for 100 epochs with annealing learning rate. The best checkpoint is chosen based on the validation loss on real data (mimicing a scenario where one hospital has access to all synthetic data and one in-house validation dataset).

Image Generation Benchmark: For benchmarking, we use the recently established EDM [25] and its autoguidance extension EDM-AG [24], along with DiADM, a diversity-aware diffusion model designed to improve diversity over the unconditional baseline [11]. We set the learning rate to 0.0003, apply decay after 17,000 steps, and disable half-precision training due to observed inaccuracies. All models are trained for two days on four Nvidia H100 GPUs, selecting the best EDM-2 and EDM-2 AG models based on FID. For compression, we use the VAE from Stable Diffusion v2 (SDv2) without fine-tuning but compute dataset-specific latent statistics following [25]. Conditional models are trained for 83886 steps, and unconditional models for 100663 steps. DiADM does not use guidance (equivalent to a strength of 1.0), but we observe that adding guidance improves IRS and FID scores. We compare guidance strategies using an unconditional model [25], an earlier checkpoint of the same model [24], and a combination of both.

Results: First we investigate our proposed changes to the general architecture and sampling of DiADM introduced in Sect. 3. Our best-performing model uses a fully trained unconditional model with a guidance strength of 1.2. The results are shown in Table 1. While previous methods exhibit a gap of more than three percentage points in downstream AUCROC, our method reduces this gap to below one percentage point compared to real data. Our approach achieves the best performance in both image fidelity and diversity. Notably, it even surpasses an IRS value of one, indicating that conditioning on c_s is effective, as the sampling exceeds the expected diversity of a perfect unconditional model.

Table 1. IRS and FID scores for $\mathcal{D}'$ generated from different state of the art class-conditional approaches without ensuring PSO-secure synthetic data. No augmentation or balancing technique was used

Name	FID ↓	IRS$_{\infty,a}$ ↑	Real-Snth Gap (AUCROC ↑)
EDM-2 (CVPR24) [25]	15.0	0.19	−4.49 (80.44)
EDM-2 AG (T/10) (Neurips24) [24]	14.7	0.23	−3.50 (81.49)
DiADM (CVPR25) [11]	8.9	0.33	−3.68 (81.31)
DiADM + SwAV (Ours)	**5.0**	**1.58**	**−0.95 (84.04)**
Real	—	—	84.99

Now, to investigate how our PSO-secure sampling impacts model performance, we examine the results of downstream models trained on all three datasets separately and on a combination of them. The results are shown in

Table 2. Generalization to new datasets. Data sharing (DS) means we combine privacy-preserving synthetic datasets to a large synthetic dataset

Test	PSO-s.	NIH			CXR			CXP		
Train		NIH	CXR	CXP	NIH	CXR	CXP	NIH	CXR	CXP
Real		85.41	81.78	79.62	77.07	82.71	76.98	74.18	76.23	79.99
Rec. (SDv2)		85.38	82.47	81.61	77.82	82.89	77.85	74.45	76.21	79.90
EDM-2		80.44	77.89	**77.23**	73.85	80.31	**75.81**	67.56	70.74	73.94
EDM-2 AG		81.49	73.17	76.24	74.90	76.12	74.46	68.21	70.59	75.02
DiADM		81.31	78.52	74.97	72.88	80.41	73.12	67.40	73.97	73.97
Ours	✓	**83.65**	**79.60**	76.16	**75.98**	**80.92**	74.12	**72.57**	**74.88**	**77.87**
Ours + DS.	✓	**83.83**			**81.31**			**77.94**		

Table 2. We observe that our model outperforms all others by a large margin. To statistically verify our results, we perform a ten-fold cross-validation using the training dataset. Each generative model samples one synthetic dataset, $\mathcal{D}'$, which is then split according to the ten-fold cross-validation. We ignore subject overlap for this experiment, which results in higher scores for real data. The results are presented in Fig. 3. Importantly, we see a significant improvement in our method compared to all previously proposed methods. However, the model is still not on par with real data. We believe this may be because pseudo-conditional labels capture visual features well but do not fully represent the underlying distribution of the diseases.

To better understand why this works so well, we visualize the generated samples in Fig. 4 together with their privacy prediction and their predicate alignment. As we can see, all samples share key visual characteristics but differ in smaller details such as ribs, support devices, or heart shape. Clearly, the model does not

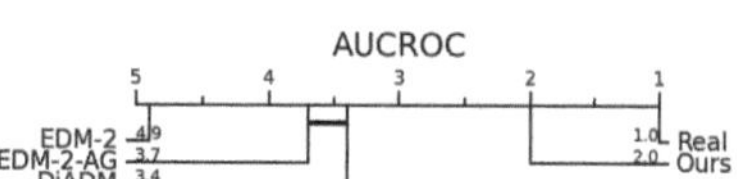

Fig. 3. Critical difference diagram of different generation methods [21]

memorize entire samples, but the visual appearance is very similar across all samples. While different memorization detection methods might lead to different results, the privacy filter we use achieves a combined test performance of 96% AUCROC on re-identification, which is much harder than simple memorization detection. Visual inspection also gives us insight how this method ensures PSO-secure datasharing. Despite knowing all predicates about the patient (such as gender, size, existence of support devices, presence of a disease etc.) it is impossible to say which image comes from the real patient.

Given the promising results of using domain-agnostic feature encoders for pseudo-conditional generation we also experiment with using models trained on medical data. Specifically, we experiment with using $\mathcal{C}_r(x)$ as feature extractor.

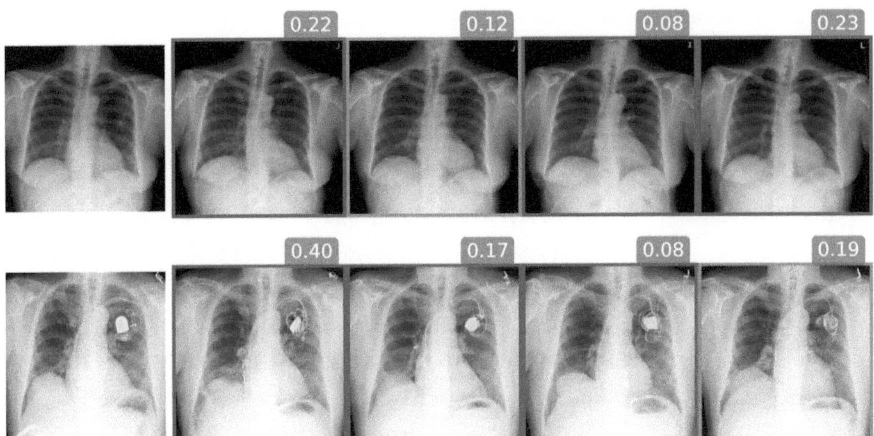

Fig. 4. Two random examples of four generated samples using our proposed generation method. The left-most image shows the training image. All other images have a boundary indicating the prediction of $\mathcal{P}(x, x')$, with red indicating privacy issues. The scores indicate the agreement of real and PSO-secure image according to 1 (Color figure online)

Suprisingly, the model does not properly learn to generate images from these features. Both IRS and FID increase by a magnitude and the downstream performance is worse than all the results presented in Table 1. We believe that this is because the pseudo-conditional features extracted by this domain-specific model are visually not meaningful enough for the diffusion model.

Limitations: Using our framework could lead to synthetic datasets that are as good as real datasets. However, we did not demonstrate how a generative model can outperform real data, limiting the impact of our approach in typical applications of generative models, such as data augmentation. Additionally, the effectiveness of our approach relies heavily on the privacy filtering mechanism and, unlike differential privacy, it does not provide formal guarantees. While our results demonstrate that the filter can produce synthetic images sufficiently different from real ones to support generalization, other privacy risks such as membership inference attacks may still remain possible. Furthermore, filtering increases the sampling time by a factor of b. We consider this overhead acceptable given the resulting privacy benefits in the generated datasets.

5   Conclusion

We propose a method for generating synthetic, privacy-preserving datasets that retain competitive downstream performance on image classification tasks compared to real data. Our approach outperforms state-of-the-art class-conditional methods across multiple metrics and datasets. To ensure privacy, we formalize the concept of "singling-out", *i.e.*, the risk of identifying individuals based solely on predicates, and explicitly prevent it, paving the way for a new paradigm in secure data sharing.

Acknowledgments. This work was supported by the High-Tech-Agenda Bavaria. HPC resources were provided by the Erlangen National High Performance Computing Center (NHR@FAU) of the Friedrich-Alexander-Universität Erlangen-Nürnberg (FAU) under the NHR project b143dc and b180dc. NHR funding is provided by federal and Bavarian state authorities. NHR@FAU hardware is partially funded by the German Research Foundation (DFG)   440719683. Support was also received by the ERC - projects MIA-NORMAL 101083647 as well as DFG 513220538, 512819079.

Disclosure of Interests. The authors have no competing interests to declare that are relevant to the content of this article.

References

1. GDPR Brief: when are synthetic health data personal data? https://www.ga4gh.org/news_item/when-are-synthetic-health-data-personal-data/
2. Opinion 4/2007 on the concept of personal data. https://www.pdp.ie/docs/1030.pdf
3. Recital 26 - Not Applicable to Anonymous Data. https://gdpr-info.eu/recitals/no-26/
4. Caron, M., Misra, I., Mairal, J., Goyal, P., Bojanowski, P., Joulin, A.: Unsupervised learning of visual features by contrasting cluster assignments. In: NeurIPS (2020)
5. Chebykin, A., Bosman, P.A.N., Alderliesten, T.: Hyperparameter-Free Medical Image Synthesis for Sharing Data and Improving Site-Specific Segmentation (2024)
6. Cohen, A., Nissim, K.: Towards formalizing the GDPR's notion of singling out. Proc. Natl. Acad. Sci. **117**(15), 8344–8352 (2020). https://doi.org/10.1073/pnas.1914598117. arXiv:1904.06009
7. Deshpande, T., Prakash, E., Ross, E.G., Langlotz, C., Ng, A., Valanarasu, J.M.J.: Auto-Generating Weak Labels for Real & Synthetic Data to Improve Label-Scarce Medical Image Segmentation (2024)
8. Dombrowski, M., Kainz, B.: Can diffusion models generalize? Privacy and fairness trade-offs for medical data sharing. In: Medical Imaging with Deep Learning (2025)
9. Dombrowski, M., Reynaud, H., Baugh, M., Kainz, B.: Foreground-background separation through concept distillation from generative image foundation models. In: ICCV (2023)
10. Dombrowski, M., Reynaud, H., Kainz, B.: Uncovering Hidden Subspaces in Video Diffusion Models Using Re-Identification (2024). arXiv:2411.04956
11. Dombrowski, M., Zhang, W., Cechnicka, S., Reynaud, H., Kainz, B.: Image generation diversity issues and how to tame them. In: CVPR, pp. 3029–3039 (2025)
12. Elbatel, M., Kamnitsas, K., Li, X.: An Organism Starts with a Single Pix-Cell: A Neural Cellular Diffusion for High-Resolution Image Synthesis (2024). arXiv:2407.03018
13. Frisch, Y., et al.: Synthesising Rare Cataract Surgery Samples with Guided Diffusion Models (2023). arXiv:2308.02587
14. Han, K., et al.: MedGen3D: A Deep Generative Framework for Paired 3D Image and Mask Generation (2023). arXiv:2304.04106

15. Ho, J., Jain, A., Abbeel, P.: Denoising diffusion probabilistic models. NeurIPS **33**, 6840–6851 (2020)
16. Ho, J., Salimans, T.: Classifier-Free Diffusion Guidance (2022). arXiv:2207.12598
17. Hou, Z., Yan, R., Wang, Q., Lang, N., Zhou, X.: Diversity-preserving chest radiographs generation from reports in one stage. In: MICCAI 2023, vol. 14224, pp. 482–492. Springer, Cham (2023)
18. Huang, G., Liu, Z., Maaten, L.V.D., Weinberger, K.Q.: Densely Connected Convolutional Networks (2018)
19. Huang, K., et al.: Memory-efficient High-resolution OCT Volume Synthesis with Cascaded Amortized Latent Diffusion Models (2024). arXiv:2405.16516
20. Irvin, J., et al.: CheXpert: A Large Chest Radiograph Dataset with Uncertainty Labels and Expert Comparison (2019)
21. Ismail Fawaz, H., Forestier, G., Weber, J., Idoumghar, L., Muller, P.-A.: Deep learning for time series classification: a review. Data Min. Knowl. Disc. **33**(4), 917–963 (2019). https://doi.org/10.1007/s10618-019-00619-1
22. Johnson, A.E.W., et al.: MIMIC-CXR, a de-identified publicly available database of chest radiographs with free-text reports. Sci. Data (2019)
23. Karras, T., Aittala, M., Aila, T., Laine, S.: Elucidating the Design Space of Diffusion-Based Generative Models (2022). arXiv:2206.00364
24. Karras, T., et al.: Guiding a Diffusion Model with a Bad Version of Itself (2024)
25. Karras, T., Aittala, M., Lehtinen, J., Hellsten, J., Aila, T., Laine, S.: Analyzing and Improving the Training Dynamics of Diffusion Models (2024)
26. Kumar, A., et al.: Cross-modulated Few-shot Image Generation for Colorectal Tissue Classification (2023)
27. Liu, Z., Zhang, T., He, Y., Zhang, G.: Generating progressive images from pathological transitions via diffusion model. In: MICCAI 2024, vol. 15011. Springer, Cham (2024)
28. Na, I., Kim, J., Ko, E.S., Park, H.: RadiomicsFill-Mammo: Synthetic Mammogram Mass Manipulation with Radiomics Features (2024)
29. Oh, H.J., Jeong, W.K.: Controllable and Efficient Multi-Class Pathology Nuclei Data Augmentation using Text-Conditioned Diffusion Models (2024)
30. Packhäuser, K., Gündel, S., Münster, N., Syben, C., Christlein, V., Maier, A.: Deep learning-based patient re-identification is able to exploit the biometric nature of medical chest X-ray data. Sci. Rep. **12**(1) (2022)
31. Peng, Q., et al.: Advancing H&E-to-IHC virtual staining with task-specific domain knowledge for HER2 scoring. In: MICCAI 2024, vol. 15004. Springer, Cham (2024)
32. Rajpurkar, P., et al.: CheXNet: Radiologist-Level Pneumonia Detection on Chest X-Rays with Deep Learning (2017)
33. Reynaud, H., et al.: EchoNet-Synthetic: Privacy-preserving Video Generation for Safe Medical Data Sharing (2024)
34. Reynaud, H., et al.: Feature-Conditioned Cascaded Video Diffusion Models for Precise Echocardiogram Synthesis, vol. 14229 (2023)
35. Rombach, R., Blattmann, A., Lorenz, D., Esser, P., Ommer, B.: High-Resolution Image Synthesis with Latent Diffusion Models (2022). arXiv:2112.10752
36. Shen, Z., Cao, M., Wang, S., Zhang, L., Wang, Q.: CellGAN: Conditional Cervical Cell Synthesis for Augmenting Cytopathological Image Classification (2023)
37. Wang, F., Ren, Z., Lian, C., Ma, J.: Controllable counterfactual generation for interpretable medical image classification. In: MICCAI 2024. Springer, Cham (2024)

38. Wang, X., Peng, Y., Lu, L., Lu, Z., Bagheri, M., Summers, R.M.: ChestX-ray8: Hospital-Scale Chest X-Ray Database and Benchmarks on Weakly-Supervised Classification and Localization of Common Thorax Diseases (2017)
39. Ye, J., Ni, H., Jin, P., Huang, S.X., Xue, Y.: Synthetic Augmentation with Large-scale Unconditional Pre-training (2023). arXiv:2308.04020
40. Yuan, Z., et al.: Adapting pre-trained generative model to medical image for data augmentation. In: MICCAI 2024, vol. 15005. Springer, Cham (2024)
41. Zhao, Z., et al.: Label-preserving data augmentation in latent space for diabetic retinopathy recognition. In: MICCAI 2023, vol. 14222 (2023)

Three Countries, Three Continents: AI Medical Device Regulation and Certification Comparison in the US, EU, and South Korea

Kanjar De$^{(\boxtimes)}$ and Alireza Salehi M.

RISE Research Institutes of Sweden, Stockholm, Sweden
{kanjar.de,alireza.salehi}@ri.se

Abstract. The rapid integration of artificial intelligence into medical devices has created unprecedented regulatory challenges, requiring novel certification frameworks that balance innovation with patient safety across major global markets. This paper provides a comparative analysis of AI medical device certification pathways in three leading jurisdictions: the United States (FDA), the European Union (AI Act and MDR/IVDR) and South Korea (Medical Devices Act), examining risk classification systems, approval processes, and post-market requirements through systematic review of regulatory frameworks and guidance documents. Although all jurisdictions adopt risk-based approaches, implementation strategies vary significantly. The FDA emphasizes adaptive frameworks with predetermined change control plans, the EU combines horizontal AI Act requirements with sector-specific medical device regulations, and South Korea introduces novel high-impact AI provisions with incentivized impact assessments for medical applications. These regulatory differences create complex compliance landscapes for global manufacturers, making understanding of jurisdiction-specific pathways essential for strategic market entry and product development. The analysis in this paper provides actionable insights for optimizing certification strategies while ensuring patient safety across these critical markets.

Keywords: Artificial Intelligence · Medical Devices Regulation · EU AI Act · EU MDR · EU IVDR · Risk based Regulation

1 Introduction and Need for Regulation in AI Based Medical Devices

Artificial intelligence is transforming modern medicine through enhanced diagnostic accuracy, accelerated drug discovery, and personalized treatment protocols. AI systems now assist radiologists in early cancer detection, predict patient deterioration, and automate administrative workflows across clinical settings. However, the sophisticated and adaptive nature of AI systems creates regulatory challenges that traditional medical device frameworks cannot adequately address. This has prompted major global health authorities to develop comprehensive AI-specific governance structures for medical devices, as documented by Onitiu et al. [23]. Real-world deployment failures demonstrate the inadequacy of conventional regulatory approaches for data-driven technologies. The IDx-DR system, one of the first FDA-cleared autonomous AI systems for the detection of diabetic retinopathy, showed strong trial results but experienced significant performance degradation in practice, specificity dropped to 82% and positive predictive value fell to just 19%, causing unnecessary excessive referrals. This case highlighted the limitations of static pre-market evaluation and underscored the need for adaptive regulatory frameworks [4]. Analysis of 266 safety events with FDA-approved ML devices revealed that 66% posed potential harm and 16% caused actual patient injury, with data input problems contributing to 82% of problems [15]. Although device malfunctions were the most common, user-related problems were four times more likely to cause harm, emphasizing the need for comprehensive system-wide approaches to the safety of ML devices. Recent comparative analysis of AI medical device regulation demonstrates that each jurisdiction's approach reflects distinct technological maturity levels and cultural norms, precluding a one-size-fits-all regulatory standard [24]. This underscores the critical need for balanced regulatory frameworks that reconcile compliance requirements with objectives of ensuring safety, efficacy, and innovation in AI medical devices [24]. This comparative analysis focuses on three pivotal jurisdictions: the United States as the world's largest medical device market, the European Union with its pioneering AI Act, and South Korea as the first Asian nation to enact comprehensive AI legislation, representing distinct regulatory philosophies that collectively influence global AI governance standards. The following sections examine each jurisdiction's certification pathways, risk classification frameworks, and post-market surveillance requirements to identify best practices and regulatory gaps that will inform future AI medical device policy worldwide.

2   Definition of Medical Devices and AI System

The official definitions presented in Tables 1 and 2 demonstrate remarkable consistency in the definition of AI systems and medical devices between jurisdictions, allowing a meaningful comparison of how each jurisdiction translates these common definitions into distinct certification pathways.

3   AI Specific Regulations

The following comparison draws insights from established comparative studies [12] while focusing on key regulatory distinctions between the jurisdictions. While the EU established comprehensive AI regulation through its horizontal legislative approach with the AI Act entering force in August 2024, South Korea quickly followed as the first Asian jurisdiction to enact AI-specific legislation with its Basic Act passed in December 2024. Both regulatory frameworks

Table 1. Official Definitions of "AI System" in the EU, US and South Korea

Region	Official Definition of "AI System"
European Union	"AI system" means a machine-based system that is designed to operate with varying levels of autonomy and that may exhibit adaptiveness after deployment, and that, for explicit or implicit objectives, infers, from the input it receives, how to generate outputs such as predictions, content, recommendations, or decisions that can influence physical or virtual environments [6]
United States	A machine-based system that can, for a given set of human-defined objectives, make predictions, recommendations, or decisions influencing real or virtual environments. Artificial intelligence systems use machine- and human-based inputs to perceive real and virtual environments; abstract such perceptions into models through analysis in an automated manner; and use model inference to formulate options for information or action [32]
South Korea	An artificial intelligence-based system that infers results such as predictions, recommendations and decisions that affect real and virtual environments for a given goal with various levels of autonomy and adaptability [11]

Table 2. Official Legal Definitions of Medical Device in EU, US and South Korea

Region	Official Definition of Medical Device
European Union	"medical device" means any instrument, apparatus, appliance, software, implant, reagent, material or other article intended by the manufacturer to be used, alone or in combination, for human beings for medical purposes: diagnosis, prevention, monitoring, prediction, prognosis, treatment or alleviation of disease; diagnosis, monitoring, treatment, alleviation of, or compensation for, an injury or disability; investigation, replacement or modification of the anatomy or physiological/pathological process; providing information by means of in vitro examination of specimens derived from the human body; and which does not achieve its principal intended action by pharmacological, immunological or metabolic means. Products for conception control and cleaning/disinfection/sterilisation of medical devices are also included [8]
United States	The term "device" means an instrument, apparatus, implement, machine, contrivance, implant, in vitro reagent, or similar article, including component parts or accessories which is: (A) recognized in official formularies, (B) intended for diagnosis, cure, mitigation, treatment, or prevention of disease, or (C) intended to affect body structure or function, and which does not achieve primary purposes through chemical action or metabolism [31]
South Korea	The term "medical device" means an instrument, machine, apparatus, material, software, or similar product used alone or in combination for: 1. diagnosing, curing, alleviating, treating, or preventing disease; 2. diagnosing, curing, alleviating, or correcting injury or impairment; 3. testing, replacing, or transforming structure or function; 4. control of conception [16]

emerged from similar policy motivations—balancing innovation promotion with risk mitigation—but reflect distinct regional approaches to AI governance, as detailed in Table 3. The EU's strict regulatory model emphasizes prohibited practices and substantial penalties, while South Korea adopts a more industry-collaborative approach focused on supporting domestic AI development alongside measured oversight. These parallel developments in 2024 demonstrate the global momentum toward establishing comprehensive AI regulatory frameworks, with both acts serving as influential models for other jurisdictions considering AI legislation.

4   Overview of Regulatory Frameworks for AI Medical Devices

This section examines the regulatory approaches of three leading jurisdictions for AI-powered medical devices. Table 4 provides a detailed comparison of their frameworks Additionally, data protection requirements vary across jurisdictions: the EU enforces GDPR compliance for medical AI systems [10], South Korea applies the Personal Information Protection Act (PIPA) [21], while the US lacks comprehensive federal data privacy legislation specific to medical devices beyond HIPAA for covered entities [25].

Table 3. Comparison of EU AI Act and South Korea AI Basic Act

Aspect	EU AI Act	South Korea AI Basic Act
Legal Framework	Regulation (EU) 2024/1689 - Entered into force August 1, 2024, with staggered implementation: prohibited practices (February 2, 2025), GPAI obligations (August 2, 2025), full application (August 2, 2026) [2]	Basic Act on the Development of Artificial Intelligence and Establishment of Trust - Passed December 26, 2024, taking effect January 22, 2026 [22]
Risk Classification	Four-tier system: (1) Prohibited AI practices (Article 5), (2) High-risk AI systems (Article 6), (3) Limited risk AI with transparency obligations, (4) General-purpose AI models with systemic risk [2]	Risk-based approach with two main categories: (1) High-impact AI systems (Article 2), (2) Generative AI systems, plus obligations for AI systems exceeding computational thresholds [22]
Prohibited Practices	Article 5 explicitly bans eight AI practices including: cognitive behavioral manipulation, social scoring, real-time biometric identification in public spaces (with limited exceptions), and AI systems predicting future criminality [2]	No explicit prohibition of AI practices. Instead focuses on ensuring safety and reliability of high-impact AI and transparency regulations for generative AI [11,22]
Penalties	Maximum penalties: €35 million or 7% of global annual turnover for prohibited AI practices (Article 99(3)); €15 million or 3% for other violations; €7.5 million or 1% for providing misleading information [2]	Fines up to KRW 30 million (~ $20,870 USD) for violations. Significantly lower than EU penalties [22]
Governance	European AI Office within European Commission for oversight (Article 65), AI Board for coordination (Article 66), Scientific Panel of independent experts (Article 68), and national competent authorities (Article 70) [2]	National AI Committee chaired by the President (Article 7), AI Policy Center (Article 11), AI Safety Research Institute, and Korea AI Promotion Association for comprehensive governance framework [22]

European Union. The EU operates dual regulatory compliance: MDR/IVDR for medical device approval and the 2024 AI Act for AI system oversight. The AI Act classifies systems into four risk levels (unacceptable, high, limited, minimal risk), with medical devices Class IIa and above automatically designated as high-risk AI systems requiring additional conformity assessments [3].

United States. The FDA utilizes risk-based pathways (510(k), De Novo, PMA) with Predetermined Change Control Plans (PCCPs) enabling pre-authorized modifications for adaptive AI systems without requiring new submissions [33].

South Korea. South Korea's MFDS led comprehensive digital health regulation through the Digital Medical Products Act (2024), establishing the world's first framework specifically for digital medical products including AI devices [17].

5   Risk Class in Medical Devices

Risk classification systems fundamentally shape the commercial viability and development trajectory of AI-enabled medical devices, where higher risk classifications require exponentially more resources and longer development timelines compared to lower-risk classifications. As shown in Table 5, the United States

Table 4. High-level comparison of regulatory frameworks for AI in medical devices.

Attribute	European Union	United States	South Korea
Lead Agency	European Commission, NCAs, NBs	FDA	MFDS
Core Medical Device Law	MDR (EU 2017/745); IVDR (EU 2017/746)	FD&C Act; 21 CFR 807, 814, 860	Medical Device Act; DMPA (2024)
AI-Specific Regulation	AI Act (EU 2024/1689) high-risk systems; MDR/IVDR compliance	FDA Final Guidance for AI-DSF (Dec 2024); PCCP framework	DMPA (2024); AI/ML guidelines; Generative AI guideline (2025)
Risk Classification	Class I–III (MDR); A–D (IVDR); AI Act high-risk designation	Class I–III with AI change management	Class 1–4 with algorithm maturity criteria
Approval Pathways	CE Marking via NB; Dual MDR/AI Act conformity	510(k), De Novo, PMA + PCCP	Standard/expedited (80-day); Third-Party Reviewer
Post-Market Requirements	Vigilance (MDR/IVDR), Art. 73 (AI Act) reporting	MDR, QSR, real-world monitoring, PCCP updates	Adverse event reporting, DMPA monitoring, cybersecurity
AI/Software Definitions	MDSW (MDR/IVDR); AI system (Art. 3)	IMDRF SaMD/SiMD; AI-DSF	AIMD; Digital medical products (AI/ML)

operates a three-tier system (Classes I, II, III) while South Korea employs a four-tier system (Classes I, II, III, IV), creating strategic decisions about market entry sequencing for global manufacturers. The European Union presents unique regulatory complexity through its dual classification system [1], where AI-enabled medical devices must simultaneously satisfy traditional medical device regulations (MDR/IVDR) and AI Act requirements, a layered compliance burden not present in other jurisdictions. South Korea's four-tier classification system includes a Class IV category for the highest-risk devices, while the US and EU address similar high-risk devices within their existing three-tier frameworks, creating different regulatory pathways for equivalent risk levels.

Table 5. Risk Classification of AI-Based Medical Devices in EU, US, and South Korea

Region	Risk Classes & Criteria
European Union [2,7,8]	**MDR:** Class I (Low Risk), IIa/IIb (Moderate/High Risk), III (Highest Risk). **IVDR:** Class A (Low Risk), B, C, D (Highest Risk). **AI Act High-Risk:** Any AI system that is a medical device or IVD requiring Notified Body review under MDR/IVDR is automatically "high-risk" under AI Act Article 6 and Annex II.
United States [31]	**Class I (Low Risk):** General controls. **Class II (Moderate Risk):** 510(k) clearance. **Class III (High Risk):** Pre Market Approval required.
South Korea [18]	**Class 1 (Low Risk):** Non-invasive, minimal risk. **Class 2 (Moderate Risk):** Moderate risk, non-critical diagnostics. **Class 3 (High Risk):** Critical diagnostics. **Class 4 (Highest Risk):** Life-sustaining/autonomous AI.

6 Regulatory Approval of AI-Enabled Medical Devices: Requirements and Pathways by Region

Table 6 compares certification requirements for AI-based medical devices across the United States (FDA), European Union (MDR/IVDR with AI Act), and South Korea (MFDS with Digital Medical Products Act). The US uses a 3-tier classification system (Class I-III) while the EU and South Korea utilize 4-tier frameworks. Regulatory approaches differ significantly: the US relies on FDA pathways with Predetermined Change Control Plans (PCCP) for adaptive AI systems; the EU requires dual compliance with medical device regulations and the AI Act, including mandatory CE marking and automatic high-risk classification for devices requiring Notified Body assessment; South Korea implemented the Digital Medical Products Act (effective January 24, 2025) with specific cloud

Table 6. Certification Pathways for AI-Based Medical Devices: EU, US and South Korea

Region	Certification Pathway	Legal Basis/Article Numbers
European Union (MDR/IVDR + CE Marking + AI Act)	**MDR:** Class I: Self-declaration by manufacturer. Class IIa/IIb/III: Notified Body review required. **IVDR:** Class A: Self-declaration. Class B/C/D: Notified Body review required. **CE Marking:** All medical devices and IVDs must bear the CE mark after successful conformity assessment (MDR Art. 20, IVDR Art. 18, AI Act Art. 48). **AI Act:** Any device requiring Notified Body assessment under MDR/IVDR is automatically "high-risk" (AI Act Art. 6, Annex II) and must comply with all AI Act obligations (risk management, transparency, human oversight, etc.). **Post-market:** Surveillance required under MDR/IVDR (Art. 83–86 MDR; Art. 78–81 IVDR) and AI Act (Art. 72–73).	MDR: Art. 52, Annex VIII [8] IVDR: Art. 48, Annex VIII [7] CE Marking: MDR Art. 20, IVDR Art. 18, AI Act Art. 48 [2, 9] AI Act: Art. 6, Annex II, Art. 48 [2]
United States (FDA)	**Class I:** General controls. Most are exempt from premarket notification (510(k)). **Class II:** 510(k) premarket notification showing substantial equivalence to a predicate device. Most AI/ML-enabled SaMD are Class II. **Class III:** Premarket Approval (PMA) required for high-risk devices; extensive clinical evidence required. **AI-specific:** For adaptive AI, a Predetermined Change Control Plan (PCCP) must be submitted. All AI-enabled devices must include algorithm description, validation, and performance metrics. **Post-market:** Surveillance required for all classes; PCCPs allow some pre-authorized software updates.	FD&C Act, 21 U.S.C. §360c (Sect. 513) [26] 21 CFR Part 860 [29], 807 [27], 814 [28] FDA AI/ML Guidance (2024) [30]
South Korea (MFDS, DMPA)	**Class I:** Notification pathway; no clinical data required. **Class II:** Pre-market certification; performance data required. **Class III:** Pre-market approval; clinical validation required. **Class IV:** Pre-market approval; clinical validation and Summary Technical documentation required. **AI-specific:** Algorithm description, training/validation data, and cybersecurity documentation required. **Post-market:** Ongoing monitoring and reporting required for all classes, especially for adaptive AI and Class 4 devices. **Latest Acts:** The Digital Medical Products Act (DMPA, effective January 24, 2025) primarily regulates digital medical products, with the Medical Devices Act applying where DMPA has no corresponding provisions.	MFDS Medical Device Act, "Classification of medical devices" [20] MFDS Approval Process Overview [19] MFDS AI-Based Medical Device Guidance [18] DMPA: Digital Medical Products Act (2025) [5]

infrastructure and cybersecurity requirements. All jurisdictions require algorithm description and post-market surveillance. Table 6 provides specific legal references and article numbers to enable manufacturers to navigate regulatory pathways for AI medical device market access.

7   Discussion and Insights

Regulatory affairs professionals must navigate unprecedented complexity with EU dual compliance (MDR + AI Act) while US PCCP frameworks enable pre-authorized algorithm updates. Academic researchers and policy makers should prioritize regulatory science development for adaptive AI validation methodologies and international harmonization frameworks addressing fundamental technology governance questions. Healthcare practitioners require enhanced AI literacy training to understand system limitations, maintain clinical oversight authority, and implement appropriate patient communication strategies for AI-assisted medical decisions.

Kearney and McDermott [13] listed the main challenges faced by manufacturers when generating MDR-compliant clinical evaluation reports are determining the quantity and quality of clinical data required to generate sufficient clinical evidence and understanding the expectations of the MDR, making the EU market more challenging for medical device manufacturers. Enhanced communication with FDA represents a challenge as academics and small start-ups often do not know how or when to initiate contact and may fear sharing information about early prototype failures, while communication between and among stakeholders is identified as a critical factor for successful medical device translation [14]. Regulatory harmonization, the process of aligning regulatory requirements and standards across different jurisdictions to create consistency in how medical devices are regulated, is essential to reduce regulatory burden on manufacturers, accelerate global market access, improve patient access to innovative technologies, and enhance regulatory efficiency through shared expertise, yet significant research gaps remain in understanding optimal harmonization frameworks, addressing cultural and legal differences between jurisdictions, developing effective implementation strategies, and creating sustainable mechanisms for ongoing coordination, and this work shows limited regulatory harmonization, making further comprehensive research in this area critically important for advancing global medical device regulation. This work indicates that launching medical devices in multiple geographies requires collaborative efforts among clinicians, researchers, industry, and regulators, prompting a multi-stakeholder group to develop this review for enhancing regulatory knowledge and improving medical device translational success.

Funding Information. The authors acknowledge funding by the EU project TEF-Health. The project TEF-Health has received funding from the European Union's Digital Europe programme under grant agreement no. 101100700.

References

1. Aboy, M., Minssen, T., Vayena, E.: Navigating the EU AI act: implications for regulated digital medical products. NPJ Digit. Med. **7**(1), 237 (2024)
2. Regulation (EU) 2024/1689 on artificial intelligence (2024). https://eur-lex.europa.eu/eli/reg/2024/1689/oj/eng. Article 6, Annex III

44   K. De and A. Salehi M.

3. Busch, F., et al.: Navigating the European union artificial intelligence act for healthcare. NPJ Digit. Med. **7**(1), 210 (2024)
4. Cuadros, J.: The real-world impact of artificial intelligence on diabetic retinopathy screening in primary care. J. Diabetes Sci. Technol. **15**(3), 664–665 (2021)
5. Digital medical products act (DMPA) (2025). `https://www.law.go.kr/ëšŢëăź/ ëŤŤiğĂíĐÿiİŸëčŒiãœíŠĹëšŢ`
6. Regulation (EU) 2024/1689 on artificial intelligence (AI act), article 3 (2024). https://artificialintelligenceact.eu/article/3/
7. Regulation (EU) 2017/746 of the European parliament and of the council of 5 April 2017 on in vitro diagnostic medical devices (2017). https://eur-lex.europa.eu/legal-content/EN/TXT/?uri=CELEX:32017R0746. Annex VIII, Rules 1–7
8. Regulation (EU) 2017/745 of the European parliament and of the council of 5 April 2017 on medical devices (2017). https://eur-lex.europa.eu/legal-content/EN/TXT/?uri=CELEX:32017R0745. Annex VIII, Rules 1–13
9. European Commission: Ce marking for medical devices (2024). https://health.ec.europa.eu/medical-devices-topics-interest/reprocessing-devices/manufacturers-md_en
10. European Parliament and Council: General data protection regulation (2016). https://eur-lex.europa.eu/eli/reg/2016/679/oj/eng. Regulation (EU) 2016/679, Official Journal of the European Union, L 119, pp. 1–88
11. Future of Privacy Forum: South Korea's new AI framework act: a balancing act between innovation and regulation (2024). https://fpf.org/blog/south-koreas-new-ai-framework-act-a-balancing-act-between-innovation-and-regulation/
12. Future of Privacy Forum: Comparison table: South Korea AI framework act and EU AI act (2025). https://fpf.org/wp-content/uploads/2025/05/SK-AI-Framework-Act-Comparison-Table.pdf
13. Kearney, B., McDermott, O.: The challenges for manufacturers of the increased clinical evaluation in the European medical device regulations: a quantitative study. Ther. Innov. Regul. Sci. **57**(4), 783–796 (2023)
14. Lottes, A., et al.: Navigating the regulatory pathway for medical devices–a conversation with the FDA, clinicians, researchers, and industry experts. J. Cardiovasc. Transl. Res. **15**(5), 927–943 (2022)
15. Lyell, D., Wang, Y., Coiera, E., Magrabi, F.: More than algorithms: an analysis of safety events involving ml-enabled medical devices reported to the FDA. J. Am. Med. Inform. Assoc. **30**(7), 1227–1236 (2023)
16. Medical device act of the republic of Korea (English translation) (2023). https://elaw.klri.re.kr/eng_service/lawView.do?hseq=67025&lang=ENG
17. Ministry of Food and Drug Safety: Ministry of food and drug safety official website (2024). https://www.mfds.go.kr/eng/index.do
18. Ministry of Food and Drug Safety: MFDS AI-based medical device guidance (2025). https://www.mfds.go.kr/eng/brd/m_40/view.do?seq=72627
19. Ministry of Food and Drug Safety: MFDS approval process overview (2025). https://www.mfds.go.kr/eng/wpge/m_39/denofile.do
20. Ministry of Food and Drug Safety: MFDS medical device classification system (English) (2025). https://www.mfds.go.kr/mfds/eng/html/sub04/MFDS-DE01-10-26-L0001.jsp
21. National Assembly of the Republic of Korea: Personal information protection act (2011). https://elaw.klri.re.kr/eng_service/lawView.do?hseq=53044&lang=ENG. Act No. 10465, enacted September 30, 2011

22. National Assembly of the Republic of Korea: Basic act on the development of artificial intelligence and establishment of foundation for trust (2025). https://likms.assembly.go.kr/bill/billDetail.do?billId=PRC_R2V4H1W1T2K5M1O6E4Q9T0V7Q9S0U0
23. Onitiu, D., Wachter, S., Mittelstadt, B.: How AI challenges the medical device regulation: patient safety, benefits, and intended uses. J. Law Biosci. lsae007 (2024)
24. Tang, D., Xi, X., Li, Y., Hu, M.: Regulatory approaches towards AI medical devices: a comparative study of the united states, the EU and china. Health Policy 105260 (2025)
25. United States Congress: Health insurance portability and accountability act of 1996 (1996). https://www.hhs.gov/hipaa/for-professionals/privacy/laws-regulations/index.html. Public Law 104-191
26. United States Congress: 21 U.S. code §360c - classification of devices intended for human use (2022). https://www.govinfo.gov/content/pkg/USCODE-2022-title21/html/USCODE-2022-title21-chap9-subchapV-partA-sec360c.htm
27. U.S. Food and Drug Administration: 21 CFR part 807 - establishment registration and device listing for manufacturers and initial importers of devices (2024). https://www.ecfr.gov/current/title-21/chapter-I/subchapter-H/part-807
28. U.S. Food and Drug Administration: 21 CFR part 814 - premarket approval of medical devices (2024). https://www.ecfr.gov/current/title-21/chapter-I/subchapter-H/part-814
29. U.S. Food and Drug Administration: 21 CFR part 860 - medical device classification procedures (2024). https://www.ecfr.gov/current/title-21/chapter-I/subchapter-H/part-860
30. U.S. Food and Drug Administration: Artificial intelligence and machine learning in software as a medical device (2024). https://www.fda.gov/medical-devices/software-medical-device-samd/artificial-intelligence-and-machine-learning-software-medical-device
31. U.S. Food and Drug Administration: Classify your medical device (2024). https://www.fda.gov/medical-devices/overview-device-regulation/classify-your-medical-device
32. U.S. Food and Drug Administration: FDA digital health and artificial intelligence glossary (educational resource) (2024). https://www.fda.gov/science-research/artificial-intelligence-and-medical-products/fda-digital-health-and-artificial-intelligence-glossary-educational-resource
33. U.S. Food and Drug Administration: Predetermined change control plan for AI-enabled device software functions - final guidance (2024). https://www.fda.gov/regulatory-information/search-fda-guidance-documents/marketing-submission-recommendations-predetermined-change-control-plan-artificial-intelligence

From Data to Value: Gaps in Federated Learning Evaluation for Clinical Deployment in Medical Imaging

Beatriz Garcia Santa Cruz(✉) [ID], Jaleh Shoshtarian Malak[ID],
Hanna Cwiek-Kupczynska[ID], and Venkata Satagopam(✉) [ID]

Clinical and Translational Informatics Group, Centre for Systems Biomedicine
(LCSB), University of Luxembourg, Esch-sur-Alzette, Luxembourg
`{beatriz.garcia,jaleh.malak,hanna.cwiek,venkata.satagopam}@uni.lu`

Abstract. Federated Learning (FL) offers a promising solution to the dual challenges of data privacy and multi-institutional collaboration in medical imaging. However, despite strong benchmark performance, FL models rarely reach routine clinical deployment. We hypothesize that this "last-mile" gap stems from a misalignment between current FL evaluation-focused on technical metrics-and the priorities of value-based healthcare (VBHC). We conduct a structured gap analysis comparing current FL practices with VBHC principles and emerging regulatory frameworks. Seven critical deployment axes are identified; six show high-severity gaps, and one a medium-severity gap. Supporting literature is limited: only one axis is backed by strong evidence, three by moderate, one by weak, and two by very weak reviews. Based on these findings and insights from real-world pilots, we propose a practical roadmap to align FL development with clinical and regulatory expectations. By identifying key evidence gaps and outlining actionable next steps, this work aims to inform translational strategies and support the deployment challenges addressed by the BRIDGE Workshop.

Keywords: Federated Learning · Value-Based Healthcare · Global regulatory frameworks · Quality Management System · Trustworthy AI

1   Introduction

Federated Learning (FL) has emerged as a promising paradigm for collaborative model training without centralising sensitive patient data [1]. In medical imaging, FL is often seen as a privacy-preserving alternative that bypasses legal and logistical barriers to inter-institutional data sharing. Over the past five years, several landmark initiatives have demonstrated the technical feasibility of FL for key medical imaging tasks such as segmentation, classification, and anomaly

---

Supplementary Information The online version contains supplementary material available at https://doi.org/10.1007/978-3-032-05663-4_5.

detection. Notable examples include the FeTS Challenge (2021) for brain tumour segmentation [2], the EXAM study (2021) for COVID-19 prognosis across 20 institutions [3], and a recent peer-reviewed study on melanoma detection using dermoscopic images [4]. Yet, despite its growing popularity, the clinical deployment of FL-based models remains rare. For instance, fewer than 5% of published FL models in medical imaging have been tested in prospective clinical trials or real-world settings [5]. This gap raises important questions about the alignment between FL methods and the broader goals of health systems, particularly those rooted in Value-Based Health Care (VBHC), where clinical relevance, patient-centred outcomes, and cost-effectiveness outweigh technical performance alone [6]. In this framework, technical performance alone is insufficient; models must demonstrate impact on clinical decision-making, quality of care, patient satisfaction, and system sustainability.

This includes cost-utility analyses, longitudinal tracking of clinical benefit, and the routine use of validated patient-reported outcome measures (PROMs) and patient-reported experience measures (PREMs). Instruments such as the EQ-5D-5L and PROMIS-29 quantify health-related quality of life and enable calculation of quality-adjusted life years (QALYs), thereby anchoring economic evaluations in VBHC [7]. PREMs, exemplified by the HCAHPS survey [8] or the NHS Friends and Family Test—capture patients' perceptions of access, communication and overall care experience [9]. For example, *a model may achieve a high AUC in detecting pulmonary nodules, yet fail to improve diagnostic accuracy or workflow efficiency in practice.* Recent work advocates for moving "beyond accuracy" to include explainability, fairness, external validity, and stakeholder engagement as core dimensions of trustworthy AI [10].

Meanwhile, regulatory bodies worldwide, including the United States Food and Drug Administration (FDA) [11], Japan's Pharmaceuticals and Medical Devices Agency (PMDA) [12], the European Union Artificial Intelligence Act (EU AI Act) [13], China's National Medical Products Administration (NMPA) [14], and South Korea's Ministry of Food and Drug Safety (MFDS) [15], are imposing increasingly stringent requirements for real-world validation, continuous safety monitoring, and explainability of AI-driven medical technologies. Nevertheless, many FL studies still prioritise internal technical metrics [16], often overlooking clinical utility, interpretability, equity, and sustainability.

In this preliminary study, we first perform a gap analysis of existing reviews and meta-reviews and, in parallel, distil our own internal lessons learned; together, these insights underpin an initial roadmap to align federated learning with the demands of value-based, regulation-ready healthcare AI.

2 Gap Matrix: FL vs VBHC

To identify key misalignments between current FL practice, VBHC expectations and emerging regulatory frameworks, we conducted a structured gap analysis across **seven critical axes**: regulation/traceability, external validation, clinical co-design, equity/bias, sustainability, evaluation metrics, and clinical integration.

The axes were distilled from recurring topics in the scientific literature, international policy documents (e.g., FDA GMLP, EU AI Act) and real-world deployments reports. For each axis we compared prevailing FL practices with the corresponding VBHC or regulatory requirement and assigned a gap-severity label.

Evidence identification and grading:

1. *Literature search.* For each axis we searched PubMed, Embase, Scopus, Web of Science, and IEEE Xplore (January 2019–10 May 2025) using the query ("federated learning" OR "medical imaging AI") combined with axis-specific terms. Eligible records were systematic reviews, scoping reviews, or structured surveys that reported PRISMA-like methods. Searches were run without language filters; however, only English full-text articles were considered for inclusion. One reviewer screened titles, abstracts, and full texts, resolving borderline cases through discussion with the study team.
2. *Selection.* For this preliminary study, we retained the five highest-quality reviews per axis (n = 35).
3. *Gap-severity scoring.* For each axis we tallied the number of eligible primary studies that explicitly highlighted the existence of that gap. High—3 or more independent studies reported the gap. Medium—one or two studies reported the gap. Low—no published study reported the gap.
4. *Evidence-strength grading* Each review was evaluated with the abbreviated AMSTAR-2 checklist [17]. For every axis we counted the number of High + Moderate reviews: Strong $\geq$ 3; Moderate = 2; Weak = 1; Very Weak = 0. Gap severity was then cross-checked against this evidence level to highlight where conclusions rest on limited data. Note that "Medium" or "Low" here refers to the *quality of the supporting reviews*, not to the importance of the gap itself. A gap can be high-severity yet rest on very weak evidence, highlighting an urgent research need.

The results of the analysis are summarised in Table 1. Gap severity was determined according to the predefined rubric; decision logs of all the steps are available in Supplyment A.[1]

3   Real-World Case Snapshots

Real-world evidence shows both the promise and the pitfalls of FL. On the success side, a multi-centre cardiac-risk study raised every participating hospital's Area Under the Receiver-Operating-Characteristic curve (AUROC) by up to 8% without any data transfer, confirming that FL can lift under-performing sites while preserving privacy [18]. Likewise, the EXAM consortium trained an oxygen-demand predictor for COVID-19 across 20 institutions on six continents, achieved AUROC > 0.92 ($\approx$ 16 % better than local models) and validated it prospectively in a regulatory sandbox [3].

Conversely, a recent meta-analysis reported Dice-score drops of up to 25% whenever imaging protocols varied significantly between sites, stressing the

---

[1] https://doi.org/10.5281/zenodo.15742397.

Table 1. Structured gap analysis of FL practices against the expectations of VBHC and regulatory frameworks.

Axis	Typical FL Practice	VBHC/Regulatory Requirement	Gap Severity	Evidence Strength	Quick Interpretation
Regulation/Traceability	Heterogeneous reporting; few post-market surveillance or versioning plans.	Auditability, traceability and early regulatory engagement.	High	Strong (4)	Four high/moderate-quality reviews agree gap and severity are well-substantiated.
External Validation	Internal validation or similar datasets only; real-world prospective testing scarce.	Multicentric, longitudinal external and real-world validation.	High	Moderate (2)	Two moderate-quality reviews converge; the gap is credible but would benefit from at least one high-quality systematic review.
Clinical Co-design	Engineering-driven design; minimal structured involvement of clinicians or patients.	Stakeholder engagement from project inception.	High	Moderate (2)	Acceptable evidence base; additional high-quality qualitative or mixed-methods studies would add certainty.
Equity/Bias	Rarely reports subgroup performance; observed disparities ≥ 5 percentage points.	Explicit measurement and mitigation of demographic bias.	High	Moderate (2)	Consistent findings across reviews; guidelines for standardised fairness reporting are still lacking.
Sustainability	Carbon footprint rarely reported; distributed training infrastructure can be costly.	Cost-effective, environmentally responsible solutions.	Medium	Weak (1)	Only one moderate-quality review supports this gap; conclusions should be treated with caution.
Evaluation Metrics	Relies almost exclusively on Dice/AUC/F1; no PROMs, QALY or economic endpoints reported.	Demonstrate clinical impact and cost-effectiveness (e.g., QALY, PROMs).	High	Very Weak (0)	The gap looks plausible but is underpinned only by low-quality reviews; a rigorous systematic review is urgently needed.
Clinical Integration	Standalone prototypes with poor FHIR/HL7 interoperability; limited workflow integration.	Seamless plug-and-play integration into HIS/EHR systems.	High	Very Weak (0)	Severity is based on scant, low-quality literature; stronger empirical or review evidence is required.

still-unresolved non-Independent and Identically Distributed (non-IID) challenge [19]. Even when overall accuracy is retained, fairness gaps can persist: age- and race-dependent error rates were observed in hospital Machine Learning (ML) systems, a risk that vanilla FedAvg does not mitigate unless equity metrics are audited explicitly [20]. These mixed outcomes support our roadmap pillars on heterogeneous validation and fairness-aware auditing.

While the technical soundness of FL algorithms is no longer in doubt, a second wave of large European programmes is now translating these algorithms into day-to-day healthcare research infrastructures. Four notable examples illustrate how this transition is being operationalised across complementary layers:

IDERHA ("Integration of Heterogeneous Data and Evidence towards Regulatory and HTA Acceptance", 20232028) [21] addresses the data and analysis layer. It builds a platform aligned with the forthcoming European Health Data Space (EHDS)—the EU's legal framework for cross-border sharing and secondary use of health data—and is specifically designed to generate HTA-relevant evidence, using lung cancer as a pilot case. **Clinnova** tackles the workflow layer [22]. Its cross-border lung cancer programme integrates chest CT imaging with routine clinical data to enhance early diagnosis and risk stratification, all without moving patient data across national boundaries. **EPND** ("European Platform for Neurodegenerative Diseases", 20212026) [23] focuses on discovery and access infrastructure. It federates over 100 neurodegeneration cohorts and supports biomarker discovery and therapeutic trials by funding privacy-preserving analytics and harmonised metadata pipelines. **EUCAIM**, the flagship federation project under the European Cancer Imaging Initiative, operates at the scale-out layer [24]. It provides an ontology-driven common data model and "hyper-ontology" that already aligns more than 25 cancer imaging repositories, enabling validated federated queries in domains such as prostate and breast cancer. Together, these programmes demonstrate how investment in data quality, workflow integration, cohort harmonisation, and continental-scale federation can transform FL from a promising prototype into a regulated clinical reality. Similar momentum is visible globally. In North America, the *NIH's Bridge2AI* initiative is standardising consent and metadata for multi-modal datasets [32]. In the Asia-Pacific region, Japan's *MED-AI-Cloud* [33] and Australia's *Federated Imaging Network* [34] are developing national infrastructures to connect tertiary hospitals through privacy-preserving analytics. These converging efforts signal a global shift—from algorithmic feasibility to real-world, policy-ready deployment of federated medical imaging AI.

3.1 Lessons Learned

Experience from several large federated pilots suggests that the technical plumbing (containers, GPUs, secure aggregation) is only part of the story. Long-term success also requires strategic design and thoughtful evaluation to ensure these tools are both clinically useful and ethically defensible. Ultimately, sustained progress depends on robust data work, as outlined below.

Data-Discovery and Metadata Depth. Before any model is trained, sites must expose layered metadata that lets a prospective analyst "zoom" from catalogue-level counts to table- and field-level descriptors (coding system, temporal granularity, missingness, consent tags). Comparing these rich summaries across partners is the fastest way to forecast whether a candidate architecture will generalise, spotlight hidden selection bias and decide whether extra harmonisation effort is justified. Case studies applying the FAIR framework into their workflows inside hospitals confirm that machine-actionable metadata is what ultimately enables cross-border, privacy-preserving queries in practice [25].

Common Data Models: Necessary but not Sufficient. Mapping EHRs to the OMOP-CDM or Digital Imaging and Communications in Medicine (DICOM) remains the most scalable route [27] to interoperable analytics, but the core standard still omits whole modalities and fine-grained units. Imaging projects therefore rely on the new Medical-Imaging CDM tables [26] while community discussions highlight persistent vocabulary gaps (e.g. intraday events, genomics) and the need for site-specific unit agreements before federated code will run reproducibly. In other words, agreeing to "use OMOP" alone does not guarantee semantic alignment. Reaching agreement on project-specific harmonization protocols is an essential, though time-consuming, step for successful federation.

Data Harmonisation is Fundamental but Often Slow, Tedious, and Occasionally Infeasible. Even with a CDM in place, source data that have degraded through lossy exports, inconsistent units, or missing provenance may never be fully recovered. Budgeting sufficient time and resources for iterative ETL cycles, validation, and re-extraction is therefore critical.

Regulation, Ethics and Machine Readability. FL networks increasingly embed consent codes and data-use constraints directly in their metadata using ontologies such as GA4GH's Data-Use Ontology (DUO) [29], allowing access rules to be enforced automatically at query time and audited afterwards—an essential step toward EHDS compliance and trustworthy AI. Projects that ignore this layer risk building technically elegant yet legally unusable solutions.

Capacity-Building and Quality Culture. Even the best schema fails without people who can implement it. Initiatives like the EHDEN Academy [28] provide structured learning paths on ETL, SQL and OMOP conventions, certifying both SMEs and data partners to ensure harmonisation work is done once and done right. Our experience echoes theirs: underestimating data quality and harmonisation tasks is one of the biggest cause of cost overruns in federated roll-outs. Moreover, the lack of standardised, truly interoperable data models means every new site must repeat the same mapping and validation work from scratch, driving up both timelines and costs.

4   Discussion

FL has already demonstrated that it can raise accuracy curves and safeguard patient privacy; however, those achievements have not translated into routine care. The explanation lies less in algorithmic maturity than in a persistent misalignment between the questions FL researchers ask and the evidence clinicians, research, data scientist, bioinformaticians, payers and regulators require. Our gap matrix exposes three structural faults.

First, metric myopia: internal scores such as Dice or AUROC dominate publications, yet they are silent on cost, time-to-decision, and patient-reported benefit. *Second, siloed design*: prototypes are still built far from the day-to-day realities of radiology worklists and hospital IT, so integration costs surface late and kill momentum. *Third, evidence fragility*: most studies stop at retrospective testing, leaving regulators without prospective or longitudinal data to judge safety. Bridging these faults demands a research programme that treats clinical value and regulatory readiness as primary design constraints, not afterthoughts.

Our proposed roadmap converts those constraints into five tangible workstreams. Aligning these streams in parallel not sequentially may assist in turning FL projects into regulation-ready, value-generating clinical tools rather than polished proofs of concept.

4.1   Roadmap for Value-Aligned Federated Learning

To bridge current FL practices and the expectations of VBHC and regulatory frameworks, we propose a roadmap built around five strategic pillars (see Fig. 1).

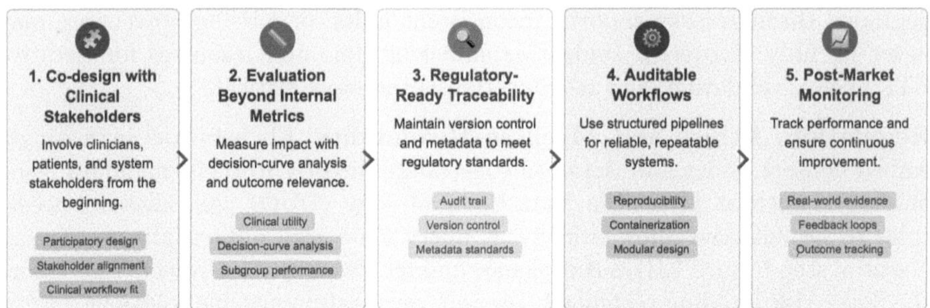

Fig. 1. Proposed roadmap to align FL with clinical and regulatory needs

These recommendations aim to guide the development of FL systems technically robust, clinically meaningful, ethically grounded, and regulation-ready.

1: Engage stakeholders from project inception: Early and sustained involvement of clinicians, patients, bio-medical-informatics and regulatory experts via co-design workshops, participatory prototyping and iterative feedback loops ensures that FL models address real clinical needs, align with workflow constraints and reflect patient priorities, fostering trust and downstream adoption.

2: Expand evaluation beyond technical metrics: FL studies should go beyond technical scores such as Dice score and AUC, with (A) patient-reported outcomes to capture perceived benefit, such as PROMs and PREMs. (B) health-economic metrics such as cost-utility and time savings; (C) workflow-impact assessments covering clinician burden and decision latency; and (D) decision-curve analysis to gauge clinical utility.

3: Validate in diverse and longitudinal settings: Robust external validation across multiple institutions, patient populations and time periods should include (A) testing in low-resource, high-variability environments; (B) longitudinal performance tracking to detect model drift; and (C) real-world-evidence collection aligned with regulatory expectations.

4: Embed equity and sustainability audits: Evaluate FL systems for impact on health equity and resource use by (A) reporting stratified performance across demographics; use equal-opportunity, demographic-parity, and subgroup-calibration metrics to identify potential disparities in model performance. (B) computing fairness metrics such as equal opportunity and demographic parity; and (C) assessing infrastructure feasibility in under-resourced settings.

5: Establish transparent and auditable workflows: To meet regulatory standards, FL pipelines must be (A) traceable, with version-controlled models, data lineage, audit logs and unit tests; (B) explainable, providing interpretable outputs and prediction rationales; and (C) monitored post-deployment through continuous performance and safety tracking. Mapping each traceability element to ISO 13485 (Quality management systems for medical devices) [30] clauses could help to strengthen regulatory alignment.

5   Limitations

The literature search was conducted by a single reviewer, which may introduce bias. Future updates will involve dual review and consensus scoring. The roadmap remains conceptual and aims to generate hypotheses. Empirical validation via pilots and regulatory sandbox trials is a logical next step. While interpretability was not the focus, it remains vital for regulatory alignment. Tools like Grad-CAM and SHAP can enhance traceability pipelines and clinician trust.

Future work should define success indicators for real-world FL—such as clinical integration time, inter-site variability, and regulatory readiness scores—to support evidence-based adoption.

6   Conclusions and Future Directions

FL in medical imaging has moved from proof-of-concept to multi-centre pilots, but marginal AUC gains no longer persuade clinicians or regulators. Future systems must demonstrate patient benefit, integrate into workflows, ensure fairness, and meet regulatory demands across their life cycle. Our gap-matrix shows that while FL methods are advancing, their evidentiary support for clinical use remains fragile. We exercised caution where evidence was weak or inconsistent. High-severity gaps—especially around sustainability and evaluation metrics—often rely on sparse literature. Addressing this requires: (i) rigorous updates of existing reviews and (ii) new, high-quality primary studies. Systematic reviews integrating FL with clinical integration, evaluation, and environmental impact are also needed to build a robust evidence base. Key lessons include: (1) Early stakeholder co-design surfaces equity and workflow issues before they become regulatory blockers; (2) Risk calibration, decision-curve analysis, and subgroup reporting better capture clinical value than internal accuracy metrics; (3) Sustainability is now a policy concern, with CO_2-equivalent reporting increasingly required [31]. To address these challenges, we distilled global guidance (FDA, EU AI Act, VBHC) into a five-pillar roadmap spanning co-design to post-market monitoring. It includes practical checkpoints (e.g., calibration reports, carbon disclosures) to help align FL systems with SaMD pathways and patient-centred value. Rather than presenting new case studies, this paper provides a cross-cutting framework to derive generalisable principles from efforts like Clinnova and EUCAIM. We aim to formalise indicators such as calibration drift, integration timelines, and regulatory readiness. This is a starting point. Future versions will build toward a systematic, consensus-driven framework. We invite collaborators—including clinical sites, research teams, and policy experts—to help refine and expand this work. Contributors to evaluation, workflow, or critique are warmly encouraged to contact the authors.

Acknowledgments. This work was supported by the IDERHA project (Innovative Health Initiative Joint Undertaking, grant No. 101112135), the EPND project (Innovative Medicines Initiative 2 Joint Undertaking, grant No. 101034344), and the Clinnova project (FNR NCER, grant No. NCER/23/16695277).

Disclosure of Interests. The authors have no competing interests to declare that are relevant to the content of this article.

References

1. McMahan, B., Moore, E., Ramage, D., Hampson, S., Arcas, B.: Communication-efficient learning of deep networks from decentralized data. Artif. Intell. Stat. (2017)
2. Pati, S., Baid, U., Zenk, M., et at.: The federated tumor segmentation (FeTS) challenge. arXiv Preprint arXiv:2105.05874 (2021)
3. Dayan, I., Roth, H., Zhong, A., et at.: Federated learning for predicting clinical outcomes in patients with COVID-19. Nat. Med. (2021)
4. Agbley, B., Li, J., Haq, A., et at.: Multimodal melanoma detection with federated learning. In: ICCWAMTIP (2021)
5. Kaissis, G., Ziller, A., Passerat-Palmbach, J., et at.: End-to-end privacy preserving deep learning on multi-institutional medical imaging. Nat. Mach. Intell. (2021)
6. Teisberg, E., Wallace, S., O'Hara, S.: Defining and implementing value-based health care: a strategic framework. Acad. Med. (2020)
7. Pan, T., Mulhern, B., Viney, R., et at.: Evidence on the relationship between PROMIS-29 and EQ-5D: a literature review. Qual. Life Res. (2022)
8. Molta, M.: Assessing the Patient Experience Evaluation Methodology: A Review of the HCAHPS Survey and Related Processes (2023)
9. Stirling, P., Jenkins, P., Clement, N., et at.: The net promoter scores with friends and family test after four hand surgery procedures. J. Hand Surg. (Eur. Vol.) (2019)
10. Rajkomar, A., Hardt, M., Howell, M., et at.: Ensuring fairness in machine learning to advance health equity. Ann. Internal Med. (2018)
11. Joshi, G., Jain, A., Araveeti, S., et at.: FDA-approved artificial intelligence and machine learning (AI/ML)-enabled medical devices: an updated landscape. Electronics (2024)
12. Pharmaceuticals and Medical Devices Agency (PMDA). Points to Consider for the Utilization of Artificial Intelligence (AI) in the Medical Field (2019). https://www.pmda.go.jp/files/000266100.pdf
13. European Commission. Proposal for a Regulation on Artificial Intelligence (AI Act) (2021). https://eur-lex.europa.eu/legal-content/EN/TXT/?uri=CELEX:52021PC0206
14. NMPA. Guiding Principles of Artificial Intelligence Medical Device Product Registration (2021). https://www.nmpa.gov.cn/xxgk/ggtg/qtggtg/20210706171636185.html
15. MFDS. Guidelines on Review and Approval of Medical Devices Utilizing Artificial Intelligence Technology (2020). https://www.mfds.go.kr/eng/index.do?nMenuCode=64
16. Sarma, K., Harmon, S., Sanford, T., et at.: Federated learning improves site performance in multicenter deep learning without data sharing. J. Am. Med. Inform. Assoc. (2021)
17. Shea, B., Reeves, B., Wells, G., et at.: AMSTAR 2: a critical appraisal tool for systematic reviews. BMJ (2017)
18. Randl, K., Lladós Armengol, N., Mondrejevski, L., Miliou, I.: Early prediction of the risk of Intensive Care Unit mortality with Deep Federated Learning. arXiv Preprint arXiv:2212.00554 (2022)

19. Crowson, M., Moukheiber, D., Arévalo, A.: A systematic review of federated learning applications for biomedical data. PLOS Digit. Health (2022)
20. Salazar, T., Araújo, H., Cano, A., Abreu, P.: A Survey on Group Fairness in Federated Learning: Challenges, Taxonomy of Solutions and Directions for Future Research. arXiv Preprint arXiv:2410.03855
21. Hussein, R., et at.: Getting ready for the European Health Data Space (EHDS): IDERHA's plan to align with the latest EHDS requirements for the secondary use of health data. Open Res. Eur. **4**, 160 (2024)
22. Alekseenko, J., et al.: Clinnova Federated Learning Proof of Concept: Key Takeaways from a Cross-Border Collaboration. arXiv Preprint arXiv:2410.02443 (2024)
23. Bose, N., Scordis, P., Vos, S., et at.: Data and sample sharing as an enabler for large-scale biomarker research – the EPND perspective. Front. Neurol. (2023)
24. EUCAIM Consortium Deliverable D5.2: The EUCAIM CDM and Hyper-Ontology for Data Interoperability (2025). https://cancerimage.eu/wp-content/uploads/2025/05/D5.2-EUCAIM-CDM-and-Hyper-Ontology.pdf
25. Wilkinson, M., et al.: The FAIR Guiding Principles for scientific data management and stewardship. Sci. Data **3**, 160018 (2016)
26. Park, C., You, S., Jeon, H., Jeong, C., Choi, J., Park, R.: Development and validation of the radiology common data model (R-CDM) for the international standardization of medical imaging data. Yonsei Med. J. **63**, S74–S83 (2022)
27. Hallinan, C., et al.: Seamless EMR data access: integrated governance, digital health and the OMOP-CDM. BMJ Health Care Inform. **31**, e100953 (2024)
28. European Health Data and Evidence Network (EHDEN) EHDEN Academy (2025). https://academy.ehden.eu
29. Cabili, M., et al.: The GA4GH data use ontology (DUO): enabling responsible and scalable data-access governance. Cell Genomics **1**, 100028 (2021)
30. International Organization for Standardization ISO 13485:2016 Medical devices – Quality management systems – Requirements for regulatory purposes. ISO Standard. (2016). https://www.iso.org/standard/59752.html
31. ISO/IEC JTC 1/SC 42 & Green Software Foundation Standards Working Group ISO/IEC 21031:2024 — Information Technology — Software Carbon Intensity (SCI) Specification. International Organization for Standardization (2024). https://sci.greensoftware.foundation/. ISO-approved standard defining the SCI sustainability metric
32. Clark, T., Caufield, H., Parker, J., Al. AI-readiness for Biomedical Data: Bridge2AI Recommendations. BioRxiv (2024). Preprint
33. Kakihara, D., Nishie, A., Machitori, A., Honda, H.: The Japan medical imaging database (J-MID). In: Epidemiologic Research on Real-World Medical Data in Japan, vol. 1, pp. 87–93 (2022)
34. Mehnert, A., et al.: Putting the trust into trusted data repositories: a federated solution for the Australian national imaging facility. Int. J. Digit. Curation **14**, 102–113 (2019)

FDA's PCCP: Opportunities and Gaps

Niklas Babendererde[1]([✉])[iD], Amin Ranem[1][iD], Moritz Fuchs[1][iD],
Camila González[2][iD], Henry John Krumb[1][iD], and Anirban Mukhopadhyay[1][iD]

[1] Technical University Darmstadt, Darmstadt, Germany
`niklas.babendererde@gris.tu-darmstadt.de`
[2] Stanford University, Stanford, USA

Abstract. The dynamic nature of medical imaging data poses a significant regulatory challenge for AI-based Software as a Medical Device (SaMD), as it requires constant adaptation. Traditionally, each of these modifications would require the SaMD to go through the complete approval process again, limiting the real-world deployment of AI-assisted SaMDs. The U.S. FDA's Predetermined Change Control Plan for Artificial Intelligence-Enabled Device Software Functions (PCCP) aims to bridge this gap. It allows, under certain conditions, a significantly simplified approval process for updated AI-enabled SaMDs. In this work, we discuss the great potential that this brings for the dynamic reality of medical imaging, but also explain three potential gaps in the current regulation. These concern an "evaluation gap" that poses a potential loophole from modified test data, an "intended use gap" that limits flexibility for unexpected and time-critical events such as a pandemic, and the "foundation model gap" that limits the applicability of this emerging technology. For each of those gaps, we present a solution to fully leverage the potential of PCCP as a regulatory framework enabling technologies that address the dynamic reality of medical imaging.

Keywords: PCCP · Continual Learning · Medical Imaging

1   Introduction

The demand for deploying Artificial Intelligence (AI) models for medical imaging is increasing, but the dynamic reality of medical image data poses a significant challenge [6,10,14,18]. Existing technical solutions such as Continual Learning [9] allow to effectively train on data that is constantly changing. However, *real-world deployment is hindered by the current state of regulations that so far does not acknowledge this potential, as most authorities require for already certified models to pass through the whole certification process again upon receiving training on additional data,* often making it impractical due to the long process that entails with an average duration of 338 d for a medium risk device [5] and high costs.

The U.S. Food & Drug Administration (FDA) has recently published the final version for the Marketing Submission Recommendations for a Predetermined Change Control Plan for Artificial Intelligence-Enabled Device Software

G. Zamzmi et al. (Eds.): MICCAI 2025, LNCS 16135, pp. 56–64, 2026.
https://doi.org/10.1007/978-3-032-05663-4_6

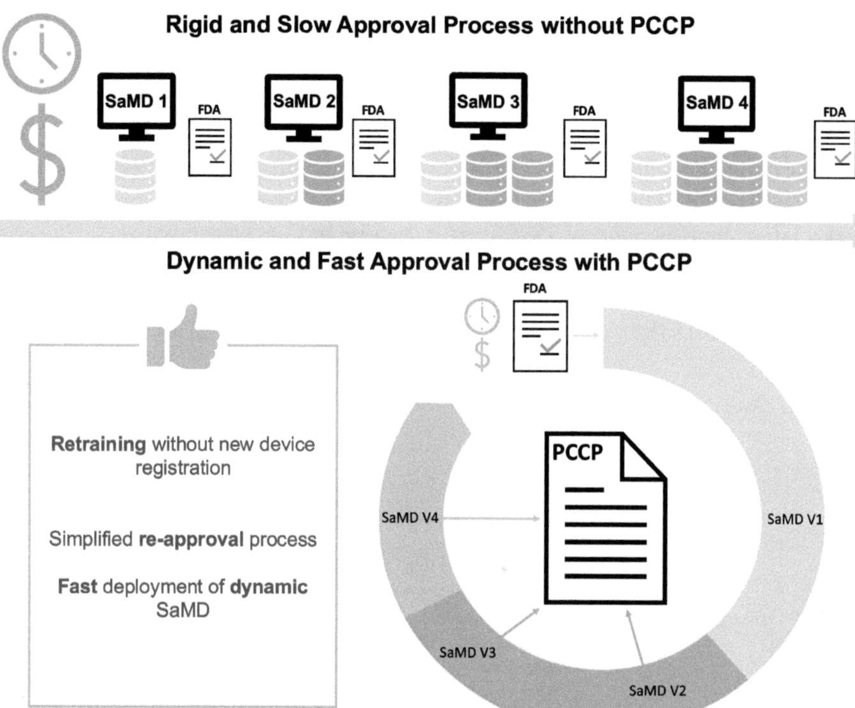

Fig. 1. *Opportunities of PCCP:* The traditional approval process for SaMDs (top) is slow and inflexible, as it requires a new marketing submission for each model update. This does not align with the dynamic reality of medical imaging, where training data constantly changes. PCCP improves the efficiency of the approval process in these dynamic scenarios

Functions (PCCP) [3] that serves as a framework for a more dynamic certification process. It explains the process of only reviewing the changes to the model that were previously announced in the marketing submission, instead of requiring it to pass through the whole certification process again.

This is a significant step towards regulatory-compliant deployment of continual learning models that are robust to the dynamic reality of medical imaging. Figure 1 gives an overview of the improvements of PCCP compared to the traditional regulatory process.

However, there are also some potential issues in the current state of PCCP that we point out in this work, such as:

1. *Evaluation Gap:* This could potentially allow getting an update of a SaMD approved despite performance degradation on the test set that was used on the initial marketing submission.
2. *Intended Use Gap:* Limitations in flexibility that hinder the potential of PCCP for time-critical adaptations, such as in the case of a pandemic.

3. *Foundation Model Gap:* Due to the strict definition of the intended use, PCCP cannot be applied for Foundation Models, even though these are an important step to improve robustness of models on dynamic medical images.

Table 1 provides an overview of these issues and possible solutions to them. To the best of our knowledge, no existing publications are addressing these technical aspects of PCCP. Therefore, in the following, we provide details on these issues in the latest final version of PCCP as it was issued on December 4, 2024.

Moreover, we highlight potential changes that would mitigate these issues and allow to fully leverage the potential of PCCP for enabling an efficient approval process for SaMD that pays justice to the dynamic reality of medical imaging.

Table 1. Overview of the issues of PCCP and their corresponding suggested solutions

Gap	Example	Solution
Evaluation Gap	Potential approval of model despite performance degradation on the earlier test set.	During marketing submission, define a performance goal for the initial test set
Intended Use Gap	Narrow intended use in urgent cases like pandemics with unknown diseases at marketing submission	Use alternative definition of intended use which defines manifestations of conditions and modalities
Foundation Model Gap	Intended use cannot be clearly defined for Foundation Models	Define performance goals for each initially defined use case and make sure to fulfill them during the evaluation of the PCCP

2   Background

The Predetermined Change Control Plan (PCCP) is a novel regulatory framework, issued by the FDA on December 4, 2024, that allows AI-based SaMDs to be updated after the initial marketing submission unlike these other existing regulations. For the approval of such updates, a PCCP consists of the following three main components:

- *Description of Modifications*: Describes the future updates, such as retraining on additional data or other improvements.
- *Modification Protocol*: Defines how these changes stated in the description of modifications should be implemented safely. This includes information such as training data details, learning methods and performance benchmark methods.
- *Impact Assessment*: Assesses how each of the proposed modifications and the corresponding implementations might affect the safety and performance by providing components such as a risk analysis, clinical performance assessment, mitigation strategies, monitoring plans and rollback strategies.

The PCCP poses great potential to improve the regulatory process for SaMDs that require constant updates during their life cycle such as models that will be trained on additional data to adapt to the dynamic reality of medical imaging that might include population or acquisition shifts or new tasks. This is an important improvement compared to the traditional process that would require a new marketing submission for all changes, potentially taking too long for time-critical applications and binding significant resources. Existing regulations from other countries' regulatory bodies for SaMDs such as those from the European Union [4], China [1] and India [2] do not allow such simplified approval processes for updated medical devices, highlighting the novelty of the FDA's approach with PCCP.

3   The Evaluation Gap

Issue: As mentioned before, PCCP poses great potential to enable a significantly simplified approval process of updated SaMDs that are trained in a offline Continual Learning process. For example, if new training data becomes available and the manufacturer is training the existing model on these additional training data, this new version of the model would have to be tested on a separate test set to confirm that the performance can be reliably achieved. Naturally, as part of the Continual Learning process, the test set would change as well compared to the initial training. However, *PCCP does not clearly define, what kind of changes are restricted for the test set.* Specifically, in section VII.B (1) (Data management practices) on page 25 it only requires providing an overview of the methods for collecting, organizing, storing, retaining and controlling the new data. A *manipulated, updated test set can potentially help to pretend a better performance of the model than it can actually provide*: For example, let us imagine a company that marks an approved SaMD capable of classifying pulmonary embolisms. This company wants to get an updated version of the model approved using PCCP. Section VII B (3) (Performance Evaluation) of PCCP on page 27 requires "AI model testing protocols comparing the newly modified device to both the original device (the version of the device without any modifications implemented) and the last modified version of the device". As visualized in Fig. 2, this potentially allows changes to the SaMD to get approved that actually lead to a performance degradation on the initial test set, potentially compromising the safety of patients.

Possible Improvements: To mitigate this risk and avoid this loophole, we suggest adding the requirement for an *additional mandatory evaluation on the initial test dataset and all following datasets from previous already approved updates.* It should be required to retain a minimum performance that needs to be defined in the marketing submission for any future updates. This allows to tolerate a certain limited performance degradation as it is normal in Continual Learning while ensuring to stay in a margin that was approved by the FDA. Specifically, we would add in Section VII B (3) (Performance Evaluation) on page 27 of PCCP that the performance evaluation not only has to be conducted

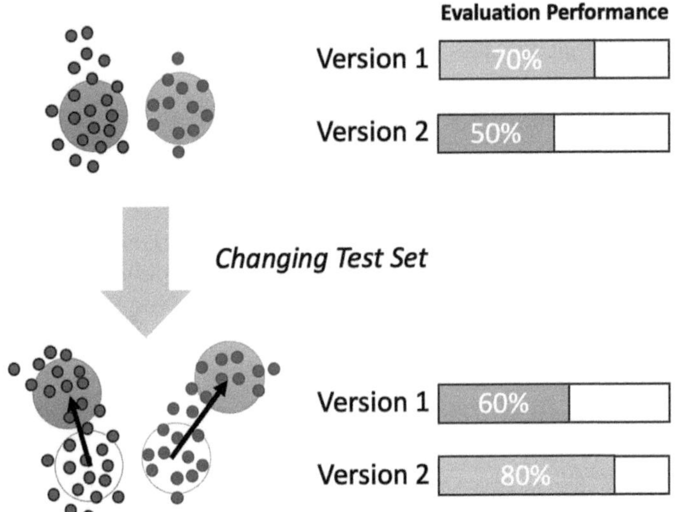

Fig. 2. *The evaluation gap:* By changing the distribution of the test data in a way that improves performance of the updated model on it, the manufacturer can create the impression that the update to the SaMD improved the performance while it could actually potentially still degrade on other test set distributions such as the distribution from the initial marketing submission

on the previous and new version of the product, but also on the previous and the potential new dataset. If the new version of the model does not retain the performance margin stated in the marketing submission on all datasets that it was previously evaluated on, its approval should be denied. This small change to the performance evaluation section of PCCP allows improving patient safety compared to the current PCCP, while still fully leveraging the potential of the significantly simplified regulatory approval process for continual model updates.

4   Intended Use Gap

Issue: Offline Continual Learning approaches that allow to adapt models to new data distributions and new tasks, have great potential to quickly and reliably adapt existing AI models to changing environments and tasks, such as induced by the occurrence of a pandemic. For example, we assume to have a SaMD for classification of pulmonary embolisms (PE) and lung tumors captured in a CT successfully registered at the FDA. When time-critical scenarios like a pandemic, such as COVID-19 occurs where doctors face the challenge of distinguishing between Ground Glass Opacities (GGO) and COVID-19 cases that shares the manifestation with these previously covered diseases, this device could potentially be a promising foundation for a new revision of the device that was continually trained on the new train set with this new task and the pandemic data distribution. Specifically, the existing model could be trained in a Continual Learning setup on a third task (COVID-19) additionally to the already approved classification of lung tumor and PE.

This would technically require minimal effort, but unfortunately PCCP Section VI C on page 22 limits such a modification as it states, "Modifications included in a PCCP must maintain the device within the device's intended use". This "intended use" is defined in Sects. 515C(a)(2) and 515C(b)(2) of the FD&C Act. Adding a new task such as COVID-19 detection would violate this requirement and also would be unknown during the initial approval process that happened before this new disease occurred for the first time. *Therefore, it would still be required to go through the whole approval process again and register this extended version of the model as a new SaMD.* This limitation is *problematic as a situation such as a pandemic requires a quick response* and the re-approval process could potentially take too long to help during the critical phase of the pandemic. Figure 3 visualizes this problem.

Possible Improvements: Even though it is not easy to have a full proof regulation for this kind of complex problem, that requires to balance the goal of preserving performance on old data while also allowing improved performance on new data or covering new tasks/diseases. A possible solution would be to *add an exception for PCCP regarding the definition of the intended use beyond the currently used definitions that are defined in Sects. 515C(a)(2) and 515C(b)(2) of the FD&C Act*: It should additionally allow defining a list of diseases and their manifestations combined with a list of modalities during the marketing submission.

To improve flexibility, it should be possible, as part of PCCP, to add new diseases that share manifestations and risk levels with the initially submitted list. For safety, the modified definition of the intended use should still require keeping the initial data modality or task type (classification, segmentation etc.). In the previously described pandemic scenario, this would allow benefiting from the simplicity of a PCCP, as the modality (lung CTs), type of task (classification) and manifestation would remain the same as in the initially approved marketing submission of the SaMD. As only the training data changed by adding a new class of COVID-19, with this suggested broader definition of the intended use, the updated SaMD would now be eligible for a PCCP instead of going through a new complete approval process. This would allow to quickly react to new changes such as a pandemic while preserving patient safety.

5   Foundation Model Gap

Issue: As stated in section V (Policy for Predetermined Change Control Plans) on page 10, the FDA demands precise specifications for the intended use of a device and generally requires a new marketing submission in case of any changes of it ("Manufacturers should evaluate the impact of modifications to their devices and must generally submit a marketing submission when device modifications affect the intended use of the device or [...]"). This makes sense for traditional

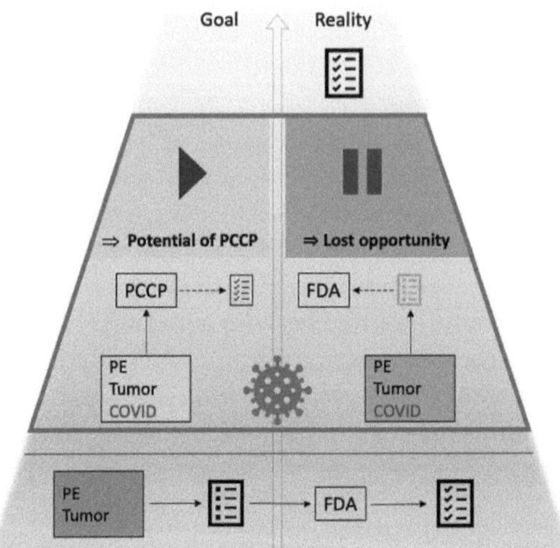

Fig. 3. *The intended use gap:* In time-critical events such as a pandemic, the PCCP could potentially accelerate the approval process by training an existing and similar FDA-approved SaMD on the new pandemic datasets. However, the current version of PCCP strictly requires preserving the device's intended use, which currently blocks PCCP to being applied in this scenario. This is a lost opportunity, as a swift approval is required during pandemics

applications and models but hinders the use of modern, emerging concepts such as Foundation Models as they are trained on highly diverse datasets of various modalities and diseases rather than for specific intended use cases. The recent fast growth of medical Foundation Models [7,12,13,17] shows the demand and importance of this technology for the field. They bring significant potential for SaMDs as they enable advanced capabilities like image interpretation and predictive analytics. Their ability to learn from vast, diverse datasets helps improve diagnostic accuracy and support clinical decision-making across a wide range of conditions. Moreover, there are already applications to deploy Foundation Models such as the Segment Anything Model (SAM) [8], Medical SAM [16] and to enable domain-incremental Continual Learning [11] with a strong potential for task-incremental learning [15].

Unfortunately, due to this wide range of conditions, modalities and data, the current definition of the intended use cannot be clearly defined in a marketing submission for a medical Foundation Model. However, the current version of the PCCP requires a clear definition of a device's intended use during marketing submission, *making it impractical to get Foundation Models approved.* This means that the *significant potential of this important trend in AI-assisted SaMDs cannot be leveraged in FDA-approved real-world applications, hindering progress in the field.*

Possible Improvements: To mitigate this limitation, we suggest broadening the definition of the intended use of SaMDs: If a group of modalities and tasks could be mentioned in the initial marketing submission combined with the information that the SaMD is based on a Foundation Model, it should be possible to evaluate the performance and safety on exactly these data and tasks. Even though, the evaluation would be complex, it would enable the deployment of limited Foundation Models, balancing the demand for safety and flexibility. If additional modalities or tasks should be added, a *PCCP must allow adding these under the condition that the updated SaMD fulfills the performance range on all the tasks from the initial evaluation as defined in the initial marketing submission.* This change would enable the safe and regulated deployment of these emerging techniques in the clinical reality.

6   Conclusion

We gave a technical overview of the PCCP framework and explained what potential it brings for training in dynamic environments with dynamically changing medical imaging data. We explained three potential issues that we see with the current version of PCCP for these dynamic applications.

The first issue concerns a potential manipulation to the advantage of the manufacturer by *modifying the test set* for the evaluation of the updated SaMD. We suggested an additional evaluation on old test data as a potential improvement to close this loophole while still reporting evaluations on updated test sets.

The second stated issue is that the definition of the "intended use" of the SaMD is *too strict to swiftly react to time-critical and unexpected events such as pandemics.* We suggested broadening the definition of the "intended use" for PCCP in a way that allows to leverage PCCP in such time-critical situations while still ensuring patients' safety.

The third and last stated issue is that the current version of PCCP is *conflicting with the important trend in AI on medical imaging that is Foundation Models*, as their intended use cannot be defined precisely enough as required by PCCP. Our suggested change to the definition of the intended use mitigates this problem.

All the proposed improvements described in this work make it possible to fully leverage the great potential that PCCP offers as a regulatory framework to support these technologies that address the dynamic reality of medical imaging.

Acknowledgements. This work has been partially funded by the Federal Ministry of Education and Research as part of the Software Campus project "FedVS4Hist" (grant 01IS23067) and as part of the project "FED-PATH" (grant 01KD2210B).

Disclosure of Interests. The authors have no competing interests to declare that are relevant to the content of this article.

References

1. China medical devices regulations 2002. https://www.gov.cn/gongbao/content/2021/content_5595920.htm, Accessed 25 June 2025
2. India medical devices rules, 2017. https://cdsco.gov.in/opencms/resources/UploadCDSCOWeb/2022/m_device/Medical%20Devices%20Rules,%202017.pdf Accessed 25 June 2025
3. Marketing submission recommendations for a predetermined change control plan for artificial intelligence-enabled device software functions. https://www.fda.gov/media/166704/download, Accessed 23 June 2025
4. Regulation (eu) 2017/745 of the european parliament and of the council of 5 april 2017 on medical devices. https://eur-lex.europa.eu/eli/reg/2017/745/oj/eng, Accessed 25 June 2025
5. Aboy, M., Crespo, C., Stern, A.: Beyond the 510 (k): the regulation of novel moderate-risk medical devices, intellectual property considerations, and innovation incentives in the fda's de novo pathway. NPJ Digital Med. **7**(1), 29 (2024)
6. Fuchs, M., et al.: Harp: unsupervised histopathology artifact restoration. In: Medical Imaging with Deep Learning, pp. 465–479. PMLR (2024)
7. He, Y., et al.: Vista3d: a unified segmentation foundation model for 3d medical imaging. In: Proceedings of the Computer Vision and Pattern Recognition Conference, pp. 20863–20873 (2025)
8. Kirillov, A., et al.: Segment anything. In: Proceedings of the IEEE/CVF International Conference on Computer Vision, pp. 4015–4026 (2023)
9. Lee, C.S., Lee, A.Y.: Clinical applications of continual learning machine learning. Lancet Digital Health **2**(6), e279–e281 (2020)
10. Raj, A., Bresler, Y., Li, B.: Improving robustness of deep-learning-based image reconstruction. In: International Conference on Machine Learning, pp. 7932–7942. PMLR (2020)
11. Ranem, A., Aflal, M.A.M., Fuchs, M., Mukhopadhyay, A.: Uncle sam: unleashing sam's potential for continual prostate mri segmentation. Med. Imaging Deep Learn. **2** (2024)
12. Sepehri, M.S., Fabian, Z., Soltanolkotabi, M., Soltanolkotabi, M.: Mediconfusion: can you trust your ai radiologist? probing the reliability of multimodal medical foundation models. arXiv preprint arXiv:2409.15477 (2024)
13. Shi, P., Qiu, J., Abaxi, S.M.D., Wei, H., Lo, F.P.W., Yuan, W.: Generalist vision foundation models for medical imaging: a case study of segment anything model on zero-shot medical segmentation. Diagnostics **13**(11), 1947 (2023)
14. Stacke, K., Eilertsen, G., Unger, J., Lundström, C.: Measuring domain shift for deep learning in histopathology. IEEE J. Biomed. Health Inform. **25**(2), 325–336 (2020)
15. Ven, G.M., Tuytelaars, T., Tolias, A.S.: Three types of incremental learning. Nat. Mach. Intell. **4**(12), 1185–1197 (2022)
16. Wu, J., et al.: Medical sam adapter: adapting segment anything model for medical image segmentation. Med. Image Anal. **102**, 103547 (2025)
17. Zhang, S., Metaxas, D.: On the challenges and perspectives of foundation models for medical image analysis. Med. Image Anal. **91**, 102996 (2024)
18. Zhang, Y., Sun, Y., Li, H., Zheng, S., Zhu, C., Yang, L.: Benchmarking the robustness of deep neural networks to common corruptions in digital pathology. In: International Conference on Medical Image Computing and Computer-Assisted Intervention. pp. 242–252. Springer Nature Switzerland (2022). https://doi.org/10.1007/978-3-031-16434-7_24

Proceedings of the Sixth MICCAI Workshop on Distributed, Collaborative and Federated Learning (DeCaF 2025)

DeCaF Preface

Deep learning (DL), the fastest-growing field within artificial intelligence (AI), continues to drive remarkable advances across science and real-world applications. There is broad consensus that the performance of DL models can be significantly enhanced by leveraging larger, more diverse datasets. However, a persistent challenge in this field is how to utilize data effectively while safeguarding user privacy. This challenge is particularly pronounced in the medical domain, where stringent privacy regulations and concerns about data ownership frequently make centralized data sharing impractical, if not impossible. In industrial applications, machine learning encounters two primary issues: accessing diverse, relevant user data to facilitate continuous model improvement and addressing privacy and security concerns associated with data usage.

The focus on developing innovative methods for acquiring, managing, and utilizing data while ensuring privacy and security has become more critical than ever. Many existing approaches rely on centralized data storage, which often places sensitive information beyond the direct control of users. This is particularly problematic in privacy-sensitive domains like healthcare, where centralized strategies can restrict model development and application. Additionally, privacy concerns extend to the core mathematical frameworks of machine learning, especially DL techniques, as models can inadvertently retain sensitive training data in their parameters. Ongoing research is actively addressing these challenges, which are intrinsically linked to distributed and collaborative learning methods.

The Sixth MICCAI Workshop on Distributed, Collaborative, and Federated Learning (DeCaF 2025) aimed to create a platform for academic and practical discussions around these pressing issues. The workshop focused on the comparative analysis, evaluation, and exploration of methodological innovations and practical solutions in machine learning, particularly in scenarios where centralized data storage is infeasible. These include situations where privacy is paramount, requiring strong guarantees about the extent and nature of private information exposed during model training, as well as environments that demand effective coordination and management of distributed nodes participating in collaborative learning tasks.

At the sixth edition of DeCaF, 10 submissions were received and underwent a rigorous evaluation process. Each submission was carefully reviewed by at least three independent experts in a double-blind review process, ensuring fairness and scientific rigor. Following this process, 9 papers were accepted for presentation. The decisions on acceptance were based on reviewer feedback, with conditional acceptances requiring authors to address significant comments to enhance the clarity and scientific validity of their work.

The continued success of the DeCaF workshop reflects the dedication of the contributors and the growing importance of distributed, collaborative, and federated learning in the MICCAI community. We extend our deepest gratitude to the authors for their valuable contributions and to the reviewers for their diligence and constructive feedback. Their efforts ensured the high quality of the presented works and the workshop's relevance to current challenges in the field.

We hope that the discussions and insights from DeCaF 2025 inspire further research, collaboration, and innovation. By addressing critical challenges in data privacy, fairness, and distributed learning, we can accelerate the application of machine learning in real-world medical imaging and healthcare settings, ensuring meaningful benefits to both academia and society at large.

October 2025

Shadi Albarqouni
Spyridon Bakas
Xiaoxiao Li
Meirui Jiang
Nicola Rieke
Holger Roth

DeCaF Organization

Workshop Chairs

Shadi Albarqouni	University Hospital Bonn, Germany
Spyridon Bakas	Indiana University, USA
Xiaoxiao Li	University of British Columbia, Canada
Meirui Jiang	Chinese University of Hong Kong, China
Nicola Rieke	NVIDIA, Germany
Holger Roth	NVIDIA, USA

Program Committee

Anabik Pal	IISER Berhampur, India
Anna Banaszak	Technical University of Munich, Germany
Chamani Shiranthika Jayakody Kankanamalage	Simon Fraser University, Canada
Di Fan	University of Southern California, USA
Hervé Delingette	Inria, France
Jonny Hancox	NVIDIA, UK
Kevinminh Ta	Yale University, USA
Lucia Innocenti	Inria, King's College London, UK
Moritz Fuchs	TU Darmstadt, Germany
Nikhil J. Dhinagar	University of Southern California, USA
Onat Dalmaz	Stanford University, USA
Shunxing Bao	Vanderbilt University, USA
Tolga Çukur	Bilkent University, Turkey
Xiangyi Yan	University of California, Irvine, USA
Zhao Wang	Chinese University of Hong Kong, China

Outreach Committee

Elodie Germani	University Hospital Bonn, Germany
Yuan Zhong	Chinese University of Hong Kong, China

Federated Fine-Tuning of SAM-Med3D for MRI-Based Dementia Classification

Kaouther Mouheb[1(✉)], Marawan Elbatel[2], Janne Papma[3], Geert Jan Biessels[4], Jurgen Claassen[5], Huub Middelkoop[6], Barbara van Munster[7], Wiesje van der Flier[8], Inez Ramakers[9], Stefan Klein[1], and Esther E. Bron[1]

[1] Department of Radiology and Nuclear Medicine, Erasmus MC, Rotterdam, The Netherlands
k.mouheb@erasmusmc.nl
[2] The Hong Kong University of Science and Technology, Sai Kung, Hong Kong SAR
[3] Department of Neurology, Erasmus MC, Rotterdam, The Netherlands
[4] Department of Neurology, UMC Utrecht, Utrecht, The Netherlands
[5] Department of Geriatrics, Radboud UMC, Nijmegen, The Netherlands
[6] Department of Neurology, Leiden UMC, Leiden, The Netherlands
[7] Department of Internal Medicine, UMC Groningen, Groningen, The Netherlands
[8] Department of Neurology, Amsterdam UMC location VUmc, Amsterdam, The Netherlands
[9] Department of Psychiatry and Psychology, Maastricht UMC, Maastricht, The Netherlands

Abstract. While foundation models (FMs) offer strong potential for AI-based dementia diagnosis, their integration into federated learning (FL) systems remains underexplored. In this benchmarking study, we systematically evaluate the impact of key design choices: classification head architecture, fine-tuning strategy, and aggregation method, on the performance and efficiency of federated FM tuning using brain MRI data. Using a large multi-cohort dataset, we find that the architecture of the classification head substantially influences performance, freezing the FM encoder achieves comparable results to full fine-tuning, and advanced aggregation methods outperform standard federated averaging. Our results offer practical insights for deploying FMs in decentralized clinical settings and highlight trade-offs that should guide future method development.

Keywords: Federated learning · Foundation models · Dementia · MRI

1 Introduction

The accurate and early diagnosis of dementia is crucial for effective intervention and care [3]. Training AI models for this task requires diverse, multi-center

---

Supplementary Information The online version contains supplementary material available at https://doi.org/10.1007/978-3-032-05663-4_7.

G. Zamzmi et al. (Eds.): MICCAI 2025, LNCS 16135, pp. 69–79, 2026.
https://doi.org/10.1007/978-3-032-05663-4_7

datasets to capture patient variability. However, centralizing such data raises significant privacy concerns [22]. Federated learning (FL) addresses this challenge by allowing collaborative training while preserving data privacy [14,17]. However, FL faces challenges such as inter-client heterogeneity, which can hinder model convergence and performance [4]. Foundation models (FMs) are large-scale models pre-trained on extensive datasets, capable of generalizing across diverse tasks. Integrating FMs into FL offers a promising approach to improve performance, as they act as powerful feature extractors, allowing efficient transfer learning for down-stream tasks [5,7]. Fine-tuning FMs in federated settings involves critical design decisions, including the selection of the classification head, fine-tuning strategy, and aggregation method. While prior research has explored some of these aspects in medical image segmentation [18] and 2D classification [2], their impact on 3D medical image classification remains unexplored.

Transfer learning from FMs have shown strong promise in medical imaging. Baharoon et al. found that DINOv2, a general-purpose 2D FM, shows high performance in various medical tasks, including MRI-based classification [5,23]. Wang et al. built SAM-Med3D, an FM trained fully on 3D medical images using a multimodal dataset of 140,000 scans [29]. In dementia research, Xue et al. built a multimodal FM for dementia diagnosis using public datasets [30], building on the SwinUNETR model [28]. The intersection of FL and FMs in medical tasks is gaining attention [16]. For instance, Rate-My-LoRA was proposed to fine-tune FMs for cardiac MRI segmentation [12]. Comparing these studies highlights key design choices that can impact model performance and efficiency. For example, Xue et al. integrated a convolutional adapter on top of Swin-UNETR, while Baharoon et al. used a simple linear layer as a classification head [5,30]. Fine-tuning methods vary, with some freezing the FM backbone [30], while others use parameter-efficient fine-tuning (PEFT) methods such as low-rank adaptation (LoRA) to reduce communication overhead [12,13]. Aggregation methods also differ, from traditional algorithms such as FedAvg [20], to more advanced methods such as Rate-My-LoRA [12]. Existing work on federated FMs mainly focuses on 2D modalities and segmentation tasks. Moreover, many use simulated federations due to limited multi-center datasets, raising concerns about their clinical relevance and viability in medical practice. Thus, the impact of the different design choices on the performance and efficiency of federated FM fine-tuning for dementia diagnosis is poorly understood, highlighting the need for a rigorous and systematic evaluations on real-world multi-center datasets.

In this work, we present a comprehensive empirical study on federated fine-tuning of a 3D FM (SAM-Med3D) for MRI-based dementia diagnosis. Our key contributions are: (i) We develop an open-source framework for evaluating federated fine-tuning of 3D FMs in medical image classification. (ii) We conduct a systematic analysis of three key design factors: classification head architecture, fine-tuning strategy, and federated aggregation technique, demonstrating their impact on diagnostic performance and efficiency. (iii) We benchmark the methods on a large dataset of 6076 samples from multiple cohorts of diverse sources, offering actionable insights into deploying federated FMs in clinical settings.

2   Materials and Method

2.1   Problem Formulation

We aim to fine-tune an FM for a classification task using FL. The training data is distributed across a number of clients N, with the i-th client having a local dataset $\mathcal{D}_i = \{(\mathbf{x}_{i,j}, y_{i,j})\}_{j=1}^{n_i}$ where $\mathbf{x}_{i,j}$ represents the input 3D scan, and $y_{i,j} \in \{1, 2, \ldots, C\}$ is the corresponding class label. The model $f(\mathbf{x}; \boldsymbol{\theta})$ comprises two main components: a pre-trained FM that serves as a feature extraction backbone $g(\mathbf{x}; \boldsymbol{\theta}_g)$ and a classification head $h(\mathbf{z}; \boldsymbol{\theta}_h)$, where $\mathbf{z} = g(\mathbf{x}; \boldsymbol{\theta}_g)$ is the feature representation. The overall model is expressed as $f(\mathbf{x}; \boldsymbol{\theta}) = h(g(\mathbf{x}; \boldsymbol{\theta}_g); \boldsymbol{\theta}_h)$, with $\boldsymbol{\theta} = \{\boldsymbol{\theta}_g, \boldsymbol{\theta}_h\}$ denoting the model parameters. In FL, the model is trained at each client. The resulting local models $f_i(\mathbf{x}; \boldsymbol{\theta}_i)$ are aggregated on the server into a global model $f(\mathbf{x}; \boldsymbol{\theta}_{\text{glob}})$, computed as a weighted average of the local models: $\theta_{\text{glob}} = \sum_{i=1}^{N} \omega_i \boldsymbol{\theta}_i$ where ω_i denotes the aggregation weight for client i, determined by the aggregation method. The global model is sent back to the clients for the next round. This process is repeated for a number of rounds R.

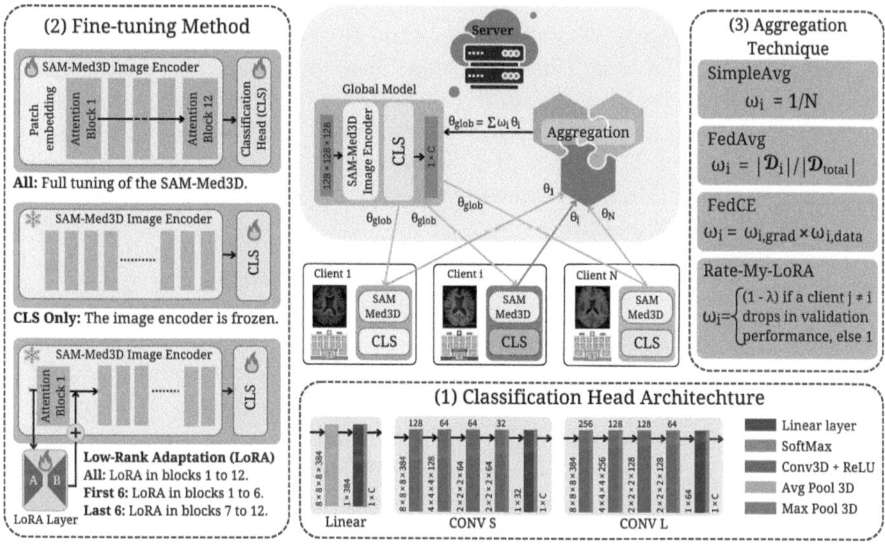

Fig. 1. The framework explores three design choices: (1) Classification Head Architecture: linear, small CNN adapter (CONV S), and large CNN adapter (CONV L); (2) Fine-tuning Method: full model tuning, classifier-only (linear probing), and LoRA with selective attention block adaptation; (3) Aggregation Strategy: including SimpleAvg, FedAvg, and the advanced methods FedCE and Rate-My-LoRA.

2.2   Evaluation Framework

We identify three design choices that can impact performance and efficiency: the classification head architecture, the fine-tuning technique, and the aggregation method. To systematically assess their impact, each element is evaluated independently under consistent conditions. SAM-Med3D's image encoder [29] is used as the backbone $g(\mathbf{x}; \boldsymbol{\theta}_g)$. This choice is motivated by the 3D nature of the model and its large medical training set. The framework is illustrated in Fig. 1.

Classification Head Architecture: The output of SAM-Med3D's encoder is 384 feature maps of shape $(8 \times 8 \times 8)$. To classify samples based on this output, we evaluate three classification head architectures: (1) *Linear:* an average pooling layer followed by a linear layer; (2) *CONV S:* a lightweight 4-layer convolutional block with 128, 64, 64, and 32 kernels, followed by a linear layer; and (3) *CONV L:* a 4-layer convolutional block with 256, 128, 128, and 64 kernels, followed by a linear layer. These architectures are selected based on prior work [5,30] to explore a trade-off between representational capacity and efficiency.

Fine-Tuning Method: We compare 3 methods: (1) *Full:* tuning all parameters in the model. (2) *CLS Only* (linear probing): freezing the backbone $g(\mathbf{x}; \boldsymbol{\theta}_g)$ and training only the classifier $h(\mathbf{z}; \boldsymbol{\theta}_h)$. (3) *LoRA:* a technique that reduces the number of parameters to be trained. Let $\boldsymbol{\theta}_g$ denote the pre-trained parameters of the backbone $g(\mathbf{x}; \boldsymbol{\theta}_g)$. Suppose a linear layer in the encoder has a weight matrix $\mathbf{W} \in \mathbb{R}^{d \times k}$. LoRA introduces a trainable low-rank update $\Delta\mathbf{W} \in \mathbb{R}^{d \times k}$ as:

$$\mathbf{W}_{\mathrm{LoRA}} = \mathbf{W} + \Delta\mathbf{W} = \mathbf{W} + \mathbf{AB}, \quad \mathbf{A} \in \mathbb{R}^{d \times r}, \quad \mathbf{B} \in \mathbb{R}^{r \times k}, \quad r \ll \min(d, k)$$

where only the weights $\mathbf{A}$ and $\mathbf{B}$ are trainable. The backbone function becomes: $g_{\mathrm{LoRA}}(\mathbf{x}) = g(\mathbf{x}; \boldsymbol{\theta}_g, \Delta\boldsymbol{\theta}_g)$, where $\Delta\boldsymbol{\theta}_g$ consists of the low-rank parameters $\{\mathbf{A}^{(l)}, \mathbf{B}^{(l)}\}_{l \in \mathcal{L}}$ for a subset of layers $\mathcal{L}$ to which LoRA is applied. We test configurations where LoRA is applied to all, the first 6, or the last 6 attention blocks of the encoder. We focus on linear probing and LoRA as they are the most commonly used PEFT methods, known for preserving pre-trained representations while reducing computational cost, making them well-suited for FL [9].

Aggregation Technique: We evaluate two traditional aggregation methods, *simple averaging*, which assigns equal weights to all clients ($\omega_i = 1/N$), and *FedAvg* which weights clients based on their dataset size ($\omega_i = |\mathcal{D}_i| / \sum_{j=1}^{N} |D_j|$). Furthermore, we explore two advanced methods: (1) *FedCE* [15]: the aggregation weight is given as $\omega_i = \omega_i^{\mathrm{grad}} \times \omega_i^{\mathrm{data}}$, where ω_i^{grad} measures the alignment of client i's gradient with those of other clients, reflecting its contribution in gradient space, and ω_i^{data} is the validation error of the model obtained by aggregating all clients excluding client i. A higher error is assumed to reflect greater contribution in the data space. (2) *Rate-My-LoRA* [12]: validation performance is monitored and higher weights are assigned to clients whose performance declines from the previous round. FedCE and Rate-My-LoRA were selected because they are designed to address client heterogeneity in 3D medical imaging, and Rate-My-LoRA specifically addresses federated fine-tuning of 3D FMs.

2.3   Implementation Details

We used Nvidia-Flare and MONAI [8,26], with training distributed over 4 H100 GPUs. MRI scans were registered to the MNI template and skull-stripped [10,27] and resized to 128^3 (SAM-Med3D's input size). Models were trained for $R = 10$ rounds with a batch size of 8, learning rate of 0.001 and the AdamW optimizer. LoRA rank was set to $r = 8$, which outperformed other tested values ($r = 4, 16$). The code is available at gitlab.com/radiology/neuro/fedmedsam_ad.

Table 1. Diagnosis distribution per client for the train, validation and test splits

Client	ADNI		NIFD		OASIS		NACC		BrainLAT		PND		Total
Label	DE	CN	DE	CN	DE	CN	DE	CN	DE	CN	DE	CN	
Training	240	516	98	74	224	28	683	1262	210	106	119	82	3642
Validation	40	86	17	12	37	5	113	211	35	18	20	13	607
Test	121	258	49	38	113	14	342	632	105	54	60	41	1827

2.4   Baselines

We compare against three baselines: (1) a 3D CNN (ResNet18) trained from scratch using FedAvg, following current FL practices for dementia diagnosis [11]; (2) centralized fine-tuning with a frozen encoder and 'CONV S' classifier; and (3) a nearest centroid classifier (NCC) using frozen encoder features, where clients share class-wise feature sums and counts. The global centroid for class c is $\mu_c = \frac{1}{n_c} \sum_{i=1}^{N} \sum_{j:y_{i,j}=c} g(\mathbf{x}_{i,j}; \boldsymbol{\theta}_g)$, with n_c the total number of samples in class c.

2.5   Datasets

We compiled a large dataset of 6,076 brain MRI scans from multiple sources reflecting a realistic and heterogeneous setting. The dataset consists of the Alzheimer's Disease Neuroimaging Initiative (ADNI) [21], a clinical cohort of the Open Access Series of Imaging Studies (OASIS-4) [19], the Neuroimaging in Frontotemporal Dementia Study (NIFD) [25], the National Alzheimer's Coordinating Center (NACC) cohort [6], the Latin American Brain Health Institute dataset (BrainLAT) [24], as well as the Health-RI Parelsnoer Neurodegenerative Diseases Biobank (PND) [1] which consists of data acquired from 8 medical centers in the Netherlands. These sources cover a wide range of dementia subtypes, geographical location and demographic variability, providing a robust benchmark for evaluating dementia diagnosis models in a federated setting. In our experiments, each cohort is treated as a client in the federation. The task is to classify dementia patients (DE) and cognitively normal (CN) individuals. Subjects without T1-weighted brain MRI scans were excluded from the analysis. Table 1 shows the label distribution per client. To illustrate inter-client variability in image appearance, we provide intensity histograms (Fig. S1, Appendix).

3   Experimental Results

We assess diagnostic performance using AUC, communication efficiency via average message size and latency, and computational efficiency via GPU memory, energy usage, and FLOPs per sample. AUC per client is reported in Table S.1. We compute 95% confidence intervals (CI) from 10,000 test-set bootstraps; non-overlapping CIs indicate statistical significance.

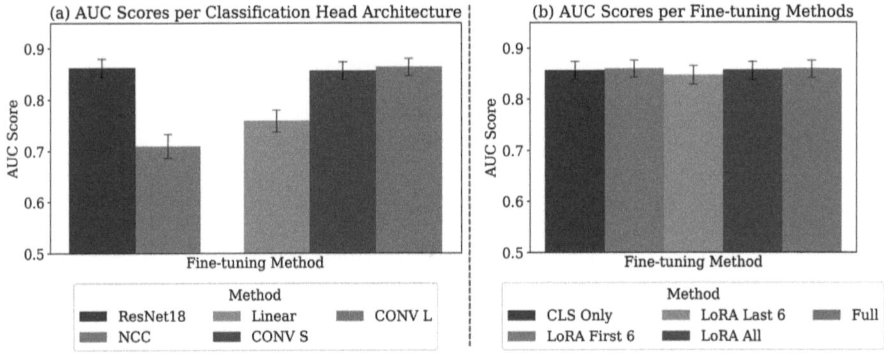

Fig. 2. (a) AUC per classification head architecture for each dataset. ResNet18 and NCC are included as a reference, (b) AUC per fine-tuning method. Error bars show the 95% CI obtained by bootstrapping on the test set.

3.1   Classification Head Architecture

In this experiment, the SAM-Med3D encoder is frozen and FedAvg is used for aggregation. Classification performance is reported in Fig. 2 (a) and efficiency metrics are reported in Table 2.

Training the classifier significantly outperforms the NCC (AUC = 0.71, 95% CI: 0.69–0.73). Both convolutional heads significantly outperform the linear classifier (AUC = 0.76, 95% CI: 0.74–0.78), with "CONV S" and "CONV L" achieving similar performance (AUC = 0.86, 95% CI: 0.84–0.87 vs. 0.86, 95% CI: 0.85–0.88), both matching ResNet18 (AUC = 0.86, 95% CI: 0.84–0.88) while using <13% of its parameters and 75% of its FLOPs. Larger heads increase message size (0.5 kB for linear vs. 36 kB for "CONV L") and latency (1.3 ms for linear vs. 3.0 ms for "CONV L"); and minimally impact computational efficiency. "CONV S" offers the best trade-off, retaining high AUC with lower communication cost.

3.2 Fine-Tuning Method

This experiment uses "CONV S" as a classifier and FedAvg for aggregation. Diagnostic performance is shown in Fig. 2 (b) and efficiency metrics in Table 2.

None of the fine-tuning methods yielded higher performance than that obtained by linear probing (AUC = 0.86, 95% CI: 0.84âĂŞ0.87). No significant differences are observed between LoRA configurations: LoRA All (AUC = 0.86, 95% CI: 0.84âĂŞ0.87), LoRA First 6 (AUC = 0.86, 95% CI: 0.84âĂŞ0.88), and LoRA Last 6 (AUC = 0.85, 95% CI: 0.83âĂŞ0.86). Full-tuning achieves a similar performance (AUC = 0.86, 95% CI: 0.84-0.88) despite the larger number of trained parameters (92M). Fine-tuning the encoder increases computational cost compared to linear probing due to higher parameter counts and gradient computations.

Table 2. Efficiency metrics for experiments on classification head (CLS) architecture and fine-tuning technique. Efficiency for CLS is assessed with the CLS-only finetuning setting, efficiency for fine-tuning techniques with the "CONV S" classification head.

Experiment	Trainable Params (p)	Message Size (kB)	Latency (ms)	GPU Mem (GB)	Energy (MJ)	FLOPs (G)
ResNet18	33M	232	6.1	44	2.5	251
NCC	0	0.5	1.2	14	0.2	184
Linear	770	0.5	1.3	14	0.4	184
CONV S	1.7M	16	1.9	14	2.9	185
CONV L	4.2M	36	3.0	14	2.9	186
All	92M + 1.7M	424	6.9	44	4.1	185
LoRA ALL	294k + 1.7M	19	2.0	40	4.0	186
LoRA First 6	147k + 1.7M	18	2.0	40	4.0	185
LoRA Last 6	147k + 1.7M	18	2.0	26	3.8	185

3.3 Federated Aggregation Technique

Figure 3 shows the performance per client for each aggregation method, alongside the results of centralized training for comparison. The aggregation weights obtained with each method per round are presented in Fig. S.2 in the Appendix.

Across the entire test set, both Rate-My-LoRA and FedCE match the performance of centralized training, with an AUC of 0.87 (95% CI: 0.86âĂŞ0.89). These methods slightly outperform FedAvg (AUC = 0.86, 95% CI: 0.84âĂŞ0.87) and significantly outperform simple averaging (AUC = 0.84, 95% CI: 0.82âĂŞ0.85). At the client level, ADNI and NACC show the highest gain with advanced aggregation methods, particularly when compared to simple averaging. Although not statistically significant, FedCE outperforms Rate-My-LoRA on PND (AUC = 0.92 vs. 0.88) and NIFD (AUC = 0.89 vs. 0.84). In particular, BrainLAT, which exhibits a slightly different intensity distribution, consistently yields lower AUCs across methods and does not benefit from advanced aggregation strategies.

4   Discussion

In this work, we implemented a framework for a systematic evaluation of federated FM fine-tuning for dementia classification using T1-weighted MRI. We investigated three key design choices and their impact on model performance and efficiency, leveraging a large dataset consisting of 6 different cohorts.

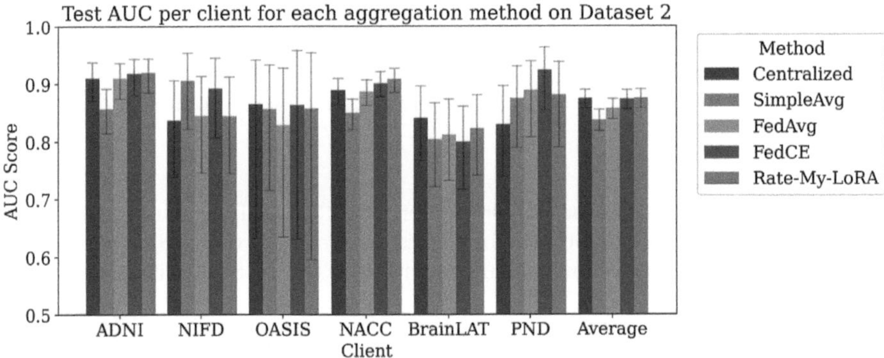

Fig. 3. Test AUC score per client with different federated aggregation methods. Error bars show the 95% CI (test set bootstrapping).

Our results show that FL enables effective fine-tuning of the SAM-Med3D segmentation model for a classification task, achieving comparable performance to conventional CNNs with higher efficiency. In addition, it approaches the performance of centralized fine-tuning, underscoring the promise of integrating FL with FMs for AI-based dementia diagnosis. Our findings indicate that the classification head architecture has a substantial impact on performance. Incorporating convolutional layers on top of SAM-Med3D enhances performance by adapting its segmentation features to the classification task. We find that fine-tuning the encoder provides no significant performance improvement over using it as a frozen backbone, highlighting the high quality of the pre-trained features. This is especially valuable in FL, as freezing the backbone greatly reduces communication overhead without compromising performance. We observe that advanced aggregation strategies improve overall diagnostic performance compared to conventional methods. However, a more detailed analysis reveals that the gain is primarily driven by clients with large datasets (e.g. NACC), while smaller clients see limited benefit. This suggests that relying solely on validation-based client weighting may be insufficient. Supporting this, we find that FedCE, which incorporates gradient information, outperforms Rate-My-LoRA, which depends exclusively on validation metrics in smaller clients. While real-world federations often involve heterogeneous hardware, we employ a homogeneous setup to minimize variability stemming from infrastructure differences. This controlled approach enables a more precise evaluation of how design choices influence efficiency.

While our study introduces a flexible framework for MRI-based dementia diagnosis with a broader applicability to other medical imaging tasks, it has a number of limitations. First, the evaluation is constrained by the scarcity of open-source 3D FMs for MRI data, limiting our experiments to SAM-Med3D and a selected set of design choices. As the field progresses and more models become available, future work will benchmark alternative FMs to determine their suitability for FL environments. Additionally, while we focus on linear probing and LoRA as the current de facto approaches in PEFT, emerging FL-specific methods could further optimize performance and communication efficiency. Exploring these techniques will be critical as FMs gain traction in FL. Finally, a deeper theoretical analysis of aggregation methods is essential. While the evaluated methods rely mostly on validation performance, integrating fairness-aware aggregation, convergence guarantees, and client-specific bias mitigation could improve both the performance and equity of the resulting models.

In essence, this work investigates federated fine-tuning of FMs within real-world, multi-source datasets, moving beyond simulated federated data to ensure clinical relevance and practical viability. By investigating foundational yet under-explored components of the federated fine-tuning paradigm, it lays the ground for broader and more in-depth future evaluations.

Acknowledgments. This project is supported by a 2022 Erasmus MC Fellowship. Esther E. Bron is recipient of TAP-dementia, a ZonMw funded project (#10510032120003). Esther E. Bron and Stefan Klein are recipients of EUCAIM, Cancer Image Europe, co-funded by the European Union under Grant Agreement 101100633. Data used in this study was partially obtained from the National Alzheimer's Coordinating Center (NACC) database. MRI imaging data are part of the SCAN initiative. The NACC database is funded by NIA/NIH Grant U24 AG072122. SCAN was funded as a U24 grant (AG067418).

Disclosure of Interests. The authors have no competing interests to declare that are relevant to the content of this article.

References

1. Aalten, P., et al.: The Dutch parelsnoer institute-neurodegenerative diseases; methods. Design Baseline Results BMC Neurol. **14**, 1–8 (2014)
2. Alkhunaizi, N., Almalik, F., Al-Refai, R., Naseer, M., Nandakumar, K.: Probing the efficacy of federated parameter-efficient fine-tuning of vision transformers for medical image classification. In: International Conference on Medical Image Computing and Computer-Assisted Intervention, pp. 236–245 (2024)
3. Alzheimer's Association: Why Get Checked? https://www.alz.org/Alzheimers-dementia/diagnosis/why-get-checked. Accessed 19 Feb 2025
4. Babar, M., Qureshi, B., Koubaa, A.: Investigating the impact of data heterogeneity on the performance of federated learning algorithms using medical imaging. PLoS ONE **19**(5), e0302539 (2024)
5. Baharoon, M., Qureshi, W., Ouyang, J., Xu, Y., Aljouie, A., Peng, W.: Towards General Purpose Vision Foundation Models for Medical Image Analysis: An Experimental Study of DINOv2 on Radiology Benchmarks (2023)

6. Beekly, D.L.: The National Alzheimer's Coordinating Center (NACC) database: an Alzheimer disease database. Alzheimer Disease Associated Disorders **18**(4), 270–277 (2004)

7. Bommasani, R., et al.: On the Opportunities and Risks of Foundation Models. arXiv:2108.07258 (2021)

8. Cardoso, M.J., et al.: MONAI: An Open-source Framework for Deep Learning in Healthcare. arXiv:2211.02701 (2022)

9. Dutt, R., Ericsson, L., Sanchez, P., Tsaftaris, S.A., Hospedales, T.: Parameter-efficient Fine-tuning for Medical Image Analysis: The Missed Opportunity. Medical Imaging with Deep Learning (2022)

10. Fischer, B., Modersitzki, J.: FLIRT: A Flexible Image Registration Toolbox. In: International Workshop on Biomedical Image Registration, pp. 261–270 (2003)

11. Guan, H., Yap, P.T., Bozoki, A., Liu, M.: Federated learning for medical image analysis: a survey. Pattern Recogn. 110424 (2024)

12. He, X., et al.: Rate-My-LoRA: efficient and adaptive federated model tuning for cardiac MRI segmentation. IEEE International Symposium on Biomedical Imaging (2025)

13. Hu, E.J., et al.: LoRA: Low–Rank Adaptation of Large Language Models. In: International Conference on Learning Representations (ICLR) (2022)

14. Huang, Y.L., Yang, H.C., Lee, C.C.: Federated learning via conditional mutual learning for Alzheimer's Disease Classification on T1w MRI. In: 2021 43rd Annual International Conference of the IEEE Engineering in Medicine & Biology Society (EMBC), pp. 2427–2432 (2021)

15. Jiang, M., et al.: Fair federated medical image segmentation via client contribution estimation. In: Proceedings of the IEEE/CVF Conference on Computer Vision and Pattern Recognition, pp. 16302–16311 (2023)

16. Jiang, Y., et al.: Privacy-Preserving Federated Foundation Model for Generalist Ultrasound Artificial Intelligence. arXiv:2411.16380 (2024)

17. Lei, B., et al.: Hybrid federated learning with brain-region attention network for multi-center Alzheimer's disease detection. Pattern Recognit. **153**, 110423 (2024)

18. Liu, Y., Luo, G., Zhu, Y.: FedFMS: exploring federated foundation models for medical image segmentation, pp. 283–293 (2024)

19. Marcus, D.S., Wang, T.H., Parker, J., Csernansky, J.G., Morris, J.C., Buckner, R.L.: Open access series of imaging studies (oasis): cross-sectional mri data in young, middle aged, nondemented, and demented older adults. J. Cogn. Neurosci. **19**(9), 1498–1507 (2007)

20. McMahan, B., Moore, E., Ramage, D., Hampson, S., y Arcas, B.A.: Communication-efficient Learning of Deep Networks From Decentralized Data. In: Artificial Intelligence and Statistics, pp. 1273–1282 (2017)

21. Mueller, S.G., et al.: The Alzheimer's disease neuroimaging initiative. Neuroimag. Clinics **15**, 869–877 (2005)

22. Murdoch, B.: Privacy and artificial intelligence: challenges for protecting health information in a new era. BMC Med. Ethics **22**, 1–5 (2021)

23. Oquab, M., et al.: Dinov2: learning robust visual features without supervision. Trans. Mach. Learn. Res. **6**, 1–25 (2025)

24. Prado, P., Medel, V., Gonzalez-Gomez, R., Sainz Ballesteros, A., et al.: The Brain-lat project, a multimodal neuroimaging dataset of neurodegeneration from under-represented backgrounds. Sci. Data **10**, 889 (2023)

25. Rosen, H.J., Boxer, A.L., Gorno-Tempini, M.L., Weiner, M.W.: Frontotemporal Lobar Degeneration Neuroimaging Initiative (FTLDNI). https://ida.loni.usc.edu/collaboration/access/appApply.jsp?project=NIFD (2010)

26. Roth, H.R., et al.: Nvidia Flare: Federated Learning From Simulation to Real-world. arXiv:2210.13291 (2022)
27. Smith, S.M.: BET: Brain Extraction Tool. FMRIB TR00SMS2b, Oxford Centre for Functional Magnetic Resonance Imaging of the Brain), Department of Clinical Neurology, Oxford University, John Radcliffe Hospital, Headington, UK p. 25 (2000)
28. Tang, Y., et al.: Self-supervised pre-training of swin transformers for 3D medical image analysis. In: Proceedings of the IEEE/CVF Conference on Computer Vision and Pattern Recognition, pp. 20730–20740 (2022)
29. Wang, H., et al.: SAM-Med3D: Towards General-purpose Segmentation Models for Volumetric Medical Images (2023)
30. Xue, C., et al.: Ai-based differential diagnosis of dementia etiologies on multimodal data. Nat. Med. **30**, 2977–2989 (2024)

Mitigating Data Exfiltration Attacks Through Layer-Wise Learning Rate Decay Fine-Tuning

Elie Thellier[(⊠)] [iD], Huiyu Li, Nicholas Ayache, and Hervé Delingette [iD]

Centre Inria d'Université Côte d'Azur, Epione Team, Sophia Antipolis, France
`elie.thellier@inria.fr`

Abstract. Data lakes enable the training of powerful machine learning models on sensitive, high-value medical datasets, but also introduce serious privacy risks due to potential leakage of protected health information. Recent studies show adversaries can exfiltrate training data by embedding latent representations into model parameters or inducing memorization via multi-task learning. These attacks disguise themselves as benign utility models while enabling reconstruction of high-fidelity medical images, posing severe privacy threats with legal and ethical implications. In this work, we propose a simple yet effective mitigation strategy that perturbs model parameters at export time through fine-tuning with a decaying layer-wise learning rate to corrupt embedded data without degrading task performance. Evaluations on DermaMNIST, ChestMNIST, and MIMIC-CXR show that our approach maintains utility task performance, effectively disrupts state-of-the-art exfiltration attacks, outperforms prior defenses, and renders exfiltrated data unusable for training. Ablations and discussions on adaptive attacks highlight challenges and future directions. Our findings offer a practical defense against data leakage in data lake-trained models and centralized federated learning.

Keywords: Data lake security · Data exfiltration mitigation

1 Introduction

To develop better AI models for medical data processing, hospitals and other data owners are creating medical data lakes [1]. These infrastructures provide controlled remote access to rare, privacy-critical data, such as dermatoscopic or x-ray images. Access to these systems is strictly regulated, as any leakage of sensitive medical information could pose a serious reputational risk for data owners and create re-identification threats for individuals [2]. Despite these safeguards, recent studies have revealed significant vulnerabilities in current defense mechanisms [3], highlighting the urgent need for effective mitigation strategies.

Defense mechanisms must consider that models trained on sensitive datasets can memorize dataset properties, intentionally or unintentionally, through

G. Zamzmi et al. (Eds.): MICCAI 2025, LNCS 16135, pp. 80–90, 2026.
https://doi.org/10.1007/978-3-032-05663-4_8

attacks like property inference [4], membership inference [5], model inversion [6], backdoor attacks [7], or simply overfitting [8]. In particular, **data exfiltration attacks** enable models to memorize and leak raw training data. Recent state-of-the-art methods such as Transpose [9] and DEC [10] highlight this risk by using neural networks as covert containers to exfiltrate data from protected environments. Transpose employs a reversible deep network to secretly memorize images while appearing to perform legitimate classification. DEC compresses target data via a pre-trained encoder, embedding it steganographically into a utility model for later extraction and reconstruction. Additionally, diffusion models have been shown to memorize and leak training data through content extraction and membership inference [11].

In response to these threats, several best practices have been proposed to protect data lakes against data theft, including differential privacy [12], model watermarking [13], and manual model inspection. However, these approaches often struggle to balance performance, robustness, and computational cost. More targeted defenses like Fine-Pruning [14] and Super-Fine-Tuning [15] address specific attacks such as backdoors, but the defense landscape remains fragmented. Broader strategies such as training on synthetic data or strong anonymization have also been explored. For example, [16] implements medical image anonymization by disentangling utility and identity in latent representations and [17] introduces identity unlearning to prevent generative models from reproducing individuals. Despite these advances, a key gap remains: to our knowledge, no prior work has specifically evaluated mitigation strategies designed for neural network-based data exfiltration attacks.

In this paper, we fill this gap by introducing a straightforward but effective method to reduce neural networks' memorization ability while keeping their performance largely intact. Our approach is based on a fine-tuning protocol that applies a decaying, layer-wise learning rate, to disrupt the early layers of the model while preserving the stability of the output layers. We evaluate our method against two state-of-the-art data exfiltration attacks, Transpose and an improved version of DEC, using several medical datasets of various resolutions. In addition, we benchmark our approach against existing mitigation baselines, design a usability test, present a detailed ablation study and explore the impact of adaptive adversaries. Those experiments show the good trade-off between privacy and accuracy that one can reach using our novel fine-tuning mitigation method. While our method is designed for post-training sanitization of models exported from centralized data lakes, a similar risk arises in centralized federated learning when local models trained on sensitive data are shared with a central server [10]. In such cases, our approach can be applied at the point of model export or aggregation to mitigate data exfiltration.

1.1 Related Mitigation Methods

This section presents fine-tuning-based defenses designed to mitigate data stealing while preserving classification utility. All baselines are then implemented with hyperparameters sourced from original papers or tuned by us.

Vanilla Fine-Tuning (Vanilla FT) retrains the full model on the utility task using original hyperparameters for 3 to 10 epochs (depending on dataset size). The goal is to adapt model weights for utility while reducing memorization: $\min_\theta \mathcal{L}_{ut}(\theta; X, y)$ starting from trained θ_0, with gradient descent updates: $\theta_{t+1} = \theta_t - \eta\nabla_\theta\mathcal{L}_{ut}(\theta_t)$, with $\eta = \eta_{training} = 1 \times 10^{-4}$. A variation of this approach is **High LR Fine-Tuning (High LR FT)**, which uses a $100 \times$ higher learning rate $(\eta = 1 \times 10^{-2})$ to escape memorization-related local minima, while optimizing for utility. Extending these elemental fine-tuning methods, **Super-Fine-Tuning [15] (Super-FT)** employs cyclical learning rates to alternate between disruption and recovery phases. The learning rate at step t follows: $\eta(t) = \eta_{\text{base}} + \left(1 - \left|2\frac{t \bmod C}{C} - 1\right|\right) \cdot (\eta_{\text{MAX}} - \eta_{\text{base}})$, where $\eta_{\text{base}} = 1 \times 10^{-4}$, C is the cycle length, and η_{MAX} is 1×10^{-1} (in phase 1) or 1×10^{-3} (in phase 2, starting after 10% of training). In contrast, **Weight Decay Fine-Tuning (WD FT)** adds L2 regularization to discourage large weights, which are often associated with memorization: $\theta_{t+1} = \theta_t - \eta\left(\nabla_\theta\mathcal{L}_{ut}(\theta_t) + \lambda\theta_t\right)$ where $\lambda = 10^{-2}$ is the weight decay coefficient.

Other techniques consist of streamlined weight modifications before a fine-tuning step. **Random Weight Perturbation (RWP)** injects Gaussian noise to parameters before fine-tuning to disrupt memorized patterns then restore task accuracy: $\theta' = \theta + \epsilon$, $\epsilon \sim \mathcal{N}(0, \sigma^2)$ where $\sigma = 10^{-2}$ controls noise magnitude. **Fine-Pruning [14]** adopts a structural approach by removing small-magnitude weights within the last convolutional layer (allowing up to 4% accuracy drop), then fine-tunes the masked model. Specifically, $\theta' = \theta \odot m$, where $m_i = 0$ if $|\theta_i| \leq \tau$ with m as a binary mask and τ the pruning threshold. Utility is recovered by optimizing over remaining weights: $\min_{\theta'} \mathcal{L}_{ut}(\theta'; X, y)$. Similarly, **Random Weight Dropout (RWD)** applies random independent binary masks to zero out weights with probability p: $\theta'_i = \theta_i \cdot z_i$, $z_i \sim \text{Bernoulli}(1 - p)$ and fine-tunes the model to restore task performance.

Finally, **Transpose Detection [9]** is a detection-only method targeting Transpose-type attacks. It optimizes a latent code to test whether the transposed model can reconstruct training-like data, success indicates memorization. While effective against Transpose attacks, it requires manual model transposition and does not provide mitigation.

2   Layer-Wise Learning Rate Decay Fine-Tuning

We introduce a novel fine-tuning mitigation approach building on strategies like LARS [18] and AutoLR [19], which assign varying learning rates across layers to enhance training. Traditional Layer-wise Learning Rate Decay, widely used in NLP and ViT, fine-tunes task-specific layers with higher rates while preserving low-level features [20].

In contrast, our Layer-Wise Learning Rate Decay Fine-Tuning (LWLRD FT) method deliberately reverses this strategy by assigning higher learning rates to early layers, where memorization tends to occur, to disrupt memorization, and lower learning rates to later layers, where task-relevant features reside, to

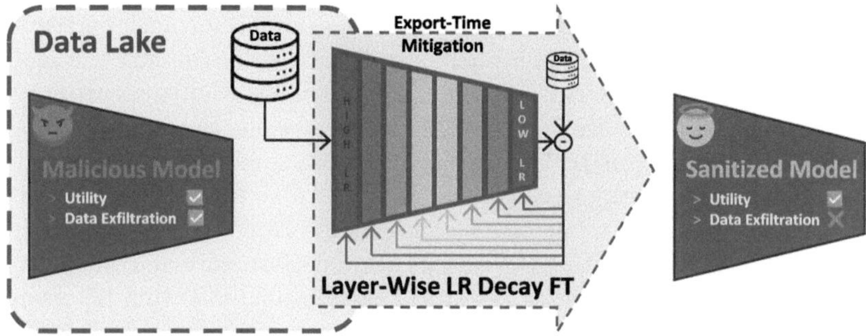

Fig. 1. Overview of our export-time mitigation. A malicious model trained on the data lake may retain both utility and private data. At export, we apply LWLRD FT using training data to disrupt early-layer memorization while preserving task performance. The sanitized model retains utility but loses reconstruction ability.

preserve their utility (see Fig. 1). The per layer learning rate η_ℓ mapping is defined as: $\eta_\ell = \eta_{\text{high}} \cdot \left(\frac{\eta_{\text{low}}}{\eta_{\text{high}}}\right)^{\frac{\ell-1}{L-1}}$ where L is the total number of layers, $\ell \in [1, L]$ is the layer index (with $\ell = 1$ at the first), $\eta_{\text{high}} = 1 \times 10^{-2}$ is the learning rate for the first layer, and $\eta_{\text{low}} = 1 \times 10^{-4}$ for the last.

LWLRD FT is especially effective against threats like Transpose and DEC, which exploit early-layer stability to reconstruct or hide training data. DEC encodes sensitive content via steganography in early-layer parameters, while Transpose models repurpose early layers as a reconstruction head because of the model inversion. By targeting updates to these early layers, LWLRD FT offers a lightweight yet effective export-time mitigation, approaching the benefits of full retraining with significantly reduced overhead and low-to-no loss in utility.

3   Experimental Setup

In our scenario (shown in Fig. 1), a data exfiltration attack produces a malicious model within the data lake capable of reconstructing sensitive medical images. To mitigate this, we apply our mitigation method during export, using only the original training data, hyperparameters and additional method-dependent settings. The resulting sanitized model is no longer able to reconstruct images.

3.1   Attacks

We focus on two prominent attacks: **Transpose** [9] and **Data Exfiltration by Compression (DEC)** [10]. For comparison, we limit the number of extracted samples to 1,000 (and 100 for Transpose on MIMIC-CXR), although, both attacks can recover more images depending on model and data size.

The Transpose attack trains a single model simultaneously on two tasks: a visible utility task and a hidden memorization task, by running the model in both directions. Yet, this malicious approach introduces implementation challenges. First, some layers are mathematically irreversible, thus not transposable, limiting the quality of memorized images. Second, the current implementation restricts the attack's utility task to classification problems only. Finally, the two-tasks learning procedure tends to restrain classification convergence in favor of memorization, thereby limiting the classification performance of Transpose models. We implement the model transposition and training following [9], using two AdamW optimizers [21] with learning rates of 1×10^{-4} for classification and 1×10^{-3} for memorization, alongside a learning rate scheduler for memorization.

The DEC attack employs a multi-task learning framework composed of a compression network and a separate utility branch, making DEC adaptable to segmentation or detection. However, vanilla DEC is limited by the output size of its HiFiC compression network and by a fragile steganography technique. To improve its reliability, we replace the compressor with an AE-GAN [16] trained on external data. The encoder converts target data into compact 512-length latent vectors in the data lake, while the utility network is trained on the classification task, using AdamW [21] at a learning rate of 1×10^{-4}, concealing the attack. Latent codes are hidden via steganography in the 16 least significant bits of the utility network's float32 parameters using a custom 16-bit format that shifts by 1, scales by 20,000, and rounds floats to integers before bit-encoding. This restricts values to the latent code range [-0.5, 2.5], matching the AE-GAN distribution, rather than the IEEE 754 float32 range, improving robustness by preventing value explosions. Finally, the model is exported, latent codes are extracted, and the AE-GAN generator decodes them to reconstruct the stolen data.

3.2   Datasets, Models, and Metrics

We evaluate our mitigation and baseline methods on three medical imaging datasets. **DermaMNIST** [22–24] is a 7-class classification task with 10,015 low-resolution (28×28) images, using a **ResNet18** [25] model, leading to a latent capacity for DEC of 21,820. While its clinical relevance is limited, DermaMNIST offers a reproducible benchmark for trend analysis and hyperparameter tuning. **ChestMNIST** [26,27] involves 14-label classification with 112,120 images of size 224×224, also using **ResNet18**. **MIMIC-CXR** [28] is a higher-resolution (512×512) 4-label classification task with 54,038 samples, using **DenseNet121** [29], with a DEC latent capacity of 14,612. These models are selected for their strong reported utility baselines [22,26,30], enabling reliable comparisons.

We evaluate mitigation methods by their effect on model utility, using average AUC and label-wise accuracy (acc) computed on the original test set. To quantify data leakage and assess the model's image reconstruction capability, we use SSIM [31], LPIPS [32] and PSNR between original training images and their stolen reconstructions. The goal is to preserve classification performance while degrading reconstruction quality. We also report mitigation duration to verify practical deployment at export. All experiments run on an H100 NVL GPU, with results averaged over multiple runs for statistical robustness.

To further evaluate privacy, we conduct a usability test simulating a practical attack scenario: an adversary reconstructs training data and is also assumed to have access to corresponding labels, then trains a new classifier from scratch on this stolen dataset. We evaluate the classifier on the original task's test set to assess whether the exfiltrated data retains enough task-relevant information to support model training, something mitigation should ideally prevent.

Table 1. Comparison of mitigation methods under the Transpose attack. Best values are bolded, second-best underlined. auc, acc and ssim are reported in %.

Method	DermaMNIST				ChestMNIST					MIMIC-CXR				
	auc	acc	ssim	psnr	auc	acc	ssim	psnr	lpips	auc	acc	ssim	psnr	lpips
No Mitigation	88.1	72.7	95.6	37.6	67.9	91.9	85.4	30.4	0.24	49.7	64.6	71.2	23.8	0.46
Vanilla FT	86.9	**71.4**	73.2	17.7	67.9	93.3	61.1	20.5	0.37	59.0	56.9	54.2	16.6	0.52
High LR FT	85.9	68.9	13.6	<u>6.3</u>	67.0	93.2	23.0	**5.0**	<u>0.72</u>	50.0	53.9	<u>30.5</u>	**4.9**	<u>0.66</u>
Super-FT	85.0	68.8	<u>12.1</u>	**5.9**	66.5	**94.7**	31.5	<u>5.3</u>	0.64	50.0	**60.9**	42.0	<u>5.0</u>	0.62
WD FT	86.8	70.9	67.3	15.9	67.9	<u>93.4</u>	59.7	20.1	0.36	59.0	56.0	54.2	16.6	0.52
RWP + FT	<u>87.1</u>	<u>71.1</u>	39.0	15.1	67.8	93.3	**20.4**	14.8	0.49	59.6	56.5	53.2	16.4	0.53
Fine-Pruning	87.0	70.9	38.1	12.4	<u>71.4</u>	**94.7**	55.1	14.5	0.44	<u>60.7</u>	53.3	49.5	14.6	0.53
RWD + FT	86.9	<u>71.1</u>	58.0	13.4	68.1	<u>93.4</u>	43.8	17.0	0.43	59.3	<u>57.0</u>	50.2	15.7	0.54
LWLRD FT	**87.8**	70.5	**11.5**	**5.9**	**74.3**	94.7	<u>20.7</u>	**5.0**	**0.74**	**66.2**	55.3	**13.3**	5.1	**0.80**

4   Results

4.1   Performance Against the Transpose Attack

Table 1 summarizes the performance of our mitigation and baselines against the Transpose attack. **LWLRD FT** achieves the strongest privacy protection (lowest SSIM and PSNR, highest LPIPS) while maintaining competitive or superior utility compared to baselines. The lower initial accuracy on ChestMNIST and MIMIC-CXR results from conflicting multi-task learning and limited convergence. The results demonstrate the effectiveness of LWLRD FT at corrupting exfiltrated images without sacrificing task performance, with mitigation time 27% longer than Vanilla FT due to the layer-wise learning rate mapping. Super-Fine-Tuning and Fine-Pruning offer reasonable defense but often reduce utility or leave higher-quality reconstructions intact; Vanilla FT is insufficient. Figure 2 visualizes the privacy-utility trade-off and includes mitigation duration, while Fig. 3 presents qualitative reconstruction examples before and after mitigation.

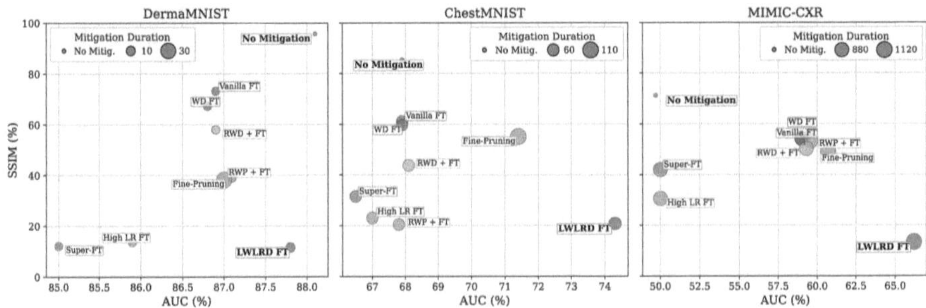

Fig. 2. Mitigation methods against the Transpose attack. Points show AUC (utility) vs. SSIM (leakage); lower-right is better. Size represents mitigation time.

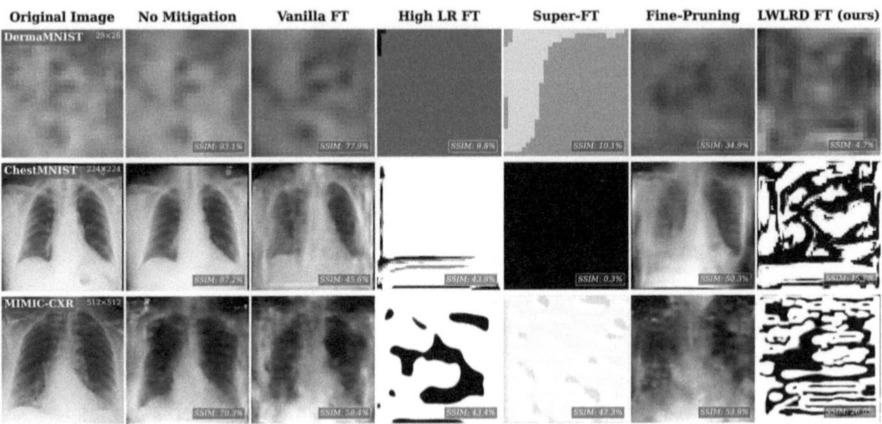

Fig. 3. Transpose reconstructions by mitigation method. Each row shows the original image (left) and mitigated reconstructions with SSIM scores.

4.2 Performance Against the DEC Attack

Figure 4 shows similar mitigation results against the DEC attack across methods, as the steganographic latent code is fragile: small bit flips or noise easily destroy the hidden data. Our adapted DEC, using a custom bit representation, reconstructs latent codes within the AE-GAN range from perturbed parameters, producing visibly distorted images and ensuring strong privacy regardless of mitigation method. Consequently, privacy metrics show minimal variation, with all methods effectively neutralizing DEC, though accuracy differs. Notably, LWLRD FT fails to recover utility on MIMIC-CXR, likely due to DenseNet121's complex dense layers being more sensitive to disruption than ResNet18's simpler structure.

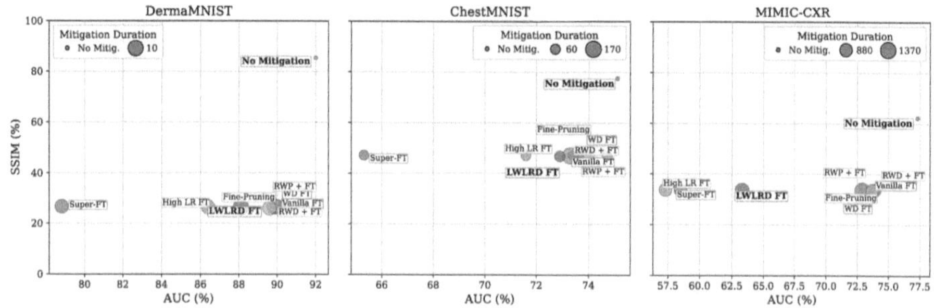

Fig. 4. Mitigation methods against the DEC attack. Points represent utility versus leakage; leakage decreases similarly across methods due to DEC's fragile steganography, while utility varies. Point size indicates mitigation duration.

4.3 Usability Test

Even when reconstructed images become visually unrecognizable after mitigation, attackers with stolen labels can sometimes train models that perform better than random guessing. Without mitigation, models trained on stolen data reach AUCs of 81.7% (DermaMNIST), 56.0% (ChestMNIST), and 50.8% (MIMIC-CXR), reflecting some retained task information, though low performance likely results from the limited amount of stolen data. With LWLRD FT, these models achieve 51.1% AUC (DermaMNIST) and below 50% (ChestMNIST, MIMIC-CXR), indicating the attacker's classifier is essentially guessing. This shows our mitigation effectively degrades the usability of stolen data for model training.

4.4 Ablation Study

We conducted an ablation study on LWLRD FT hyperparameters using the Transpose attack, examining fine-tuning duration, early-layer learning rate η_{high}, and decay strategy. Figure 5 shows that exponential decay restores classification performance faster than linear decay. Longer fine-tuning improves utility recovery but increases cost, while reconstruction is disrupted early. The learning rate $\eta_{high} = 1 \times 10^{-2}$ provides the best balance of effectiveness and stability.

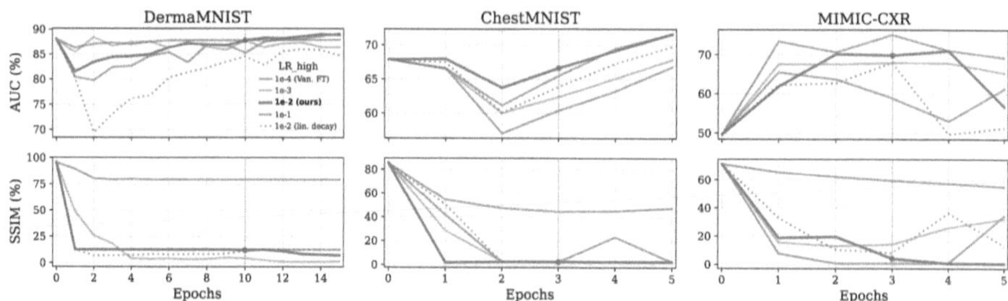

Fig. 5. LWLRD FT hyperparameter study under Transpose Attack. AUC and SSIM over epochs for varying η_{high} and decay (solid: exponential, dashed: linear).

5 Discussion and Conclusion

Our novel mitigation method disrupts current data exfiltration attacks, though adaptive techniques may improve resilience. The DEC attack produces high-fidelity reconstructions but depends on fragile steganography. Our custom float-to-bit encoding is not reversible, causing precision loss even without mitigation, which degrades latent codes into noise. More robust or error-correcting encodings could enhance recovery. As a stronger alternative to LSB steganography, we propose learned steganography, in which attackers initialize and freeze early weights with latent codes during utility training, then unfreeze later to avoid suspicion. Preliminary tests suggest it offers better image recovery and mitigation robustness, though it may be more vulnerable to random weight dropout.

To conclude, we introduced a fine-tuning strategy that perturbs early model layers during export to disrupt embedded data leakage without impacting performance. This method reduces data exfiltration success across the evaluated medical imaging datasets and shows advantages over existing mitigations. We recommend data lake owners consider this adaptive fine-tuning before model export as a practical defense against covert data theft. Similar mitigation may be applied in centralized federated learning when sharing or aggregating local models. During mitigation, performance should be monitored, with hyperparameters adjusted to preserve accuracy. Future work should extend these defenses to distributed training and address adaptive threats like learned steganography.

Acknowledgments. This work was supported by the Région PACA and France 2030 initiative through the funding of the I-Démo project PLICIA, and by the French government through the National Research Agency (ANR), under the IA Cluster projects (ANR-23-IACL-0001). Experiments in this paper were carried out using the Abaca Cluster, part of the Grid'5000 testbed, supported by a scientific interest group hosted by Inria and including CNRS, RENATER, several universities, and other organizations.

Disclosure of Interests. The authors have no competing interests to declare that are relevant to the content of this article.

References

1. Gentner, T., Neitzel, T., Schulze, J., Gerschner, F., Theissler, A.: Data lakes in healthcare: applications and benefits from the perspective of data sources and players. Proc. Comput. Sci. **225**, 1302–1311 (2023)
2. Kaissis, G.A., Makowski, M.R., Rückert, D., Braren, R.F.: Secure, privacy-preserving and federated machine learning in medical imaging. Nat. Mach. Intell. **2**(6), 305–311 (2020)
3. Gong, X., et al.: Hidden data privacy breaches in federated learning. arXiv preprint arXiv:2411.18269 (2024)
4. Wu, M., et al.: Evaluation of inference attack models for deep learning on medical data. arXiv preprint arXiv:2011.00177 (2020)
5. Xu, T., Liu, C., Zhang, K., Zhang, J.: Membership inference attacks against medical databases. In: International Conference on Neural Information Processing, pp. 15–25. Springer (2023). https://doi.org/10.1007/978-981-99-8138-0_2

6. Dibbo, S.V.: Sok: model inversion attack landscape: taxonomy, challenges, and future roadmap. In: 2023 IEEE 36th Computer Security Foundations Symposium (CSF), pp. 439–456. IEEE (2023)

7. Luzon, E., Amit, G., Weiss, R., Mirsky, Y.: Memory backdoor attacks on neural networks. arXiv preprint arXiv:2411.14516 (2024)

8. Yeom, S., Giacomelli, I., Fredrikson, M., Jha, S.: Privacy risk in machine learning: Analyzing the connection to overfitting. In: 2018 IEEE 31st Computer Security Foundations Symposium (CSF), pp. 268–282. IEEE (2018)

9. Amit, G., Levy, M., Mirsky, Y.: Transpose attack: Stealing datasets with bidirectional training. arXiv preprint arXiv:2311.07389 (2023)

10. Li, H., Ayache, N., Delingette, H.: Data stealing attack on medical images: Is it safe to export networks from data lakes? In: International Workshop on Distributed, Collaborative, and Federated Learning. pp. 28–36. Springer (2022). https://doi.org/10.1007/978-3-031-18523-6_3

11. Carlini, N., et al.: Extracting training data from diffusion models. In: 32nd USENIX Security Symposium (USENIX Security 23), pp. 5253–5270 (2023)

12. Adnan, M., Kalra, S., Cresswell, J.C., Taylor, G.W., Tizhoosh, H.R.: Federated learning and differential privacy for medical image analysis. Sci. Rep. **12**(1), 1953 (2022)

13. Giakoumaki, A., Pavlopoulos, S., Koutsouris, D.: Secure and efficient health data management through multiple watermarking on medical images. Med. Biol. Eng. Compu. **44**, 619–631 (2006)

14. Liu, K., Dolan-Gavitt, B., Garg, S.: Fine-pruning: Defending against backdooring attacks on deep neural networks. In: International Symposium on Research in Attacks, Intrusions, and Defenses, pp. 273–294. Springer (2018)

15. Sha, Z., He, X., Berrang, P., Humbert, M., Zhang, Y.: Fine-tuning is all you need to mitigate backdoor attacks. arXiv preprint arXiv:2212.09067 (2022)

16. Li, H., Ayache, N., Delingette, H.: Generative medical image anonymization based on latent code projection and optimization. In: 2025 IEEE 22nd International Symposium on Biomedical Imaging (ISBI), pp. 1–4. IEEE (2025)

17. Seo, J., Lee, S.H., Lee, T.Y., Moon, S., Park, G.M.: Generative unlearning for any identity. In: Proceedings of the IEEE/CVF Conference on Computer Vision and Pattern Recognition, pp. 9151–9161 (2024)

18. Ginsburg, B., Gitman, I., You, Y.: Large batch training of convolutional networks with layer-wise adaptive rate scaling. In: ICLR 2018 Conference (2018)

19. Ro, Y., Choi, J.Y.: Autolr: layer-wise pruning and auto-tuning of learning rates in fine-tuning of deep networks. In: Proceedings of the AAAI Conference on Artificial Intelligence (AAAI 2021), pp. 2486–2494 (2021)

20. Dong, X., Bao, J., et al.: Clip itself is a strong fine-tuner: Achieving 85.7% and 88.0% top-1 accuracy with vit-b and vit-l on imagenet. arXiv preprint arXiv:2212.06138 (2022)

21. Loshchilov, I., Hutter, F.: Decoupled weight decay regularization. In: International Conference on Learning Representations (ICLR) (2019)

22. Yang, J., Shi, R., Ni, B.: Medmnist classification decathlon: a lightweight automl benchmark for medical image analysis. In: IEEE 18th International Symposium on Biomedical Imaging (ISBI), pp. 191–195 (2021)

23. Tschandl, P., Rosendahl, C., Kittler, H.: The ham10000 dataset, a large collection of multi-source dermatoscopic images of common pigmented skin lesions. Sci. Data, 180161 (2018)

24. Codella, N., et al.: Skin lesion analysis toward melanoma detection 2018: A challenge hosted by the international skin imaging collaboration (isic). arXiv preprint arXiv:1902.03368 (2019)
25. He, K., Zhang, X., Ren, S., Sun, J.: Deep residual learning for image recognition. In: Proceedings of the IEEE Conference on Computer Vision and Pattern Recognition (CVPR), pp. 770–778 (2016)
26. Yang, J., et al.: Medmnist v2-a large-scale lightweight benchmark for 2d and 3d biomedical image classification. Scientific Data **10**(1), 41 (2023)
27. Wang, X., Peng, Y., et al.: Chestx-ray8: hospital-scale chest x-ray database and benchmarks on weakly-supervised classification and localization of common thorax diseases. In: CVPR, pp. 3462–3471 (2017)
28. Johnson, A.E., et al.: Mimic-cxr-jpg, a large publicly available database of labeled chest radiographs. arXiv preprint arXiv:1901.07042 (2019)
29. Huang, G., Liu, Z., Van Der Maaten, L., Weinberger, K.Q.: Densely connected convolutional networks. In: Proceedings of the IEEE Conference on Computer Vision and Pattern Recognition (CVPR), pp. 4700–4708 (2017)
30. Li, H.: Data exfiltration and anonymization of medical images based on generative models. Ph.D. thesis, Université Côte d'Azur (2024)
31. Wang, Z., Bovik, A.C., Sheikh, H.R., Simoncelli, E.P.: Image quality assessment: from error visibility to structural similarity. IEEE Trans. Image Process. **13**(4), 600–612 (2004)
32. Zhang, R., Isola, P., Efros, A.A., Shechtman, E., Wang, O.: The unreasonable effectiveness of deep features as a perceptual metric. In: Proceedings of the IEEE Conference on Computer Vision and Pattern Recognition, pp. 586–595 (2018)

Dynamic Hyperparameter Adjustment via Reinforcement Learning in Asynchronous Federated Learning for Medical Image Analysis

Shuang Gu[1], Zhenyu Tang[1], Song Qiu[2], and Xiaosong Wang[1]($\boxtimes$)

[1] Shanghai AI Laboratory, Shanghai, China
`gushuang@pjlab.org.cn, wangxiaosong@pjlab.org.cn`
[2] East China Normal University, Shanghai, China

Abstract. Federated learning is gaining prominence in the healthcare domain due to its ability to protect data privacy and facilitate collaboration among multiple institutions. However, the heterogeneity among clients poses a significant challenge due to differences in client data and computing facilities. Conventional synchronized federated learning, e.g., FedAvg, often leads to inefficient system utilization in training. Thus, Asynchronous Federated Learning (AFL) paradigms have been proposed to address the straggler problem. However, it also introduces the problem of model staleness, leading to significant accuracy drops. Moreover, in the context of heterogeneous client data, fixed hyperparameters (e.g., learning rate, aggregation weights, and local epochs) can detrimentally impact the convergence speed and overall model performance. To tackle these challenges, we propose a novel asynchronous federated learning architecture, AFedRL, that employs reinforcement learning to dynamically adjust hyperparameters in AFL, accelerating the convergence of the global model. It aggregates client models as soon as any client finishes its local training, while the REINFORCE algorithm is utilized to adjust hyperparameters for each client iteratively, with a reward function that considers the relative reduction in the loss of the global models across iterations and evaluates aleatoric uncertainty in the local model and epistemic uncertainty in the global model. Experiments on two multi-center medical image segmentation tasks demonstrate that AFedRL achieves competitive accuracy while significantly reducing training time. This showcases its effectiveness and practical advantages for real-world applications. The code is available at https://github.com/shuanggu0815/afedrl.

Keywords: Federated learning · Reinforcement learning · Hyperparameter optimization

1 Introduction

Recent advancements in deep learning (DL) have significantly impacted medical image analysis. However, as data scale increases, particularly in multi-center studies, privacy and security concerns have become prominent [18]. Federated Learning (FL) has emerged as a promising solution, allowing the training of global models while keeping data localized, thus enabling collaboration across institutions without compromising privacy [28]. This scheme is extremely important and flexible to enable various medical institutions to collaborate, ultimately improving the accuracy and generalization ability of medical image analysis [22].

Despite the advantages of FL, several challenges remain in its conventional scheme. First, synchronous federated learning (SFL) encounters inefficiencies due to the heterogeneity of distributed devices, which vary in factors such as network conditions, energy resources, and computational power. The "straggler problem" arises because the global update speed is determined by the slowest participating device [8], causing faster devices to remain idle while waiting for slower ones to finish local training, resulting in a loss of efficiency. Asynchronous Federated Learning (AFL) [27] addresses this by allowing updates without waiting for slower devices, but it can lead to accuracy loss due to outdated model updates [30] and non-IID data. Moreover, AFL's convergence may be hindered without proper timeliness control [25], making it crucial to determine correct aggregation weights between local and global models.

Second, in real-world scenarios, the data collected across different hospitals often exhibits heterogeneity due to varying equipment and other factors. This heterogeneity can largely degrade model performance, as evidenced by the widely adopted optimization method, FedAvg [14], which often suffers from suboptimal performance due to data variability. To mitigate this, FedProx [8] introduces regularization to manage model divergence, but its fixed aggregation weights may overlook certain specialized clients' contributions. In contrast, FedCE [6] dynamically adjusts the aggregation weights based on client contribution estimation. Furthermore, Auto-FedRL [4] not only dynamically adjusts aggregation weights but also utilizes reinforcement learning to optimize multiple hyperparameters, such as local training epochs and learning rates. While the aforementioned methods focus primarily on synchronous federated learning, in asynchronous settings, FedASMU [12] improves both the accuracy and efficiency of the system by focusing on dynamically computing whether to perform the aggregation and associate weights, which also largely increases the communication burden.

To enhance system efficiency while preserving global model performance, this paper introduces a novel AFL framework, AFedRL, which employs a policy-based reinforcement learning (RL) algorithm to dynamically optimize hyperparameters, including aggregation weights, learning rates, and local training epochs. Additional parameters could also be dynamically adjusted, but here we focus on these three important ones for the demonstration. This method allows for dynamic adjustments without prior system knowledge [20]. Specifically, each client is endowed with its own RL agent and adjusts the hyperparameters based on a reward function consisting of two components. The first represents the relative loss reduction of the global model on the client's dataset. The second quantifies the representation inconsistency of the global model and local model.

Our main contributions in this work are summarized as follows: (1) We propose AFedRL, an asynchronous federated learning framework that dynamically adjusts hyperparameters to improve system efficiency and flexibility in heterogeneous environments. (2) We introduce a novel reward function to optimize hyperparameters, improving global model performance in the presence of data heterogeneity. (3) Extensive experiments on two medical image segmentation benchmarks illustrate that AFedRL matches SFL baselines in performance while offering a significant reduction in training time.

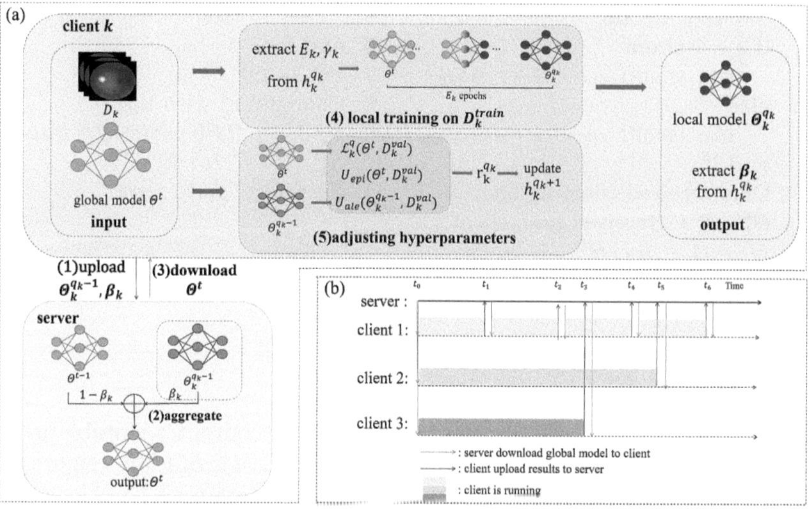

Fig. 1. (a) The schematics of AFedRL at round t. (b) AFL diagram with 3 clients.

2 Methods

In this section, we provide a comprehensive overview of the proposed AFedRL, which consists of two main components: (1) the framework of AFL presented in Sect. 2.1 and (2) the RL-based method for hyperparameter adjustment discussed in Sect. 2.2. The full algorithm is shown in Algorithm 1. The architecture details are shown in Fig. 1.

2.1 Aysnchronous System Architecture

In AFL, a central server coordinates K participating clients and the training process can be broken down into the following steps (as shown in Algorithm 1):

In the initial stage, the central server distributes the global model Θ^1 to all participating K clients, activating them to start local training. Upon receiving

---

Algorithm 1. Our proposed method AFedRL

<table>
<tr><td valign="top">

AFedRL - sever:
Input: communication rounds T,
number of clients K, initial global model
Θ^1, initial hyperparameter combinations
$\{h_i^1\}_{i=1}^K$, initial hyperparameter
distributions $\{\Phi_i^1\}_{i=1}^K$.
Output: final global model Θ.

1: Initialize server model w_0
2: **for** $t = 1, \cdots, T$ **do**
3:    **if** $t = 1$ **then**
4:        Run AFedRL-client on all clients
5:    **else**
6:        Run AFedRL-client on $client_{target}$
7:    **end if**
8:    Once received client update:
9:    $\Theta_k^{q_k}, \beta_k \leftarrow$ received from client k
10:   $\Theta^t = (1 - \beta_k) \cdot \Theta^{t-1} + \beta_k \cdot \Theta_k^{q_k}$
11:   $client_{target} \leftarrow$ client k
12: **end for**

</td><td valign="top">

AFedRL - client:
Input: global model Θ^t.
Output: local model $\Theta_k^{q_k}$, aggregation
weight β_k.

1: $\Theta_k^{q_k,0} \leftarrow \Theta^t$
2: Unpack E_k, γ_k, β_k from $h_k^{q_k}$
3: **for** $p = 1$ **to** E_k **do**
4:    Compute the gradients g
5:    $\Theta_k^{q_k,p} = \Theta_k^{q_k,p-1} - \gamma_k \cdot g \cdot \Theta_k^{q_k,p-1}$
6: **end for**
7: $\Theta_k^{q_k} \leftarrow \Theta_k^{q_k,E_k}$
8: Compute r_k^q with Eq. 7
9: $\Phi_k^{q_k+1} \leftarrow HPUpdate(r_k^{q_k})$ with Eq. 8
10: $h_k^{q_k+1} \sim P(\mathcal{H} \mid \Phi_k^{q_k+1})$
11: Send $\Theta_k^{q_k}$, β_k to server

</td></tr>
</table>

---

the global model Θ^t at global round t, each client computes suitable hyperparameters (local training epochs E_k, learning rate γ_k, aggregation weight β_k) and performs local training using the chosen hyperparameters.

Once the kth client completes its local training, it uploads the local model Θ_k and the aggregation weight β_k to the server asynchronously, *meaning that each client can upload its results as soon as its local training is finished*. When the server receives the model and aggregation weight from the client, it will perform model aggregation according to the following formula:

$$\Theta^{t+1} = (1 - \beta_k) \cdot \Theta^t + \beta_k \cdot \Theta_k^t \tag{1}$$

where Θ^t is the global model at global round t, Θ_k^t is the local model uploaded by client k, and β_k is the aggregation weight of client k.

After aggregation, the server sends the updated global model back to client k for the next round of local training.

2.2 RL-Based Hyperparameter Adjustment for AFL

We propose an online RL-based method for adjusting the hyperparameters in AFL. In this work, the search space consists of the local training epochs E_k, learning rate γ_k and aggregation weight β_k. At each local round q_k for client k, a set of hyperparameters $\{E_k, \gamma_k, \beta_k\} \in h_k^{q_k}$ is sampled from the distribution $P(\mathcal{H}|\Phi_k^{q_k})$. The goal of the RL agent at each round is to maximize the cumulative reward, which can be formulated as:

$$J_k^{q_k} = \mathbb{E}_{P(h_k^{q_k}|\Phi_k^{q_k})}[r_k^{q_k}].\tag{2}$$

The reward function design is crucial in guiding the learning process. In Auto-FedRL [4], the reward was based solely on relative loss reduction. To address the "straggler problem" and enhance generalization, we incorporate both the epistemic uncertainty of the global model and the aleatoric uncertainty of local models into the reward function, inspired by [2]. These uncertainties are quantified using a Dirichlet-based evidential model, where the classification prediction ρ is treated as a random variable following a Dirichlet distribution. For the input image x, the expected probability of class c is:

$$P(y = c|x, \theta) = \int p(y = c|\rho) \cdot p(\rho|x, \theta)d\rho = \frac{\alpha_c}{\sum_{j=1}^{C} \alpha_j} = \bar{p}_c,\tag{3}$$

where θ is the parameter of the model, and α is the Dirichlet parameter. We can use the Shannon entropy $H(\cdot)$ of the expected probability $P(y|x, \theta)$ [21] to calculate the uncertainty of predicting a sample x. The total uncertainty $U_{\text{total}}(x, \theta)$ can be decomposed into two components: epistemic uncertainty $U_{\text{epi}}(x, \theta)$ and aleatoric uncertainty $U_{\text{ale}}(x, \theta)$.

$$U_{\text{total}}(x, \theta) = H[P(y|x, \theta)]] = U_{\text{epi}}(x, \theta) + U_{\text{ale}}(x, \theta),\tag{4}$$

$$U_{\text{ale}}(x, \theta) = \mathbb{E}_{p(\rho|x,\theta)}[H[P(y|\rho)]] = \sum_{c=1}^{C} \bar{p}_c \left[\psi\left(\sum_{j=1}^{C} \alpha_j + 1\right) - \psi(\alpha_c + 1)\right],\tag{5}$$

$$U_{\text{epi}}(x, \theta) = \sum_{c=1}^{C} \bar{p}_c \left[\psi(\alpha_c + 1) - \psi\left(\sum_{j=1}^{C} \alpha_j + 1\right)\right] + \sum_{c=1}^{C} \bar{p}_c \log \bar{p}_c,\tag{6}$$

where $\psi(\cdot)$ is the digamma function. Aleatoric uncertainty captures the inherent complexity or ambiguity within the local data, while epistemic uncertainty reflects the uncertainty associated with domain shifts between the global model and local data. Consequently, a lower aleatoric uncertainty in the local model indicates greater feasibility, whereas a lower epistemic uncertainty in the global model suggests better generalization across all clients.

Finally, the reward $r_k^{q_k}$ for the RL agent at round q_k on client k is as follows:

$$r_k^{q_k} = \frac{(L_k^{q_k} \times (U_{\text{ale},k}^{q_k} + U_{\text{epi},k}^{q_k})) - (L_k^{q_k+1} \times (U_{\text{ale},k}^{q_k+1} + U_{\text{epi},k}^{q_k+1}))}{L_k^{q_k} \times (U_{\text{ale},k}^{q_k} + U_{\text{epi},k}^{q_k})}.\tag{7}$$

We update the hyperparameter distribution $\Phi_k^{q_k}$ at each round q_k. To dynamically adjust parameters in each round, we modify the REINFORCE [26] method by utilizing a moving average window to smooth the rewards over the most recent rounds rather than relying on the cumulative reward across all rounds. The update equation for $\Phi_k^{q_k}$ is:

$$\Phi_k^{q_k+1} \leftarrow \Phi_k^{q_k} - \gamma_h \sum_{\tau=q_k-Z}^{q_k} (r_k^\tau - \hat{r}_k^{q_k})\nabla_{\Phi_k^\tau} \log(P(h_k^\tau|\Phi_k^\tau)), \tag{8}$$

$$\hat{r}_k^{q_k} = \frac{1}{Z+1} \sum_{\tau=q_k-Z}^{q_k} r_k^\tau,$$

where Z is the window size, γ_h is the RL agent's learning rate.

3   Experiment

Datasets and Evaluation Metrics. We evaluate our method on two medical image segmentation datasets: the prostate MRI dataset from six institutions [7, 11,13,16] and the retinal fundus dataset from six sources [1,3,17,23]. Each source is treated as an individual client, and the data is split into 50% training, 25% validation, and 25% testing. We use the Dice coefficient to assess segmentation performance and track convergence time to evaluate efficiency.

Implemental Details. All images are resized to 256* 256 pixels. We run six clients on 2 GPUs (NVIDIA RTX 4090 with 24 GB memory), with a peak GPU utilization of approximately 85% during the execution of our method. For the model architecture, we utilize 2D U-Net [19] as the backbone. The loss function is dice loss [15], and Adam optimizer is used for each client, with a learning rate of 1×10^{-3}, betas set to (0.9, 0.99), and a batch size of 32. To ensure steady convergence of the model, The synchronous federated learning method is trained for 200 rounds with one local update epoch, while the asynchronous method is trained for 1200 rounds. Additionally, in our method, the optimizer for the RL agent is Adam with a learning rate of 1×10^{-2}. The local training epochs E_k range from 0 to 3, the learning rate γ_k ranges from 1×10^{-5} to 2×10^{-3}, and the aggregation weight β_k ranges from 0.2 to 0.7. To simulate the heterogeneity of distributed devices, we artificially introduced time delays for clients 2 and 5 in the prostate MRI segmentation task, making each epoch take twice as long.

Comparison Methods. We compare AFedRL with eight federated learning methods, including both synchronous (FedAvg [14], q-FedAvg [9], CFFL [10], FedCI [24], CGSV [29], FedCE [6]) and asynchronous (Fedasyn(const) [27], Fed-IBD(DW) [5]) approaches. Furthermore, we also compare with standalone, where local training and evaluation are performed on each client's own data. All methods share the same training configuration.

3.1   Experimental Results

We present the results for each method on two segmentation tasks in Table 1. For the retinal fundus dataset, the substantial heterogeneity in client 5's training data causes a performance drop for methods that fail to address this disparity. AFedRL, however, outperforms the second-best method by 15.46% on client 5 and significantly reduces the standard deviation. Moreover, AFedRL achieves superior average performance across all clients, outperforming all baseline methods. For the prostate dataset, when artificial time delays are introduced for two clients, all AFL methods experience performance degradation. However, AFedRL exhibits the least performance drop, especially compared to Fedasyn(const) and FedIBD(DW), demonstrating its robustness in managing data and device heterogeneity.

Table 1. Performance comparison using Dice score on two datasets. (#) represents the size of the training dataset for this client. Underlined results indicate the best performance in SFL, and **bold** results indicate the best performance in AFL.

Retinal Fundus Segmentation								
Client(#)	1(98)	2(50)	3(48)	4(600)	5(80)	6(227)	Avg.	Std.
Standalone	86.69	85.51	86.21	89.91	79.77	90.98	86.51	3.95
FedAvg [14]	81.34	85.21	83.28	88.16	40.81	90.79	78.27	18.66
q-FedAvg [9]	86.24	86.97	87.37	89.13	44.68	90.72	80.85	17.80
CFFL [10]	85.72	86.29	86.96	88.62	41.12	90.16	79.81	19.02
FedCI [24]	<u>87.02</u>	86.93	87.35	88.53	40.99	90.22	80.17	19.24
CGSV [29]	83.46	85.57	85.47	88.48	33.79	<u>91.01</u>	77.96	21.80
FedCE [6]	86.73	<u>87.45</u>	<u>87.51</u>	<u>89.26</u>	<u>57.30</u>	90.25	<u>83.08</u>	<u>12.70</u>
Fedasyn(const) [27]	85.58	85.79	82.96	86.09	51.68	88.78	80.15	15.09
FedIBD(DW) [5]	85.43	82.72	83.66	**87.93**	37.64	87.29	77.45	17.90
AFedRL	**85.67**	**85.94**	**84.24**	83.50	**72.76**	**88.89**	**83.50**	**5.09**
Prostate MRI Segmentation								
Client(#)	1(288)	2(389)	3(369)	4(251)	5(221)	6(829)	Avg.	Std.
Standalone	91.23	84.59	87.57	87.37	86.70	89.25	87.79	2.26
FedAvg [14]	91.10	84.59	89.02	89.09	83.87	<u>89.27</u>	87.82	2.90
q-FedAvg [9]	90.94	85.60	89.28	<u>89.18</u>	84.27	88.67	87.99	2.52
CFFL [10]	91.01	85.49	89.24	88.98	82.11	88.17	87.50	3.20
FedCI [24]	91.21	85.40	<u>89.49</u>	88.37	83.96	88.49	87.82	2.68
CGSV [29]	91.15	84.90	89.27	88.09	83.47	89.16	87.67	2.91
FedCE [6]	<u>91.43</u>	<u>85.79</u>	89.21	89.13	<u>85.68</u>	88.62	<u>88.31</u>	<u>2.22</u>
Fedasyn(const) [27]	88.06	78.85	84.25	83.77	84.28	86.51	84.28	3.31
FedIBD(DW) [5]	88.92	69.35	**86.56**	86.59	85.59	**88.07**	84.18	6.72
AFedRL	**89.65**	**82.46**	86.20	**86.86**	**86.13**	87.44	**86.46**	**2.34**

Additionally, as shown in Fig. 2, for both segmentation tasks, AFedRL converges faster than FedAvg on both segmentation tasks. Specifically, for the

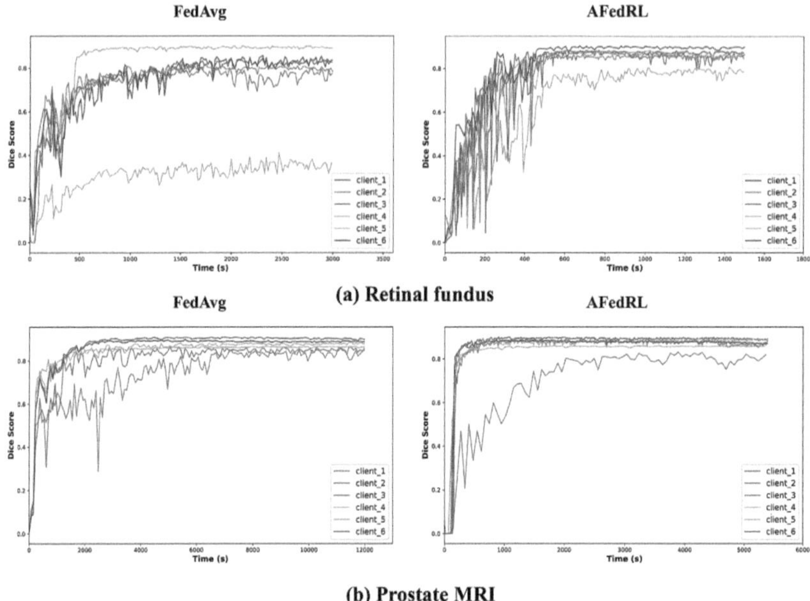

FedAvg   AFedRL

(a) Retinal fundus

FedAvg   AFedRL

(b) Prostate MRI

Fig. 2. Time vs. Dice Score curve in two tasks

prostate MRI segmentation task, the improvement in convergence speed is evident, e.g., client 5 in Retinal fundus dataset. AFedRL reaches convergence in approximately 1.11 h, while FedAvg requires roughly twice that time. This significant reduction in training time highlights the efficiency of AFedRL.

To illustrate the dynamic hyperparameter adjustments during training, we plot the aggregation weights over training rounds for the retinal fundus task in Fig. 3. In the later stages, clients 2 and 5 received larger aggregation weights, indicating that the RL agents recognize their significant contributions to the global model. This suggests that, although these clients have smaller datasets than others, they contain more valuable and informative data. This weight adjustment also leads to a notable performance improvement for AFedRL on client 5.

Table 2. Ablation of search space.

Search Space			Dice Score	
LE	AW	LR	Retinal Fundus	Prostate MRI
			80.15	84.29
✓			81.05	85.53
	✓		82.00	85.39
		✓	81.34	85.37
✓	✓		81.96	86.01
✓		✓	82.00	86.17
	✓	✓	83.44	86.00
✓	✓	✓	**83.50**	**86.46**

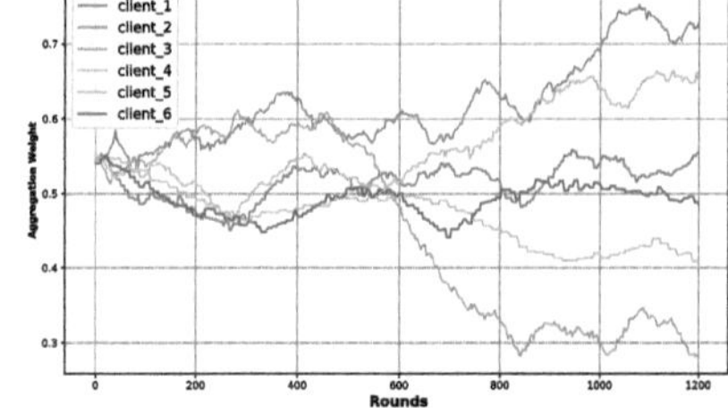

Fig. 3. The evolution of aggregation weights during the training.

3.2 Ablation Study

An extensive ablation study was conducted to investigate the impact of dynamically adjusting each hyperparameter on the performance of the two segmentation tasks. As illustrated in Table 2, the global model's performance consistently improves with the dynamic adjustment of additional hyperparameters. This highlights that, the selection of learning rate, local epochs, and aggregation weights plays a pivotal role in shaping the model's performance in AFL.

4   Conclusion

In this study, we present AFedRL, a novel asynchronous joint learning framework that allows for asynchronous client-side updates and dynamic tuning of hyperparameters using the REINFORCE algorithm, which optimizes the performance of the model, improves the efficiency and flexibility of the system and can deal with the challenges posed by the data and device heterogeneity . Through extensive experiments, we demonstrate that AFedRL achieves competitive performance while significantly reducing training time compared to traditional synchronous federated learning methods. These results highlight the effectiveness of combining reinforcement learning with federated learning for dynamic hyperparameter optimization and the potential of AFedRL for real-world applications.

Acknowledgements. This work is funded by the National Key R&D Program of China(2022ZD0160700) and Shanghai AI Laboratory.

References

1. Almazroa, A., et al.: Retinal fundus images for glaucoma analysis: the riga dataset. In: Medical Imaging 2018: Imaging Informatics for Healthcare, Research, and Applications, vol. 10579, pp. 55–62. SPIE (2018)
2. Chen, J., Ma, B., Cui, H., Xia, Y.: Think twice before selection: federated evidential active learning for medical image analysis with domain shifts. In: Proceedings of the IEEE/CVF Conference on Computer Vision and Pattern Recognition, pp. 11439–11449 (2024)
3. Fumero, F., Alayón, S., Sanchez, J.L., Sigut, J., Gonzalez-Hernandez, M.: Rimone: an open retinal image database for optic nerve evaluation. In: 2011 24th International Symposium on Computer-based Medical Systems (CBMS), pp. 1–6. IEEE (2011)
4. Guo, P., Yang, D., Hatamizadeh, A., et al.: Auto-fedrl: federated hyperparameter optimization for multi-institutional medical image segmentation. In: European Conference on Computer Vision. pp. 437–455. Springer (2022). https://doi.org/10.1007/978-3-031-19803-8_26
5. Hou, Y., Li, H., Guo, Z., Wu, W., Liu, R., You, L.: Fedibd: a federated learning framework in asynchronous mode for imbalanced data. Appl. Intell. **55**(2), 1–17 (2025)

6. Jiang, M., et al.: Fair federated medical image segmentation via client contribution estimation. In: Proceedings of the IEEE/CVF Conference on Computer Vision and Pattern Recognition pp. 16302–16311 (2023)
7. Lemaître, G., Martí, R., Freixenet, J., Vilanova, J.C., Walker, P.M., Meriaudeau, F.: Computer-aided detection and diagnosis for prostate cancer based on mono and multi-parametric mri: a review. Comput. Biol. Med. **60**, 8–31 (2015)
8. Li, T., Sahu, A.K., Zaheer, M., Sanjabi, M., Talwalkar, A., Smith, V.: Federated optimization in heterogeneous networks. Proc. Mach. Learn. Syst. **2**, 429–450 (2020)
9. Li, T., Sanjabi, M., Beirami, A., Smith, V.: Fair resource allocation in federated learning. arXiv preprint arXiv:1905.10497 (2019)
10. Lin, X., et al.: Fairness in federated learning. In: Federated Learning, pp. 143–160. Elsevier (2024)
11. Litjens, G., et al.: Evaluation of prostate segmentation algorithms for mri: the promise12 challenge. Med. Image Anal. **18**(2), 359–373 (2014)
12. Liu, J., et al.: Fedasmu: efficient asynchronous federated learning with dynamic staleness-aware model update. In: Proceedings of the AAAI Conference on Artificial Intelligence, vol. 38, pp. 13900–13908 (2024)
13. Liu, Q., Dou, Q., Yu, L., Heng, P.A.: Ms-net: multi-site network for improving prostate segmentation with heterogeneous mri data. IEEE Trans. Med. Imaging **39**(9), 2713–2724 (2020)
14. McMahan, B., Moore, E., Ramage, D., Hampson, S., y Arcas, B.A.: communication-efficient learning of deep networks from decentralized data. In: Artificial intelligence and statistics, pp. 1273–1282. PMLR (2017)
15. Milletari, F., Navab, N., Ahmadi, S.A.: V-net: fully convolutional neural networks for volumetric medical image segmentation. In: 2016 Fourth International Conference on 3D Vision (3DV), pp. 565–571. IEEE (2016)
16. Nicholas, B., Anant, M., Henkjan, H., John, F., Justin, K., et al.: Nci-proc. ieee-isbi conf. 2013 challenge: Automated segmentation of prostate structures. The Cancer Imaging Archive (2015)
17. Orlando, J.I., et al.: Refuge challenge: a unified framework for evaluating automated methods for glaucoma assessment from fundus photographs. Med. Image Anal. **59**, 101570 (2020)
18. Rieke, N., et al.: The future of digital health with federated learning. NPJ Digital Med. **3**(1), 1–7 (2020)
19. Ronneberger, O., Fischer, P., Brox, T.: U-Net: convolutional networks for biomedical image segmentation. In: Navab, N., Hornegger, J., Wells, W.M., Frangi, A.F. (eds.) MICCAI 2015. LNCS, vol. 9351, pp. 234–241. Springer, Cham (2015). https://doi.org/10.1007/978-3-319-24574-4_28
20. Ruvolo, P., Fasel, I., Movellan, J.: Optimization on a budget: a reinforcement learning approach. Adv. Neural Inform. Process. Syst. **21** (2008)
21. Shannon, C.E.: A mathematical theory of communication. Bell Syst. Tech. J. **27**(3), 379–423 (1948)
22. Sheller, M.J., et al.: Federated learning in medicine: facilitating multi-institutional collaborations without sharing patient data. Sci. Rep. **10**(1), 12598 (2020)
23. Sivaswamy, J., Krishnadas, S., Chakravarty, A., Joshi, G., Tabish, A.S., et al.: A comprehensive retinal image dataset for the assessment of glaucoma from the optic nerve head analysis. JSM Biomed. Imaging Data Papers **2**(1), 1004 (2015)
24. Song, T., Tong, Y., Wei, S.: Profit allocation for federated learning. In: 2019 IEEE International Conference on Big Data (Big Data), pp. 2577–2586. IEEE (2019)

25. Su, N., Li, B.: How asynchronous can federated learning be? In: 2022 IEEE/ACM 30th International Symposium on Quality of Service (IWQoS), pp. 1–11. IEEE (2022)
26. Williams, R.J.: Simple statistical gradient-following algorithms for connectionist reinforcement learning. Mach. Learn. **8**, 229–256 (1992)
27. Xie, C., Koyejo, S., Gupta, I.: Asynchronous federated optimization. arXiv preprint arXiv:1903.03934 (2019)
28. Xu, J., Glicksberg, B.S., Su, C., Walker, P., Bian, J., Wang, F.: Federated learning for healthcare informatics. J. Healthcare Inform. Res. **5**, 1–19 (2021)
29. Xu, X., Lyu, L., Ma, X., Miao, C., Foo, C.S., Low, B.K.H.: Gradient driven rewards to guarantee fairness in collaborative machine learning. Adv. Neural. Inf. Process. Syst. **34**, 16104–16117 (2021)
30. Zhou, C., Tian, H., Zhang, H., Zhang, J., Dong, M., Jia, J.: Tea-fed: time-efficient asynchronous federated learning for edge computing. In: Proceedings of the 18th ACM International Conference on Computing Frontiers, pp. 30–37 (2021)

MONet-FL: Extending nnU-Net with MONAI for Clinical Federated Learning

Simone Bendazzoli[1,2]([✉])(iD), Mehdi Astaraki[2,3], Antonios Tzortzakakis[2,6,7],
Andréas Abrahamsson[6], Björn Engelbrekt Wahlin[8,9], Sofia Brunori[1,5],
Maria Holstensson[2,3,6], and Rodrigo Moreno[1,4]

[1] KTH, Royal Institute of Technology, Department of Biomedical Engineering and
Health Systems, Stockholm, Sweden
`simben@kth.se`
[2] Karolinska Institutet, Department of Clinical Sciences, Intervention and
Engineering, Stockholm, Sweden
[3] Division of Medical Radiation Physics, Department of Physics, Stockholm
University, Stockholm, Sweden
[4] Department of Neurobiology, Care Sciences and Society, Karolinska Institutet,
Stockholm, Sweden
[5] Department of Electronics, Information and Bioengineering, Politecnico di Milano,
Milan, Italy
[6] Department of Nuclear Medicine and Medical Physics, Section Nuclear Medicine
Huddinge, Karolinska University Hospital, Stockholm, Sweden
[7] Department of Nuclear Medicine and Medical Physics, Theranostics Trial Center,
Karolinska University Hospital, Stockholm, Sweden
[8] Division of Hematology, Department of Medicine, Huddinge, Karolinska Institutet,
Stockholm, Sweden
[9] Medical Unit Hematology, Solna, Cancer, Karolinska University Hospital,
Stockholm, Sweden

Abstract. The widespread success of nnU-Net as a state-of-the-art tool for medical image segmentation has driven its adoption as a baseline, but its limited portability and lack of clinical integration have limited broader deployment in real-world healthcare workflows. To address these challenges, we present the MONet Bundle, extending nnU-Net within the MONAI ecosystem, providing a modular benchmarking tool for Federated Learning (FL) that is directly compatible with downstream clinical operations such as model deployment, active learning, and DICOM-based PACS integration. MONet enables federated training across distributed clinical datasets while maintaining standardized preprocessing and harmonized workflows. Its flexibility is validated on two representative segmentation tasks: lymphoma lesion segmentation in PET-CT and brain tumor segmentation from the BraTS challenge. In both settings, MONet's federated models consistently outperformed cross-site baselines and approached, or in some cases outperformed, the performance of centralized task-fusion models with minimal user intervention. The code is available at https://github.com/SimoneBendazzoli93/MONet-Bundle.

© The Author(s), under exclusive license to Springer Nature Switzerland AG 2026
G. Zamzmi et al. (Eds.): MICCAI 2025, LNCS 16135, pp. 102–110, 2026.
https://doi.org/10.1007/978-3-032-05663-4_10

Keywords: Federated Learning · Clinical Integration · Medical Image Segmentation

1   Introduction

nnU-Net [11] is a widely recognized state-of-the-art method for medical image segmentation, consistently outperforming newer architectures across diverse tasks [5,9,12]. It demonstrated robustness by winning numerous international challenges and ranking first on over 20 biomedical segmentation datasets [11], and has served as a baseline for several MICCAI winners. Comparative studies confirm that, when properly configured, it surpasses CNN-, transformer-, and Mamba-based methods [10]. Its success is largely due to its self-configuring design, enabling automatic adaptation to new tasks. As an out-of-the-box tool, it is accessible without expert knowledge and scales well with modern hardware. However, its default implementation lacks portability and integration features, limiting clinical adoption due to time-consuming workflow adaptations.

MONAI [6] addresses these limitations with an open-source framework for both research and clinical use. Specifically, it offers tools for model training, deployment via MONAI Deploy[1], and clinical integration with DICOM support and containerized inference. Furthermore, MONAI Label[2] supports smart annotation for collaborative labeling. Starting from version 1.2.0, MONAI has integrated nnU-Net into its ecosystem by developing **nnUNetV2Runner**. This class serves as a bridge for data preparation, preprocessing, training, and cross-validation using the native nnU-Net implementation through the MONAI pipeline. While this integration brings several advantages, it lacks comprehensive integration within the MONAI ecosystem for deploying nnU-Net models. Although [17] also proposed adapting the nnU-Net framework for FL, their resulting trained model still inherits the original nnU-Net's limitations in terms of adaptability and flexibility within clinical scenarios.

Addressing these limitations, we introduce MONet, a MONAI Bundle[3] developed integrating the nnU-Net framework, with the main aim to integrate it within the MONAI ecosystem and the range of available applications (active learning, deployment, PACS integration). MONet's utility has been recognized through its recent integration into the most current version of MONAI (v1.5)[4]. In this paper, we highlight the utility of MONet for FL applications.

2   MONet-FL

The MONet-FL framework represents an effort focused on federated learning for medical image segmentations, offering a modular, and flexible pipeline integrating the successful nnUNet framework. The primary goal of this effort is to

---

[1] https://monai.io/deploy.html.
[2] https://monai.io/label.html.
[3] https://docs.monai.io/en/stable/bundle_intro.html.
[4] https://docs.monai.io/en/stable/apps.html#nnunet-bundle.

enhance the performance of medical image segmentation in distributed FL settings, and provide a robust benchmarking for future developments. Furthermore, in alignment with the principles of open and reproducible science, MONet-FL is released under the GNU General Public License v3.0.

We evaluated MONet-FL on two distinct segmentation tasks from different domains: the first focuses on automated segmentation of lymphoma lesions in PET-CT volumes, while the second uses the popular BraTS [14] dataset for brain tumor segmentation in multimodal MRI.

2.1 Lymphoma Lesion Segmentation

We used two distinct PET-CT datasets acquired from different sources and scanners. The first, AutoPET [7,8], includes 1,611 whole-body scans from patients with melanoma, lymphoma, lung cancer, and negative controls. For this study, we selected the 154 scans with annotated lymphoma lesions. Each case consists of aligned 3D PET and CT volumes, along with binary lesion masks manually segmented based on the FDG-PET modality. Lesions were annotated by three expert radiologists following standardized clinical protocols.

The second dataset was collected at Karolinska University Hospital (KUH) and includes 228 PET-CT studies from lymphoma patients. Scans were acquired using a Siemens SOMATOM Definition AS scanner with FDG-18 as the radiotracer. All studies were manually annotated by two expert radiologists, each labeling a separate subset.

FL was conducted across three clients: one using the AutoPET dataset and two using the KUH dataset, reflecting the differing annotation tools and practices used by the radiologists. Accordingly, performing FL experiments within the MONet-FL framework allows for an investigation into the generalizability of lymphoma segmentation models, analyzing the impact of heterogeneity from different image acquisition protocols and annotation procedures.

2.2 Brain Tumor Segmentation

This section describes the second segmentation task, which involved the segmentation of diverse brain tumor entities utilizing multi-parametric Magnetic Resonance Imaging (MRI) data obtained from the popular Brain Tumor Segmentation (BraTS) challenge [1–4,13,15]. While the BraTS challenge initially focused on segmenting adult gliomas, its scope has expanded to include other clinically relevant tasks, including segmentation of meningioma, metastasis, and pediatric tumors.

In contrast to the described lymphoma segmentation experiments, which utilized a singular tumor entity across all participating clients, our BraTS-based experiments employed a more diverse approach. We designed an FL framework featuring three specialized clients, each dedicated to a distinct brain tumor entity from the BraTS 2023 dataset: adult glioma (1251 cases), meningioma (1000 cases), or metastasis (237 cases). This federated design enabled client-specific learning, allowing each client to independently model its designated tumor type, accounting for the highly heterogeneous, infiltrative, and poorly marginated nature of adult gliomas; the more uniform and well-defined appearance of meningiomas; and the typically small, multiple presentation of metastatic lesions. Concurrently, these clients benefited from the collective knowledge shared during subsequent aggregation rounds, which ultimately would lead to a single, more generalizable model capable of segmenting diverse brain tumor entities.

The MRI datasets utilized throughout all three tasks comprised four structural sequences: native T1-weighted (T1w), contrast-enhanced T1-weighted (T1c), T2-weighted (T2w), and T2-weighted fluid-attenuated inversion recovery (T2f). All MRI data already underwent to a series of standardized preprocessing procedures, including co-registration, atlas registration, resampling to a $1\,\text{mm}^3$ isotropic resolution, and skull stripping. The primary objective of this segmentation challenge was to accurately delineate brain tumors into their component subregions: the enhancing tumor, the non-enhancing core, and the FLAIR hyperintensity. Tumor annotations were initially performed by one to four expert raters and subsequently validated by certified neuroradiologists.

2.3 Experimental Setting

All experiments presented in this paper were executed using MONet, which wraps the original nnU-Net framework. Training hyperparameters (e.g., learning rate, scheduler, iterations, and total number of epochs) were left at their default settings with the default *nnUNetTrainer*. For the FL setup, we employed the *MONAIAlgo* mechanism, adopting the MONet Bundle for training. The FL configuration consisted of 100 global rounds, each with 10 local training epochs. To test FL in real-world conditions, we deployed three NVFlare [16] clients and a central server across two independent infrastructures: two clients in the Alvis supercomputer and one in a KTH-hosted medical AI platform integrated with KUH's PACS. The two Alvis clients used NVIDIA T4 GPUs; the client used a NVIDIA A6000 GPU. To establish a segmentation performance benchmark for the FL experiments, independent baseline nnU-Net models were trained for each dataset. These baseline models were run on a single NVIDIA T4 GPU, utilizing approximately 8 GB of virtual memory.

The evaluations of the experiments are performed and reported using a single train/validation split with a 80% - 20% ratio, ensuring consistency among all the experiments for the cases included in the train or validation split.

2.4 Federated Learning Workflow

At the initial stage of the FL workflow, we set up a three-site federation (Fig. 1) and connected the clients to a central server using the *NVFlare* toolkit. The standard nnU-Net workflow includes a preprocessing step performed before training, where the network architecture and training hyperparameters are automatically derived from the dataset. In an FL setting, aligning this preprocessing phase presents a significant challenge, as it demands a unified experimental plan that can be uniformly applied across all clients, despite possible differences in their local datasets.

Fig. 1. Dataset distribution across clients for the two segmentation tasks.

To address this, we implemented a three-step process as illustrated in Fig. 2:

1. **Experiment Planning on a Reference Client**: We first perform the planning and preprocessing steps on a designated reference client(AutoPET for the lymphoma task and adult glioma for the brain tumor task). This generates a consistent preprocessing plan based on a representative dataset.
2. **Plan Distribution and Preprocessing**: The generated plan is shared with the central server and distributed to the remaining clients. Each client then applies the shared plan to perform local preprocessing.
3. **Federated Training**: With all clients preprocessed using the unified plan, FL training is executed across the harmonized federation.

We opted to adhere to the default preprocessing configuration of nnUNet to maintain full compatibility with its established pipeline. However, the MONet-FL the framework supports the integration of more complex and customizable preprocessing techniques.

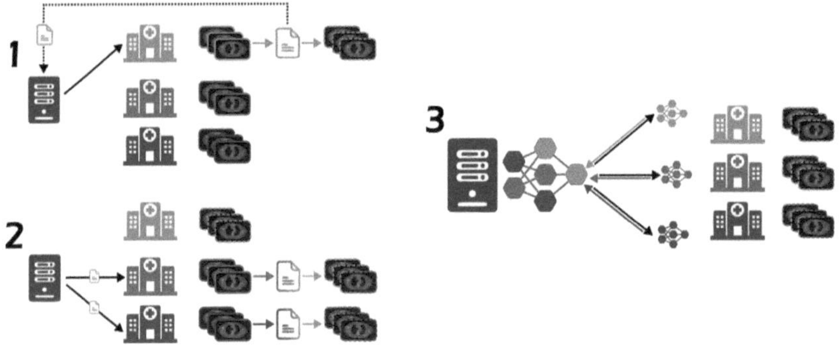

Fig. 2. Overview of the MONet-FL workflow. The process consists of three main steps: (1) Experiment planning and preprocessing, (2) Plan distribution and preprocessing, (3) Federated training.

3   Results

For each of the presented segmentation tasks (lymphoma and brain tumors), we report the validation results from the FL experiments and compare them against three baseline strategies: cross-site, task-fusion, and single-site evaluation, as follows:

- **Single-Site Evaluation (*nnU-Net-Baseline*):** Models are trained and evaluated independently on each local dataset, providing a performance estimate for the single datasets, explicitly ignoring the generalizability capability of the model.
- **Cross-site Evaluation:** Models are trained separately on each dataset and evaluated on external sites, offering a lower-bound estimate of model generalizability across institutions.
- **Task-Fusion Evaluation:** The datasets are fused together and trained as part of a single site, offering an upper-bound estimate of model generalizability in the ideal case where the data can be shared and collected in a single site for training the model.

The performance metrics included Dice similarity coefficient (DSC) and average surface distance (ASD), chosen to comprehensively evaluate segmentation performance by measuring both the overlap accuracy (DSC) and the spatial boundary agreement (ASD) between predicted and ground truth segmentations.

Table 1. Dice Similarity Coefficient (DSC) and Average Surface Distance (ASD) for each Lymphoma experiment across the three datasets (over the validation set): AutoPET, Indolent Lymphoma 1 (IL1) and Indolent Lymphoma 2 (IL2).

Dataset - Label	Experiment	DSC	ASD [mm]
AutoPET (n=27) - Lesion	Cross-Site IL1	0.445 ± 0.270	50.19 ± 95.19
	Cross-Site IL2	0.587 ± 0.251	40.06 ± 89.72
	MONet-FL	*0.694 ± 0.279*	*10.80 ± 24.61*
	LymphoFusion	0.756 ± 0.244	19.27 ± 39.78
	nnU-Net-Baseline	0.758 ± 0.252	38.50 ± 133.01
IL1 (n=16) - Lesion	Cross-Site AutoPET	0.317 ± 0.255	99.46 ± 147.08
	Cross-Site IL2	0.297 ± 0.230	111.11 ± 172.99
	MONet-FL	*0.453 ± 0.252*	*70.91 ± 127.18*
	LymphoFusion	0.421 ± 0.223	90.29 ± 143.43
	nnU-Net-Baseline	0.512 ± 0.215	12.95 ± 11.69
IL2 (n=31) - Lesion	Cross-Site AutoPET	0.534 ± 0.265	39.34 ± 71.36
	Cross-Site IL1	0.391 ± 0.247	40.03 ± 79.63
	MONet-FL	*0.610 ± 0.234*	*25.03 ± 64.44*
	LymphoFusion	0.665 ± 0.242	23.07 ± 70.48
	nnU-Net-Baseline	0.671 ± 0.275	24.09 ± 72.41

As shown in Tables 1 and 2, MONet-FL consistently outperformed cross-site models across datasets and tumor subregions, with notable gains in Dice and

Table 2. Dice Similarity Coefficient (DSC) and Average Surface Distance (ASD) for each BraTS experiment across the three datasets (over the validation set): Adult Glioma (BraTS-GLI), Meningioma (BraTS-MEN) and Brain Metastasis (BraTS-MET). The three labels are Enhancing Tumor (ET), Non Enhancing Tumor Core (NETC) and Surrounding Non-enhancing FLAIR Hyperintensity (SNFH)

Dataset - Label	Experiment	DSC	ASD [mm]
BraTS-GLI (n=251) - ET	Cross-Site BraTS-MEN	0.695 ± 0.292	3.05 ± 8.69
	Cross-Site BraTS-MET	0.729 ± 0.271	1.62 ± 4.97
	MONet-FL	*0.788 ± 0.261*	*1.57 ± 5.56*
	BraTSFusion	0.774 ± 0.271	1.61 ± 4.07
	nnU-Net-Baseline	0.796 ± 0.254	1.38 ± 3.72
BraTS-GLI (n=251) - NETC	Cross-Site BraTS-MEN	0.709 ± 0.296	2.17 ± 7.84
	Cross-Site BraTS-MET	0.787 ± 0.218	1.47 ± 2.92
	MONet-FL	*0.836 ± 0.178*	*0.88 ± 1.83*
	BraTSFusion	0.846 ± 0.153	0.84 ± 1.40
	nnU-Net-Baseline	0.871 ± 0.143	0.81 ± 1.73
BraTS-GLI (n=251) - SNFH	Cross-Site BraTS-MEN	0.823 ± 0.197	2.52 ± 8.67
	Cross-Site BraTS-MET	0.833 ± 0.167	1.29 ± 3.35
	MONet-FL	*0.884 ± 0.126*	*0.79 ± 2.21*
	BraTSFusion	0.897 ± 0.118	1.92 ± 0.08
	nnU-Net-Baseline	0.896 ± 0.116	0.48 ± 1.38
BraTS-MEN (n=200) - ET	Cross-Site BraTS-GLI	0.368 ± 0.352	8.92 ± 7.78
	Cross-Site BraTS-MET	0.366 ± 0.338	8.85 ± 12.57
	MONet-FL	*0.422 ± 0.354*	*7.14 ± 7.38*
	BraTSFusion	0.304 ± 0.308	8.45 ± 8.67
	nnU-Net-Baseline	0.367 ± 0.337	9.52 ± 8.49
BraTS-MEN (n=200) - NETC	Cross-Site BraTS-GLI	0.716 ± 0.305	6.41 ± 12.83
	Cross-Site BraTS-MET	0.714 ± 0.299	4.58 ± 7.08
	MONet-FL	*0.774 ± 0.273*	*3.25 ± 5.95*
	BraTSFusion	0.728 ± 0.349	3.97 ± 8.76
	nnU-Net-Baseline	0.774 ± 0.312	1.87 ± 3.28
BraTS-MEN (n=200) - SNFH	Cross-Site BraTS-GLI	0.763 ± 0.363	2.18 ± 10.75
	Cross-Site BraTS-MET	0.745 ± 0.345	3.47 ± 13.43
	MONet-FL	*0.911 ± 0.184*	*2.29 ± 12.21*
	BraTSFusion	0.925 ± 0.140	2.05 ± 10.11
	nnU-Net-Baseline	0.924 ± 0.168	2.35 ± 10.16
BraTS-MET (n=48) - ET	Cross-Site BraTS-GLI	0.560 ± 0.335	5.97 ± 12.76
	Cross-Site BraTS-MEN	0.358 ± 0.362	11.55 ± 23.56
	MONet-FL	*0.634 ± 0.303*	*3.47 ± 8.86*
	BraTSFusion	0.506 ± 0.313	6.79 ± 18.47
	nnU-Net-Baseline	0.677 ± 0.281	3.14 ± 8.02
BraTS-MET (n=48) - NETC	Cross-Site BraTS-GLI	0.658 ± 0.314	3.68 ± 10.01
	Cross-Site BraTS-MEN	0.547 ± 0.376	8.59 ± 19.90
	MONet-FL	*0.719 ± 0.262*	*1.48 ± 1.92*
	BraTSFusion	0.698 ± 0.256	1.42 ± 1.27
	nnU-Net-Baseline	0.727 ± 0.251	2.19 ± 5.06
BraTS-MET (n=48) - SNFH	Cross-Site BraTS-GLI	0.613 ± 0.299	0.62 ± 0.36
	Cross-Site BraTS-MEN	0.541 ± 0.338	13.51 ± 25.83
	MONet-FL	*0.763 ± 0.156*	*0.60 ± 0.66*
	BraTSFusion	0.717 ± 0.194	2.78 ± 11.49
	nnU-Net-Baseline	0.791 ± 0.147	0.53 ± 0.44

ASD. In several cases, it also matched or exceeded the fusion approach, achieving lower ASD in AutoPET (10.80 mm vs. 19.27 mm), BraTS-GLI (0.79 mm vs. 1.92 mm for SNFH), BraTS-MEN (3.25 mm vs. 3.97 mm for NETC), and BraTS-MET (1.48 mm vs. 1.42 mm for NETC). These results highlight MONet-FL's strong generalization and boundary accuracy, offering a practical advantage over fusion methods, which require central data pooling and are incompatible with FL's privacy-preserving goals.

4   Discussion

In this work, we introduced the MONet Bundle and showcased it in two FL applications. The main focus of the study was integrating the well-established nnU-Net framework into an FL setting with direct clinical integration. We show that using default configurations, using the baseline nnU-Net, a straightforward FedAvg strategy, and an out-of-the-box NVFlare setup, we achieved strong initial results without the need for additional tuning. Thus, clinical applications can potentially benefit from the advantages of nnU-Net in FL setting without much effort.

The aim of this work was to present MONet-FL as a foundational tool to support future benchmarking of preprocessing and aggregation strategies in FL. For example, using MONet-FL as a baseline, one can evaluate different strategies, as shown in [17]. By offering a standardized, modular framework, MONet aims to be the standard for systematic evaluation and comparison of novel FL aggregation methods, promoting advancements in the field.

Finally, from a clinical perspective, our pipeline supports direct integration of federated models into active learning and deployment workflows, validated through MONet Bundles with MONAI Label and MONAI Deploy, supporting rapid translation of FL advances into the clinical setting.

Acknowledgements. This study has been partially funded by the Swedish Childhood Cancer Foundation (Barncancerfonden MT2022-0008), by Vinnova through AIDA, project ID: 2319,by the Swedish Research Council (Vetenskapsrådet, grant 2022-03389), and Hjärt-Lungfonden (grant No. 2022-0492). We thank the National Academic Infrastructure for Supercomputing in Sweden (NAISS) for the computational resources at Alvis.

Ethical Approvals. The use of Indolent lymphoma data was approved by the Regional Ethics Review Board in Stockholm under approval number 2012/783-31/3. An amendment clarifying the inclusion of X-ray imaging was approved in 2020 under the reference number 2019-06366.

References

1. Baid, U., et al.: The RSNA-ASNR-MICCAI BraTS 2021 benchmark on brain tumor segmentation and radiogenomic classification (2021). arXiv: 2107.02314 [cs.CV]

2. Bakas, S., et al.: Advancing the cancer genome atlas glioma MRI collections with expert segmentation labels and radiomic features. Sci. Data **4**(1) (2017). ISSN: 2052-4463. https://doi.org/10.1038/sdata.2017.117

3. Bakas, S., et al.: segmentation labels for the pre-operative scans of the TCGA-GBM collection (2017). https://doi.org/10.7937/K9/TCIA.2017.KLXWJJ1Q, https://www.cancerimagingarchive.net/analysis-result/brats-tcga-gbm/

4. Bakas, S., et al.: segmentation labels for the pre-operative scans of the TCGA-LGG collection (2017). https://doi.org/10.7937/K9/TCIA.2017.GJQ7R0EF, https://www.cancerimagingarchive.net/analysis-result/brats-tcga-lgg/

5. Boer, M., et al.: NnU-Net versus mesh growing algorithm as a tool for the robust and timely segmentation of neurosurgical 3D images in contrast-enhanced T1 MRI scans. Acta Neurochirurgica **166**(1) (2024). ISSN: 0942-0940. https://doi.org/10.1007/s00701-024-05973-8

6. Jorge Cardoso, M., et al.: MONAI: an open-source framework for deep learning in healthcare (2022). eprint: arXiv:2211.02701

7. Gatidis, S., Kuestner, T.: A whole-body FDG-PET/CT dataset with manually annotated tumor lesions (FDG-PET-CT-Lesions) (2022). https://doi.org/10.7937/GKR0-XV29, https://www.cancerimagingarchive.net/collection/fdg-pet-ct-lesions/

8. Gatidis, S., et al.: Results from the autoPET challenge on fully automated lesion segmentation in oncologic PET/CT imaging. Nat. Mach. Intell. **6**(11), 1396–1405. ISSN: 2522-5839. https://doi.org/10.1038/s42256-024-00912-9

9. Gunawardhana, M., Xu, F., Zhao, J.: How good nnUNet for Segmenting Cardiac MRI: a comprehensive evaluation (2024). eprint: arXiv:2408.06358

10. Isensee, F., et al.: nnU-Net Revisited: a call for rigorous validation in 3D medical image segmentation. In: Medical Image Computing and Computer Assisted Intervention MICCAI 2024. Springer Nature Switzerland, 2024, pp. 488–498. ISBN: 9783031721144. https://doi.org/10.1007/978-3-031-72114-4_47, http://dx.doi.org/10.1007/978-3-031-72114-4_47

11. Isensee, F., et al.: nnU-Net: a self-configuring method for deep learning based biomedical image segmentation. Nat. Methods **18**(2), 203–211 (2020). ISSN: 1548-7105. https://doi.org/10.1038/s41592-020-01008-z, http://dx.doi.org/10.1038/s41592-020-01008-z

12. Kazaj, P.M., et al.: From Claims to Evidence: a unified framework and critical analysis of CNN vs. Transformer vs. Mamba in medical image segmentation (2025). eprint: arXiv:2503.01306

13. LaBella, D., et al.: The ASNR-MICCAI Brain Tumor Segmentation (BraTS) Challenge 2023: Intracranial Meningioma (2023). https://doi.org/10.48550/ARXIV.2305.07642

14. Menze, B.H., et al.: The multimodal brain tumor image segmentation benchmark (BRATS). IEEE Trans. Med. Imaging **34**(10), 1993–2024 (2015). https://doi.org/10.1109/TMI.2014.2377694

15. Moawad, A.W., et al.: The brain tumor segmentation (BraTS-METS) challenge 2023: brain metastasis segmentation on pre-treatment MRI (2023). https://doi.org/10.48550/ARXIV.2306.00838

16. Roth, H.R., et al.: NVIDIA FLARE: federated learning from simulation to real-world (2022). https://doi.org/10.48550/arXiv.2210.13291

17. Skorupko, G., et al.: Federated nnU-Net for privacy-preserving medical image segmentation (2025). arXiv: 2503.02549 [cs.CV]

FedGIN: Federated Learning with Dynamic Global Intensity Non-linear Augmentation for Organ Segmentation Using Multi-modal Images

Sachin Dudda Nagaraju[1(✉)], Ashkan Moradi[1], Bendik Skarre Abrahamsen[1], and Mattijs Elschot[1,2]

[1] Department of Circulation and Medical Imaging, Norwegian University of Science and Technology, Trondheim, Norway
{sachin.d.nagaraju,ashkan.moradi,bendik.s.abrahamsen,
mattijs.elschot}@ntnu.no
[2] Central Staff, St. Olavs Hospital, Trondheim University Hospital, Trondheim, Norway

Abstract. Medical image segmentation plays a crucial role in AI-assisted diagnostics, surgical planning, and treatment monitoring. Accurate and robust segmentation models are essential for enabling reliable, data-driven clinical decision making across diverse imaging modalities. Given the inherent variability in image characteristics across modalities, developing a unified model capable of generalizing effectively to multiple modalities would be highly beneficial. This model could streamline clinical workflows and reduce the need for modality-specific training. However, real-world deployment faces major challenges, including data scarcity, domain shift between modalities (e.g., CT vs. MRI), and privacy restrictions that prevent data sharing. To address these issues, we propose FedGIN, a Federated Learning (FL) framework that enables multimodal organ segmentation without sharing raw patient data. Our method integrates a lightweight Global Intensity Non-linear (GIN) augmentation module that harmonizes modality-specific intensity distributions during local training. We evaluated FedGIN using two types of datasets: a *limited dataset* and a *complete dataset*. In the limited dataset scenario, the model was initially trained using only MRI data, and CT data was added to assess its performance improvements. In the complete dataset scenario, both MRI and CT data were fully utilized for training on all clients. In the limited-data scenario, FedGIN achieved a 12-18% improvement in 3D Dice scores on MRI test cases compared to FL without GIN and consistently outperformed local baselines. In the complete dataset scenario, FedGIN demonstrated near-centralized performance, with a 30% Dice score improvement over the MRI-only baseline and a 10% improvement over the CT-only baseline, highlighting its strong cross-modality generalization under privacy constraints. Code available here https://github.com/sachugowda/FedGIN/.

G. Zamzmi et al. (Eds.): MICCAI 2025, LNCS 16135, pp. 111–120, 2026.
https://doi.org/10.1007/978-3-032-05663-4_11

Keywords: Federated Learning · Domain generalization · Multi modal data

1   Introduction

Artificial intelligence (AI) has revolutionized medical imaging by automating complex diagnostic analysis, enhancing accuracy, and improving clinical workflows. Deep learning methods, especially convolutional neural networks, have achieved expert-level performance in segmentation tasks across organs and modalities [5]. However, developing generalizable and robust models demands access to large datasets that are diverse in imaging modalities, anatomical regions, and patient populations. This requirement often conflicts with stringent privacy regulations and institutional governance policies, which restrict direct data sharing between sites [12]. Multimodal medical imaging datasets encompassing modalities such as computed tomography (CT) and magnetic resonance imaging (MRI) are crucial for developing generalizable AI models, as each modality captures distinct anatomical features. Rather than combining modalities for individual clinical cases, a more scalable and practical objective is to train unified segmentation models capable of operating across different modalities [8]. These models benefit from the diversity of multimodal data while avoiding dependence on modality-specific architectures. However, developing these models faces a fundamental barrier: multimodal datasets are isolated across institutions, limiting the ability to leverage their collective value for robust model training [12].

Federated learning (FL) [9] offers a solution for privacy and data accessibility in medical imaging by enabling collaborative model training across institutions without sharing raw data. Each client trains a local model on private data and shares only model parameters with a central server to build a global model [18]. FL has been successfully applied in tasks like brain MRI analysis and MRI-to-CT synthesis for radiotherapy planning [13]. However, challenges remain, including unpaired data (e.g., CT and MRI images from different patients), modality differences, and non-IID data [19] across institutions, which complicate the deployment of multimodal models. Recent centralized multimodal methods [3,4] improve segmentation through feature alignment. However, their reliance on complex architectures and extensive tuning limits scalability in resource-constrained clinical settings. Additionally, their performance in segmenting low-contrast, anatomically diverse organs is underexplored. Approaches like CAR-MFL [15] and other federated frameworks [10,16] address these challenges, but most require paired multimodal images, which is often impractical due to clinical protocol variations. Developing robust, generalizable solutions for unpaired multimodal data, especially with CT and MRI, remains an open challenge due to domain shifts, scanner variations, and anatomical differences, leading to performance degradation and limiting cross-site, cross-modality model reliability. In these scenarios, leveraging complementary CT data through FL could enhance MRI-based segmentation, particularly for rare cancers and anatomically complex regions [2]. To mitigate cross-modality distribution differences, domain generalization strategies have recently gained traction. Global Intensity Non-linear

(GIN) augmentation [11] has shown promise in bridging CT-MRI intensity differences under centralized settings, demonstrating the ability to train on one modality and generalize to another, its application has primarily focused on single-modality training and cross-modality testing. The potential of using GIN across multiple modalities during training to harmonize multimodal data in federated environments is underexplored. Addressing this could improve FL's generalization across modalities and institutions, enabling scalable, privacy-preserving medical AI systems.

To address these critical gaps, we propose a novel FL framework that integrates GIN augmentation for domain generalization in organ segmentation tasks using unpaired multimodal image data. Our approach specifically tackles the challenges of intensity distribution mismatches between CT and MRI data through causality-inspired augmentation techniques that expose models to synthesized domain-shifted training examples. The framework enables secure cross-modality learning under data scarcity by allowing institutions to contribute either unimodal or multimodal data while maintaining robust segmentation performance. We hypothesize that by dynamically harmonizing modality differences during training, the integration of GIN augmentation may enhance the model's ability to learn invariant representations that generalize more effectively across unseen modalities and institutions.

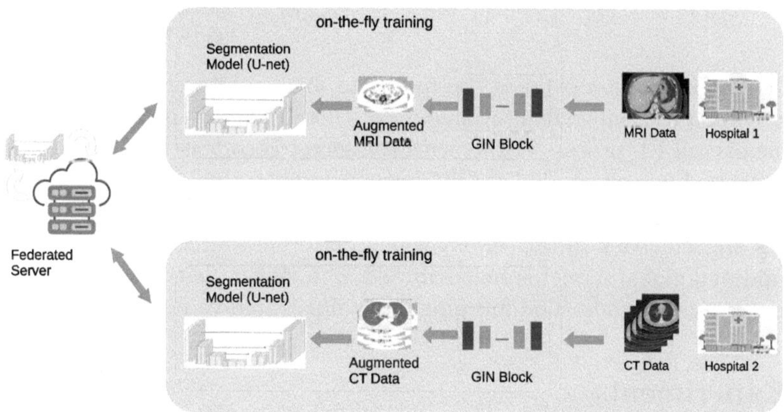

Fig. 1. Proposed FedGIN approach for FL with GIN augmentation for organ segmentation using multi-modal images

2   Methodology

We present FedGIN, a FL framework designed to build a generalizable organ segmentation model across institutions contributing different imaging modalities. Each client, which may possess unpaired data from MRI, CT, or both modalities, begins local training on its own data using the globally shared model received from the server. To facilitate cross-modality learning under these unpaired, modality-diverse conditions, we integrate a GIN augmentation module to effectively address modality-specific domain shifts; GIN applies randomized, anatomy-preserving intensity transformations during training. This encourages the model to learn modality-invariant features. After local training, model updates are sent to a central server for aggregation. This process is repeated over multiple communication rounds to iteratively refine a global model that generalizes across both modalities and different clients.

2.1 GIN Augmentation and Federated Workflow

To address modality-induced domain shifts, we use a GIN [11] module that operates on-the-fly during local training. GIN uses shallow convolutional networks with weights sampled from a Gaussian distribution $\mathcal{N}(0, I)$ at each iteration. Leaky ReLU activations are applied between layers to introduce nonlinearity, and no downsampling is used to preserve spatial resolution. The augmented image is generated by blending the shallow convolutional network's output $g_\theta^{\mathrm{Net}}(x)$ with the original input x, using a random coefficient $\alpha \sim \mathcal{U}(0, 1)$, followed by Frobenius norm normalization:

$$g_\theta(x) = \alpha \cdot g_\theta^{\mathrm{Net}}(x) + (1 - \alpha) \cdot x, \quad g_\theta(x) \leftarrow \frac{\|x\|_F}{\|g_\theta(x)\|_F} \cdot g_\theta(x).$$

This augmentation exposes the model to diverse intensity and texture variations while preserving structural content, thereby improving generalization.

The overall FL process begins with the server broadcasting the global model to all clients. Each client applies GIN-based augmentation on its local CT or MRI data and trains a U-Net model for several local epochs. After training, model weights are sent back to the server, which performs aggregation via FedAvg [9]. The updated global model is redistributed, and this cycle continues for multiple communication rounds. The full pipeline is illustrated in Fig. 1.

3 Experiments

To evaluate our method, we conducted experiments with a two-client FL setup: one client trained on CT data, the other on MRI. This allowed us to assess the model's generalization across modalities, with a centralized combination of MRI and CT data, and local models trained on individual modalities.

3.1 Dataset Details

We conducted experiments using two public 3D medical imaging datasets: TotalSegmentator [17] and AMOS2020 [7]. The TotalSegmentator dataset, containing CT and MRI images, was used for training and validation, while the

AMOS2020 dataset was reserved for testing. We aimed to evaluate generalization across modalities for five abdominal organs: liver, kidneys, spleen, pancreas, and gall bladder. Each 3D dataset was sliced along the axial plane to generate 2D training inputs. Validation was modality-specific, with separate MRI and CT splits, while testing involved 60 cases of unpaired CT and MRI images from AMOS2020. 3D Dice scores were computed after reconstructing the predicted slices into volumes. Table 1 summarizes the number of 3D volumes and 2D slices used per organ.

Table 1. Number of cases in the training and validation sets for each organ in the TotalSegmentator dataset. The numbers in parentheses indicate the total number of slices available for each organ in the respective modality.

Organ	Training		Validation	
	MRI	CT	MRI	CT
Liver	80 (28,142)	704 (112,569)	20 (2,754)	177 (25,744)
Kidneys	84 (28,142)	662 (112,018)	22 (2,865)	166 (24,648)
Gall Bladder	65 (22,701)	510 (90,805)	17 (2,330)	128 (20,556)
Spleen	81 (27,796)	687 (111,183)	21 (2,899)	172 (25,189)
Pancreas	76 (26,985)	631 (107,938)	19 (2,611)	158 (23,022)

3.2 Implementation and Experimental Setup

We implemented our proposed FedGIN using `PyTorch`, with FL handled by the `Flower` framework [1]. All experiments were run on an `NVIDIA A40 GPU` (48 GB VRAM) using `CUDA 12.4`. We used a 2D U-Net [14] as the base segmentation model, with modifications such as strided convolutions for downsampling and bilinear interpolation for upsampling, implemented explicitly via `F.interpolate` within the decoder path. This ensures accurate spatial alignment between encoder and decoder feature maps during skip connections and maintains resolution consistency in the final output. LeakyReLU activations, batch normalization, and dropout ($p = 0.3$, $p = 0.4$ in the bottleneck) were used throughout. The final layer applies a sigmoid activation function to produce binary segmentation masks. All convolutional layers in the network are initialized using Kaiming He initialization [6]. Training used a combined Focal loss and Dice loss, weighted equally, and was optimized using `AdamW` (learning rate 5×10^{-4}, weight decay 1×10^{-4}). To improve training efficiency, we used a learning rate scheduler that reduces the learning rate when the validation performance plateaus, along with automatic mixed precision to accelerate computation and reduce memory usage. In federated training, each client (CT and MRI) trained locally for 1 epochs per round across 100 communication rounds using FedAvg [9]. GIN augmentation was applied on-the-fly at each client. For centralized training, we trained the same U-Net model for 100 epochs using the combined MRI and CT data. 3D Dice scores were computed by stacking 2D predictions into full patient volumes.

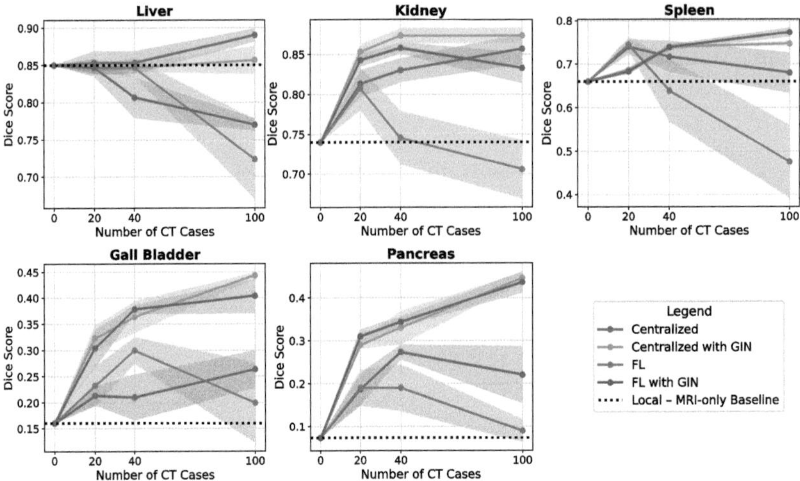

Fig. 2. 3D Dice scores on AMOS MRI test set across increasing CT cases. Comparison of local MRI-only training, centralized models with/without GIN, and FL with/without GIN (FedGIN).

3.3   Results and Analysis

We began by evaluating our FedGIN approach in a single-client setting under limited data conditions. For each organ, we first trained a baseline model using 20 MRI cases and then progressively added 20, 40, and 100 CT cases to examine whether incorporating a complementary modality can improve segmentation performance. We compared four training configurations: centralized training with and without GIN, FL with MRI and CT clients without GIN, and our proposed FedGIN setup with GIN. All experiments used the same hyperparameters and were repeated with three random seeds for fair comparison. Figure 2 displays the 3D Dice scores on the AMOS MRI test set for each organ, with the dashed line representing the local MRI-only baseline. Adding CT data improved MRI segmentation performance for most organs, except the liver. The improvement was most notable in low-contrast, complex organs like the spleen, gallbladder, and pancreas, which are challenging for segmentation tasks. In these cases, FedGIN and centralized training with GIN performed similarly, surpassing other configurations. For the spleen and pancreas, FedGIN closely matched centralized GIN models, demonstrating effective domain generalization in decentralized settings. In the case of the liver and kidneys, where anatomical consistency and intensity distribution are more homogeneous, centralized GIN training showed a slight performance advantage over FedGIN. Notably, for the liver, FedGIN did not improve performance over the local baseline or centralized counterparts. This underperformance may be due to the saturation of domain-specific characteristics in liver segmentation, where MRI-only models are already near their maximum performance. Additionally, the relatively small benefit of CT-derived variation for such organs may limit the marginal gain from GIN augmentation in the federated setting. In contrast, FL without GIN consistently underperformed and further degraded as more CT data was added. This highlights the negative effect of unharmonized modality mixing and confirms that GIN stabilizes the performance in this cross-domain federated setup. These findings support our hypothesis under specific conditions: when segmenting structurally complex and low-contrast organs (e.g., spleen, gall bladder, pancreas), the incorporation of CT data significantly enhances MRI segmentation performance. Moreover, under heterogeneous data distributions across clients, GIN augmentation proves essential for closing the performance gap between centralized and federated training. In contrast, for organs that are simpler to segment, such as the liver and kidneys, where MRI data alone already yields high baseline performance, the added benefit of CT data and GIN is more limited.

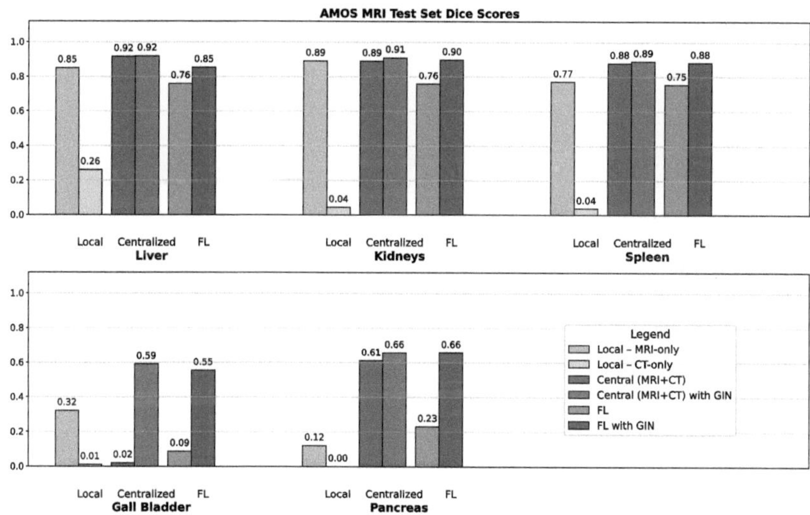

Fig. 3. Comparison of Dice Scores from AMOS MRI Test Set across TotalSegmentator-Trained Local, Centralized, and Federated Learning Models, with and without GIN, for different organs.

To assess the generalizability of our method at scale, we trained models using the complete TotalSegmentator dataset for each organ, as detailed in Table 1. These models were then evaluated on the AMOS CT and MRI test sets. We compared five training configurations: local models trained on MRI and CT data separately, centralized training on combined CT and MRI data (with and without GIN), and FL with separate MRI and CT clients (with and without GIN). Figures 3 and 4 show that models trained on unpaired multimodal data outperformed single-modality baselines in both test sets. GIN-centralized and FedGIN models achieved the best performance across all organs. In the AMOS CT test set, FedGIN and centralized GIN had comparable Dice scores in all five organs, with pancreas segmentation reaching 0.69 for FedGIN and 0.68 for centralized GIN. For gallbladder segmentation, FedGIN improved the score from 0.08 (MRI-only) and 0.51 (CT-only) to over 0.60 with multimodal training. This highlights the effectiveness of integrating CT and MRI during training, even in a federated setting. Similarly, on the AMOS MRI test set, both FedGIN and centralized GIN achieved strong and balanced generalization. In challenging cases like the gallbladder and pancreas, performance increased significantly compared to local models trained only on CT or MRI. These improvements confirm that GIN-harmonized cross-modal training leads to better generalization in both centralized and federated settings. GIN multimodal training not only outperformed local baselines but also demonstrated that FedGIN can match the performance of centralized training without requiring centralized data access.

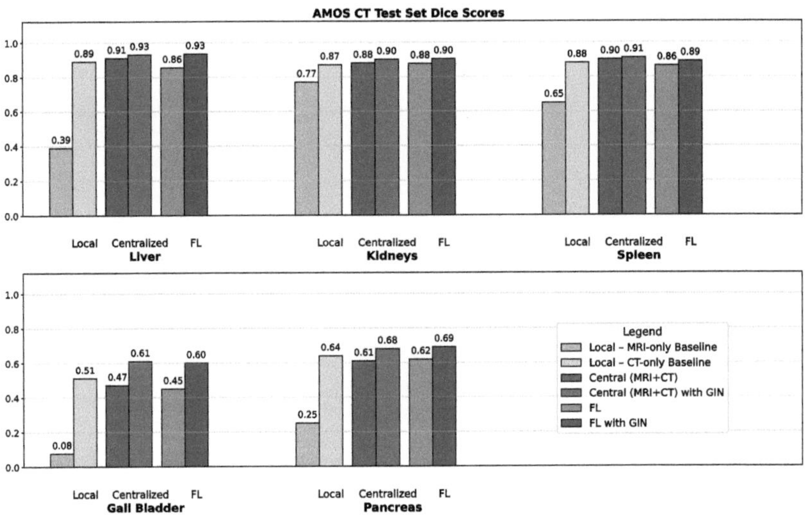

Fig. 4. Comparison of Dice Scores from AMOS CT Test Set across TotalSegmentator-Trained Local, Centralized, and Federated Learning Models, with and without GIN, for different organs.

These results show that multimodal training consistently outperformed the local baseline models across all organs. Both centralized and federated models with GIN achieved higher Dice scores, demonstrating effective modality alignment and improved generalization. Notably, FL with GIN closely matched centralized GIN performance, validating its robustness under decentralized training.

Recent studies [3,4] report the Dice scores of approximately 0.83 for the liver and up to 0.91 for the kidneys, which closely align with our results. Notably, our approach achieves comparable performance without relying on complex network architectures or centralized access to multimodal data. Instead, we employ a lightweight GIN augmentation strategy within an FL framework, offering a scalable and privacy-preserving alternative. Furthermore, our method addresses persistent segmentation challenges in low-contrast and structurally variable organs, such as the pancreas, spleen, and gallbladder, more effectively than local baseline models. These results show our framework as demonstrating competitive performance under realistic deployment constraints. As such, our work contributes a strong and generalizable baseline for future multimodal segmentation research in federated settings.

4   Conclusion

In this work, we introduced a federated multimodal organ segmentation framework that integrates unpaired CT and MRI data from multiple clients, enhanced with GIN augmentation to mitigate domain shifts. Our experiments, conducted on both small-scale and large-scale datasets, consistently demonstrate that incorporating CT data significantly enhances segmentation performance on MRI, particularly for organs that present challenging segmentation tasks, such as the pancreas and gallbladder. FedGIN shows competitive results compared to centralized training, demonstrating its potential for cross-modality learning in a federated setting. Furthermore, our large-scale evaluations reinforce the advantages of multimodal training with GIN, highlighting its ability to generalize across domains. These findings support the feasibility of scalable, federated, and modality-agnostic learning strategies for real-world clinical segmentation tasks.

References

1. Beutel, D.J., et al.: Flower: a friendly federated learning research framework. arXiv preprint arXiv:2007.14390 (2020)
2. Chen, B., et al.: Generalizable single-source cross-modality medical image segmentation via invariant causal mechanisms. In: 2025 IEEE/CVF Winter Conference on Applications of Computer Vision (WACV), pp. 3592–3602. IEEE (2025)
3. Ciausu, C., Krishnaswamy, D., Billot, B., Pieper, S., Kikinis, R., Fedorov, A.: Towards automatic abdominal MRI organ segmentation: leveraging synthesized data generated from CT labels. arXiv preprint arXiv:2403.15609 (2024)
4. D'Antonoli, T.A., et al.: Totalsegmentator MRI: sequence-independent segmentation of 59 anatomical structures in MR images. arXiv preprint arXiv:2405.19492 (2024)
5. Guan, H., Yap, P.T., Bozoki, A., Liu, M.: Federated learning for medical image analysis: a survey. Pattern Recogn., 110424 (2024)
6. He, K., Zhang, X., Ren, S., Sun, J.: Delving deep into rectifiers: surpassing human-level performance on ImageNet classification (2015). https://arxiv.org/abs/1502.01852

7. Ji, Y., et al.: AMOS: a large-scale abdominal multi-organ benchmark for versatile medical image segmentation. Adv. Neural. Inf. Process. Syst. **35**, 36722–36732 (2022)
8. Lassau, N., et al.: Three artificial intelligence data challenges based on CT and MRI. Diagn. Interv. Imaging **101**(12), 783–788 (2020)
9. McMahan, B., Moore, E., Ramage, D., Hampson, S., y Arcas, B.A.: Communication-efficient learning of deep networks from decentralized data. In: Artificial Intelligence and Statistics, pp. 1273–1282. PMLR (2017)
10. Myrzashova, R., Alsamhi, S.H., Shvetsov, A.V., Hawbani, A., Guizani, M., Wei, X.: BCFTL: blockchain-enabled multimodal federated transfer learning for decentralized Alzheimer's diagnosis. IEEE Internet Things J. (2025)
11. Ouyang, C., et al.: Causality-inspired single-source domain generalization for medical image segmentation. IEEE Trans. Med. Imaging **42**(4), 1095–1106 (2022)
12. Pati, S., et al.: Privacy preservation for federated learning in health care. Patterns **5**(7) (2024)
13. Raggio, C.B., et al.: FedSynthCT-Brain: a federated learning framework for multi-institutional brain MRI-to-CT synthesis. Comput. Biol. Med. **192**, 110160 (2025)
14. Ronneberger, O., Fischer, P., Brox, T.: U-Net: convolutional networks for biomedical image segmentation (2015). https://arxiv.org/abs/1505.04597
15. Wang, N., Deng, Y., Fan, S., Yin, J., Ng, S.K.: Multi-modal one-shot federated ensemble learning for medical data with vision large language model. arXiv preprint arXiv:2501.03292 (2025)
16. Wang, X., Zhou, R., Xie, H., Tang, X., He, L., Yang, C.: ClusMFL: a cluster-enhanced framework for modality-incomplete multimodal federated learning in brain imaging analysis. arXiv preprint arXiv:2502.12180 (2025)
17. Wasserthal, J., et al.: TotalSegmentator: robust segmentation of 104 anatomic structures in CT images. Radiol. Artif. Intell. **5**(5), e230024 (2023)
18. Yuan, L., Han, D.J., Wang, S., Upadhyay, D., Brinton, C.G.: Communication-efficient multimodal federated learning: joint modality and client selection. arXiv preprint arXiv:2401.16685 (2024)
19. Zhao, Y., Li, M., Lai, L., Suda, N., Civin, D., Chandra, V.: Federated learning with Non-IID data. arXiv preprint arXiv:1806.00582 (2018)

Validation of Various Normalization Methods for Brain Tumor Segmentation: Can Federated Learning Overcome This Heterogeneity?

Jan Fiszer[1,2(✉)], Dominika Ciupek[1], and Maciej Malawski[1,2]

[1] Sano Centre for Computational Medicine, Krakow, Poland
{j.fiszer,d.ciupek}@sanoscience.org
[2] AGH University of Krakow, Krakow, Poland

Abstract. Deep learning (DL) has been increasingly applied in medical imaging, however, it requires large amounts of data, which raises many challenges related to data privacy, storage, and transfer. Federated learning (FL) is a training paradigm that overcomes these issues, though its effectiveness may be reduced when dealing with non-independent and identically distributed (non-IID) data. This study simulates non-IID conditions by applying different MRI intensity normalization techniques to separate data subsets, reflecting a common cause of heterogeneity. These subsets are then used for training and testing models for brain tumor segmentation. The findings provide insights into the influence of the MRI intensity normalization methods on segmentation models, both training and inference. Notably, the FL methods demonstrated resilience to inconsistently normalized data across clients, achieving the 3D Dice score of 92%, which is comparable to a centralized model (trained using all data). These results indicate that FL is a solution to effectively train high-performing models without violating data privacy, a crucial concern in medical applications. The code is available at: https://github. com/SanoScience/fl-varying-normalization.

Keywords: Federated learning · Deep learning · Decentralized training · magnetic resonance imaging · MRI Intensity Normalization · Brain tumor segmentation

1 Introduction

Artificial intelligence is transforming healthcare by improving diagnostic accuracy and aiding clinical decisions [1]. In particular, deep learning excels at finding complex patterns from large datasets, achieving top performance in tasks such as tumor detection or organ segmentation [4,10]. However, its clinical adoption is limited by the need for vast amounts of high-quality annotated data–challenging to obtain due to strict privacy regulations and restricted data sharing.

© The Author(s), under exclusive license to Springer Nature Switzerland AG 2026
G. Zamzmi et al. (Eds.): MICCAI 2025, LNCS 16135, pp. 121–130, 2026.
https://doi.org/10.1007/978-3-032-05663-4_12

To address these challenges, federated learning (FL) [11] has emerged as a promising paradigm. Rather than requiring data to be centralized, FL enables institutions to collaboratively train a shared model while keeping patient data local. This approach seeks to leverage large-scale data while maintaining privacy. However, FL introduces new complexities, especially in scenarios where data across institutions (*FL clients*) is not uniformly distributed [20]. Differences in imaging protocols, scanner hardware, and preprocessing techniques can lead to variations that degrade model performance. Additionally, in magnetic resonance imaging (MRI), various intensity normalization[1] techniques have been developed [12,13,15], but none of them have been established as the superior one, becoming an additional source of heterogeneity.

This article delves into one such real-world complexity: the impact of heterogeneous MRI intensity normalization techniques on performance in brain tumor segmentation. By simulating client-specific preprocessing, the study explores how inconsistencies in data normalization can affect model training and reliability. The study evaluated different MRI normalization methods across separate data subsets, assessing their influence on the accuracy of brain tumor segmentation models. The results verify the proficiency of five normalization methods for the training and inference of segmentation models. Further, it presents the capabilities of FL models to achieve near-parity with centralized models, even under non-independent and identically distributed (non-IID) conditions.

The previous work investigated the influence of different normalization methods [7,13] on deep learning tasks, but to the best of our knowledge, it hasn't been validated for brain tumor segmentation. Further, there is a wide variety of experiments with FL for heterogeneous and non-IID data, but no publications were found regarding exactly the behavior of FL with various normalization methods between clients, a particular scenario of attribute-skew [20].

The main contributions are:

1. Verification of five normalization methods for MRI from the automatic brain tumor segmentation,
2. Proof of robustness of FL methods against variously normalized models.

2   Materials and Methods

2.1   Data

Dataset. The dataset used in this study was UCSF-PDGM-v3 [3], which includes 495 subjects diagnosed with WHO grade 2 to 4 gliomas confirmed by histopathology. Each subject had multiple MRI modalities acquired using a 3T Discovery 750 GE scanner (GE, Waukesha, WI), along with expert-validated brain tumor segmentation masks. Only T1-weighted, T2-weighted, and FLAIR images were selected, as these are compatible with the normalization techniques being evaluated. During manual filtering, two subjects were removed due to

---

[1] In the following, the word *normalization* refers to the intensity normalization.

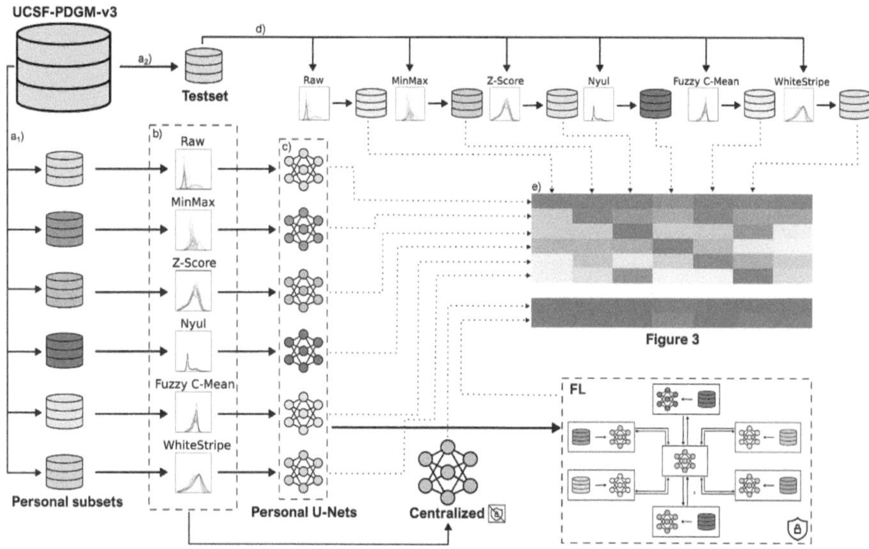

Fig. 1. The *big picture* of the pipeline used, explaining the structure of the results table in Fig. 3. Visualization of the main steps and their dependencies, including: a) the UCSF-PDGM-v3 dataset split, b) subsets normalization, c) models training, d) test sets normalization, and e) resulting evaluation table.

strong, most likely motion and reconstruction artifacts, respectively for subject with IDs 0077, 0318, leaving 493 subjects for further processing.

The dataset was divided into six equally sized personal subsets (one for each normalization and one raw—not-normalized), with a total of 82 patients each. Afterward, each of the subsets was normalized by one of the normalization methods described in subsection *Normalizations*. That procedure artificially generated six non-IID subsets, one for each client. That mimics a real-case scenario such that, during the federated learning process, collaborating institutions have very similar data, but different preprocessing methods (here, differently normalized). Furthermore, the subsets were divided into train, test, and validation sets in proportions 75:20:5, which consequently resulted in 61, 17, and 4 brain volumes for each of the sets (see Fig. 1). Since the validation set was not particularly important, this amount (4 volumes) was sufficient. It was not relevant for federated learning and was just used to monitor the process of classical training. The test sets were used during federated learning for on-site client testing.

For proper evaluation, the common test sets originated from the same subset of data (same subjects), but were differently normalized (presented in Fig. 2). The common test sets also consisted of 17 patients, equal to 1466 brain slices (division illustrated in Fig. 1) of which 1036 included brain tumors.

All volumes used were divided into 2D brain slices, resulting in 240×240 images, as the segmentation model was working on 2D data (see Sect. 2.2). The slices were filtered to contain at least 20% of brain pixels or for these having a brain tumor mask of at least 5% of the brain pixels. The segmentation task was simplified by binarization of the target tumor mask, so instead of having three possible tumor compartments, there was just one.

Normalizations. The artificial heterogeneity of the data was introduced by the use of varying normalization techniques for MR images: MinMax scaling, Z-score [13], Nyul [12], Fuzzy C-Mean [13], WhiteStripe [15]. They were applied with the help of the Python package `intensity-normalization` [13]. The Nyul method is Piecewise Linear Histogram Matching that learns the standard histogram and adjusts each volume to fit it. Fuzzy C-Mean (FCM) calculates the mean value of a specified tissue and uses it as a normalization factor. WhiteStripe performs Z-score normalization based on the white matter intensities. The hyperparameters used are the same as in the original publications [12,15].

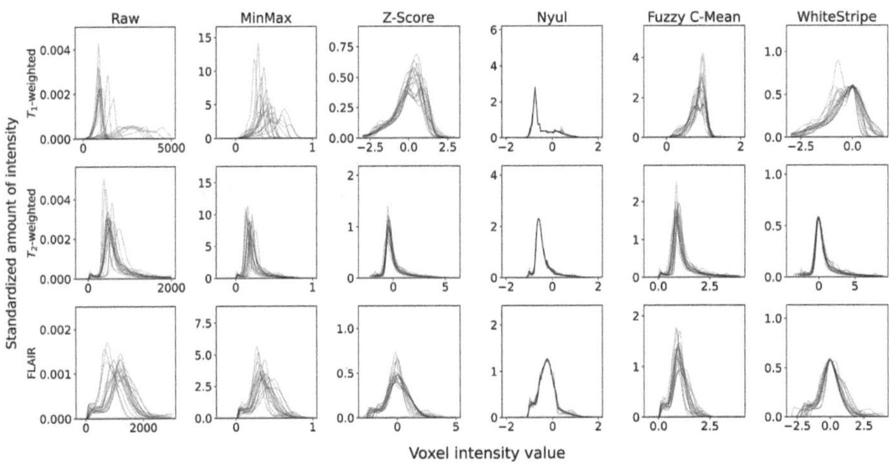

Fig. 2. The histograms for all modalities for each of the normalization methods. Each line corresponds to the brain (without the background) voxels' intensity distribution. The 17 subjects from the common test set volumes were used for this visualization.

2.2   Segmentation Model

Model Architecture. The utilized segmentation model is 2D U-Net [14], which, as input, takes 3 images (T1-weighted, T2-weighted, FLAIR) and outputs the brain tumor probability map. The encoder begins with a block containing 64 channels, progressively doubling the number of channels at each stage until it reaches 1024 at the bottleneck. The decoder then reverses this pattern, starting from the bottleneck and outputs the tumor mask. Unlike the classical implementation, here U-Net uses Group Normalization [19] instead of Batch Normalization [6], since the latter harms federated learning [18] and yielded worse performance.

Additionally, a dropout [16] layer was incorporated into the downsampling blocks with the dropout ratio of 0.3 (best performance among {0.1, 0.3, 0.5}).

Training. The neural network was trained using Adam optimizer [8] with the learning rate value of 0.001 (best performing among {0.01, 0.001, 0.0001}) with *Generalized Dice Loss (GDL)* function [17]:

$$GDL(P,T) = 1 - GDS(P,T) \tag{1}$$

$$GDS(P,T) = 2\frac{\sum_{l=1}^{2} w_l \sum_n t_{ln} p_{ln}}{\sum_{l=1}^{2} w_l \sum_n (t_{ln} + p_{ln})} \tag{2}$$

where T is the target mask image (ground truth) and P predicted probability values of the tumor throughout the image, with voxel/pixel values t_{ln} and p_{ln}, respectively. The weight w_l balances the disproportion of the pixel quantity and is equal to $\frac{1}{\left(\sum_{n=1}^{N} t_{ln}\right)^2}$.

This loss function handled the issue of a relatively small number of target pixels (sometimes even no target mask) by weighting inversely proportional to the number of brain pixels. For training, the soft Dice variant was used, meaning the values were not binarized in the calculation process.

For all classically (non-FL) trained models, the training was for 16 epochs, which led to sufficient convergence. Moreover, for the evaluation, the model with the lowest loss across the whole training process was taken, reducing the probability of overfitting. Any overfitting would be particularly undesirable due to the significant distribution skew between different test sets.

Federated Learning. Regarding FL hyperparameters, the models were trained with 2 local epochs and 32 global rounds, and in every round, all clients were used. This setup led to stabilized convergence, and the low number of local epochs prevented local overfitting during rounds. The presented aggregation methods were FedAvg and FedBN [9]. FedAvg is the FL baseline, which calculates the weighted average based on the number of samples. However, because of the similar number of data samples for each client, the averaging weights were almost alike. FedBN aggregates the model similarly, but omits the normalization layers parameters, keeping them personalized for each client. Therefore, during the evaluation, personalized models were used for the corresponding dataset. While other FL aggregation methods such as FedAdam and FedMRI were tested, only FedAvg and FedBN are reported, as the others did not improve performance and, in some cases, even yield lower *GDS*.

Quantitative Evaluations. For evaluation, the *GDS* described by Eq. 2 was used, but computed with inputs (P and T) of the entire volumes (3D Dice variant). The network was deployed for all the subject slices, then the *GDS* was calculated on the concatenated slices. Since the brain MRIs are always considered three-dimensional, that evaluation approach was more appropriate and comparable with different approaches. Furthermore, it eliminated the problem of low scores appearing for slices with only a few tumor pixels, which is particularly challenging for the network, missing spatial context (as a 2D U-Net).

Tested on:

Trained on:	Raw	MinMax	Z-Score	Nyul	Fuzzy C-Mean	WhiteStripe	Average
Centralized*	0.92 ± 0.06	0.92 ± 0.06	0.92 ± 0.06	0.90 ± 0.09	0.92 ± 0.06	0.92 ± 0.06	0.919
Single-dataset trained:							
Raw	0.90 ± 0.07	0.90 ± 0.07	0.88 ± 0.08	0.78 ± 0.13	0.89 ± 0.08	0.80 ± 0.19	0.860
MinMax	0.67 ± 0.36	0.86 ± 0.22	0.81 ± 0.23	0.75 ± 0.20	0.86 ± 0.16	0.80 ± 0.21	0.792
Z-Score	0.21 ± 0.13	0.21 ± 0.13	0.88 ± 0.15	0.68 ± 0.21	0.20 ± 0.12	0.80 ± 0.15	0.497
Nyul	0.17 ± 0.10	0.17 ± 0.10	0.63 ± 0.25	0.88 ± 0.11	0.18 ± 0.11	0.42 ± 0.22	0.408
Fuzzy C-Mean	0.50 ± 0.37	0.73 ± 0.23	0.57 ± 0.30	0.68 ± 0.23	0.86 ± 0.21	0.77 ± 0.25	0.684
WhiteStripe	0.39 ± 0.21	0.44 ± 0.23	0.86 ± 0.16	0.46 ± 0.21	0.32 ± 0.19	0.88 ± 0.12	0.558
Average	0.473	0.552	0.770	0.705	0.554	0.745	
Federated learning:							
FedAvg	0.91 ± 0.06	0.91 ± 0.09	0.92 ± 0.07	0.86 ± 0.13	0.92 ± 0.06	0.91 ± 0.07	0.906
FedBN	0.92 ± 0.05	0.91 ± 0.10	0.92 ± 0.06	0.91 ± 0.08	0.92 ± 0.08	0.92 ± 0.05	0.916

Fig. 3. 3D Dice scores for all the models (rows) and all test sets (columns) with corresponding standard deviations. The star '*' next to the *Centralized* model indicates that this model violates data privacy. The *Average* row presents the average over the *GDS* for single-dataset trained models, and the *Average* column shows the average Dice among all the test sets for the given model. The scores with pink border had **no** statistically significant difference with respect to *GDS* achieved by centralized model (p-value was greater than 0.05 for Wilcoxon test).

3   Results

The table in Fig. 3 gives a broad overview of the quality of segmentation models for all the variously normalized test sets. There is a clear diagonal for single-trained (ST) models, where high scores are obtained for models trained on identically normalized data. The highest average *GDS* among the ST models was achieved for the model trained on the raw data. For some datasets, it performed even better than the model tested with the same normalization with which it was trained[2]. However, this model convergence was unstable across different training runs, contrary to e.g. *MinMax model*[3]. The Nyul model performed the worst (probably because Nyul is the most aggressive normalization, see Fig. 2). Notably, the results might be slightly biased due to different training samples.

---

[2] This was possible thanks to the normalization layers. Without any normalization layers, there was no convergence during training on the raw dataset. However, training the same model with Z-score data was unstable, but in the end converged to similar loss values as for the model with Group Normalization.

[3] For simplicity, "*normalization_name* model" is a short version of the phrase "model trained on data normalized with *normalization_name*" e.g. here it means model trained on data normalized with MinMax. Same for the datasets.

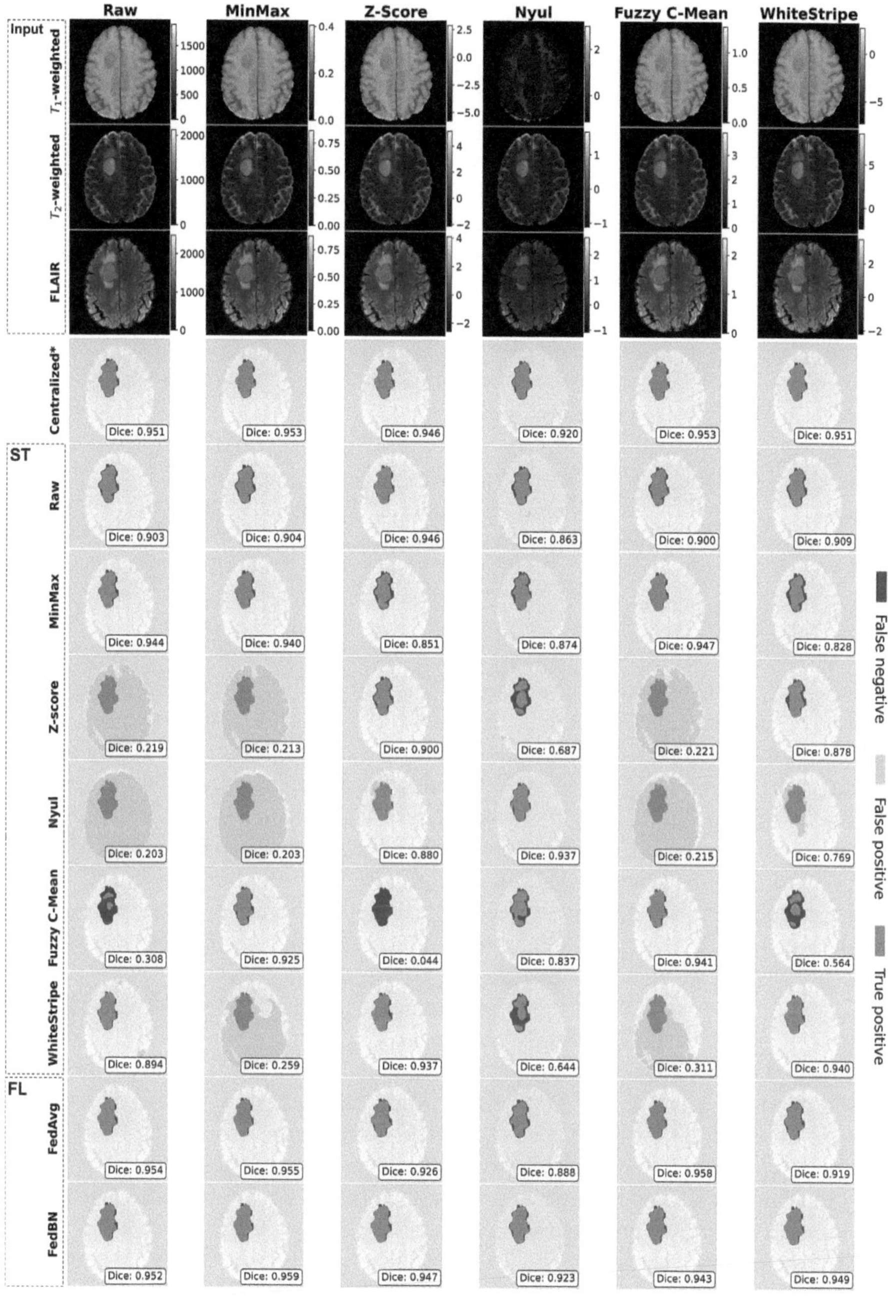

Fig. 4. Presentation of the predictions for each of the trained models on the 0229 patient. It presents the normalized inputs and the models' predictions with distinction for true positive, false negative, and false positive.

A similar pattern emerges in Fig. 4. The predictions on the ST models diagonal are satisfactory (over 90% of GDS with a little of false negatives). The worst predictions overlap with the low score values in Fig. 3, such as Z-score, Nyul, and WhiteStripe models. They were usually oversegmenting, whereas the Fuzzy-C-Mean model suffered from the opposite, many false negatives (undersegmentation). Raw and MinMax performed very well, slightly worse than the best (centralized and FL) models.

Across all models, the centralized one achieves the highest score, although violating data privacy. The models trained with FL and the centralized one obtained comparable results. FedBN yielded similar GSC to the centralized model within the margin of statistical error. The main difference between the FL methods was on the Nyul dataset, visible in both Figs. 3 and 4. Among the test sets, the Z-score normalized dataset turned out to be the most compatible with the other models (highest average score), but Fuzzy C-Mean model did not detect any tumor in the visualized slices. Also notable is the *WhiteStripe dataset* with only a low GDS for the worst model (Nyul). Furthermore, the raw datasets appeared to be the most challenging for all ST models. For FedAvg and the centralized models, the most problematic was the Nyul test set.

4   Conclusions

The results indicate some guidelines on training and running brain tumor segmentation models that can be potentially applied to other domains of deep learning and medical imaging. We could conclude that to train a well-generalizing model, which will be utilized for variously normalized data, the complicated normalization methods should be avoided and the diversity of the training set should be maintained. In the case that there are normalization layers in the neural network, the most optimal solution would be to leave the data raw. Contrary to what has been stated several times, neural networks do not have to be trained using only equally distributed data with feature values around zero (in the case of incorporating layer normalization) [6].

Using an already trained model, the most promising approach is to replicate all preprocessing steps identically to the ones applied to the training data (the diagonal). Otherwise, scenarios like the one with the Nyul sample, where even well-trained models did not handle the input properly, may occur. However, if there is no information about the steps, the go-to normalization method should be Z-score (or WhiteStripe, which is a special type of Z-score).

The federated learning models showed robustness for training with varying normalization methods between clients, achieving results comparable to the centralized model. However, the FL methods tested were the basic ones, and there is a possibility that a more sophisticated one would even outperform the centralized model. Nevertheless, the obtained results are satisfactory, and for better comparison, it might be needed to increase the complexity of the task or datasets. For example, the segmentation model could have some special context, such as 3D or 2.5D U-Net [2,5]. Furthermore, leaving all four grades of glioma and performing multi-class segmentation would be another potential challenge for the model, exploiting the presented methods' proficiency.

Acknowledgments. The numerical experiment was possible through computing allocation on the Ares and Athena systems at ACC Cyfronet AGH under the grants PLG/2023/016117 and PLG/2024/016945. This project has received funding from the European Union's Horizon 2020 research and innovation programme under grant agreement No 857533 and from the International Research Agendas Programme of the Foundation for Polish Science No MAB PLUS/2019/13. The publication was created within the project of the Minister of Science and Higher Education "Support for the activity of Centers of Excellence established in Poland under Horizon 2020" on the basis of the contract number MEiN/2023/DIR/3796.

References

1. Alowais, S.A., et al.: Revolutionizing healthcare: the role of artificial intelligence in clinical practice. BMC Med. Educ. **23**(1), 689 (2023)
2. Angermann, C., Haltmeier, M.: Random 2.5 D U-Net for fully 3D segmentation. In: International Workshop on Machine Learning and Medical Engineering for Cardiovascular Healthcare, pp. 158–166. Springer (2019)
3. Calabrese, E., et al.: The university of California San Francisco preoperative diffuse glioma MRI dataset. Radiol. Artif. Intell. **4**(6), e220058 (2022)
4. Fu, Y., Lei, Y., Wang, T., Curran, W.J., Liu, T., Yang, X.: A review of deep learning based methods for medical image multi-organ segmentation. Physica Med. **85**, 107–122 (2021)
5. Huang, H., et al.: UNet 3+: a full-scale connected UNet for medical image segmentation. In: ICASSP 2020-2020 IEEE International Conference on Acoustics, Speech and Signal Processing (ICASSP), pp. 1055–1059. IEEE (2020)
6. Ioffe, S., Szegedy, C.: Batch Normalization: accelerating deep network training by reducing internal covariate shift. In: International Conference on Machine Learning, pp. 448–456. PMLR (2015)
7. Jacobsen, N., Deistung, A., Timmann, D., Goericke, S.L., Reichenbach, J.R., Güllmar, D.: Analysis of intensity normalization for optimal segmentation performance of a fully convolutional neural network. Z. Med. Phys. **29**(2), 128–138 (2019)
8. Kingma, D.P., Ba, J.: Adam: a method for stochastic optimization. arXiv preprint arXiv:1412.6980 (2014)
9. Li, X., Jiang, M., Zhang, X., Kamp, M., Dou, Q.: FedBN: federated learning on Non-IID features via local batch normalization. arXiv preprint arXiv:2102.07623 (2021)
10. Liu, Z., et al.: Deep learning based brain tumor segmentation: a survey. Complex Intell. Syst. **9**(1), 1001–1026 (2023)
11. McMahan, B., Moore, E., Ramage, D., Hampson, S., y Arcas, B.A.: Communication-efficient learning of deep networks from decentralized data. In: Artificial Intelligence and Statistics, pp. 1273–1282. PMLR (2017)
12. Nyúl, L.G., Udupa, J.K.: On standardizing the MR image intensity scale. Magn. Reson. Med. Official J. Int. Soc. Magn. Reson. Med. **42**(6), 1072–1081 (1999)
13. Reinhold, J.C., Dewey, B.E., Carass, A., Prince, J.L.: Evaluating the impact of intensity normalization on MR image synthesis. In: Proceedings of SPIE–the International Society for Optical Engineering, vol. 10949, p. 109493H (2019)

14. Ronneberger, O., Fischer, P., Brox, T.: U-Net: convolutional networks for biomedical image segmentation. In: Navab, N., Hornegger, J., Wells, W.M., Frangi, A.F. (eds.) MICCAI 2015. LNCS, vol. 9351, pp. 234–241. Springer, Cham (2015). https://doi.org/10.1007/978-3-319-24574-4_28
15. Shinohara, R.T., et al.: Statistical normalization techniques for magnetic resonance imaging. NeuroImage: Clin. **6**, 9–19 (2014)
16. Srivastava, N., Hinton, G., Krizhevsky, A., Sutskever, I., Salakhutdinov, R.: Dropout: a simple way to prevent neural networks from overfitting. J. Mach. Learn. Res. **15**(1), 1929–1958 (2014)
17. Sudre, C.H., Li, W., Vercauteren, T., Ourselin, S., Jorge Cardoso, M.: Generalised dice overlap as a deep learning loss function for highly unbalanced segmentations. In: Deep Learning in Medical Image Analysis and Multimodal Learning for Clinical Decision Support: Third International Workshop, DLMIA 2017, and 7th International Workshop, ML-CDS 2017, Held in Conjunction with MICCAI 2017, Québec City, QC, Canada, September 14, Proceedings 3, pp. 240–248. Springer (2017)
18. Wang, Y., Shi, Q., Chang, T.H.: Why batch normalization damage federated learning on Non-IID data? IEEE Transactions on Neural Networks and Learning Systems (2023)
19. Wu, Y., He, K.: Group normalization. In: Proceedings of the European Conference on Computer Vision (ECCV), pp. 3–19 (2018)
20. Zhu, H., Xu, J., Liu, S., Jin, Y.: Federated learning on Non-IID data: a survey. Neurocomputing **465**, 371–390 (2021)

The Interplay Between Explainability and Differential Privacy in Federated Healthcare

Marc Molina Van De Bosch[1,2]($\boxtimes$), Andrea Protani[1,3], Riccardo Taiello[1],
Lorenzo Giusti[1], Matilde Carvalho Costa[1], Ioannis Stathopoulos[4],
Efstathios Efstathopoulos[4], Diogo Reis Santos[1],
Miguel Angel Gonzalez Ballester[2,5], and Luigi Serio[1]

[1] European Organization for Nuclear Research, Geneva, Switzerland
[2] Universitat Pompeu Fabra, Barcelona, Spain
marc.molina.van.den.bosch@cern.ch
[3] École Polytechnique Fédérale de Lausanne, Lausanne, Switzerland
[4] Attikon University Hospital, National and Kapodistrian University of Athens,
Athens, Greece
[5] ICREA, Barcelona, Spain

Abstract. Federated Learning (FL) enables the training of deep learning models on siloed medical data. Its real-world application is often challenged by statistical heterogeneity, privacy requirements, and the need for model transparency. This paper addresses these challenges by investigating the interplay between FL, Differential Privacy (DP), and model explainability for 3D medical image segmentation. To simulate a realistic environment, we establish a cross-silo federation of four clients, comprising data from the BraTS dataset and a distinct heterogeneous dataset from a real hospital in Europe. Our analysis characterizes and quantifies an interaction, namely the phHeterogeneity Amplifier effect, providing a metric to measure the disproportionate degradation of explanation fidelity on heterogeneous clients under DP. To address this challenge, we propose Boundary-Interior Disentangled CAM (BID-CAM), a hybrid explanation method designed for DP-awareness. Our evaluation shows that BID-CAM maintains explanation fidelity under privacy constraints with respect to standard methods, demonstrating a more robust approach to model transparency in private, federated settings applied to medical imaging.

Keywords: Federated Learning · Medical Image Segmentation · Explainable AI · Differential Privacy · Data Heterogeneity · Grad-CAM

1 Introduction

Deep learning models have achieved state-of-the-art performance in medical image analysis, including segmentation of pathological tissues [9]. However,

© The Author(s), under exclusive license to Springer Nature Switzerland AG 2026
G. Zamzmi et al. (Eds.): MICCAI 2025, LNCS 16135, pp. 131–142, 2026.
https://doi.org/10.1007/978-3-032-05663-4_13

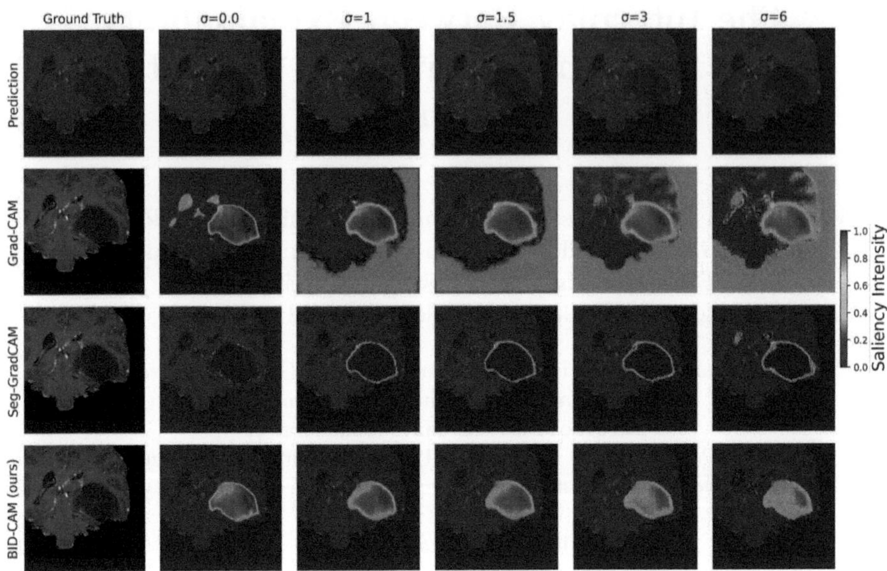

Fig. 1. Qualitative analysis of explanation methods on a sample from Client 2 under increasing Differential Privacy (DP) noise, controlled by σ. As DP noise increases, the Grad-CAM explanation becomes diffuse and Seg-GradCAM's becomes hollow, capturing only the tumor contour. In contrast, our proposed BID-CAM maintains a focused and structurally complete explanation, demonstrating superior robustness to privacy-induced noise.

their success depends heavily on large and diverse datasets, which are typically siloed within institutions due to strict patient privacy regulations (e.g., GDPR, HIPAA). Federated Learning (FL) addresses this limitation by enabling collaborative model training without centralizing raw data [18,20]. In federated environments, clinical institutions train models locally on their private data and share only model updates with a central server, which aggregates these updates to improve a shared global model [8,21]. However, FL remains vulnerable to privacy attacks, as adversaries can potentially reconstruct sensitive patient information from shared model updates [30] (Fig. 1).

While techniques like secure aggregation protect individual contributions [5, 24], using cryptographic building blocks, our work focuses on **Differential Privacy (DP)**, which offers more rigorous, quantifiable guarantees against inference attacks by injecting calibrated noise during the training process [11]. We employ *sample-level* DP via DP-SGD [1], which introduces a well-known privacy-utility trade-off [3,25]. This challenge is often exacerbated in federated settings by data heterogeneity, as *client drift* [14] can further impair the performance of standard aggregation algorithms like FedAvg [15].

In healthcare applications, model explainability is often essential for clinical adoption, enabling practitioners to trust predictions and adhere to regulatory standards like the *right to explanation* [6,13]. However, a tension exists between the mechanisms of DP and many common explanation techniques [22, 26]. Saliency-based methods, in particular, rely on precise gradients to generate explanations, but the perturbation inherent to DP-SGD can render these methods unreliable [12]. The nature of this three-way interplay among privacy, heterogeneity, and explainability is not yet fully understood, motivating the investigation in this work.

This study builds upon our prior work in federated 3D brain tumor segmentation [23], which employed our established security-by-design FL platform, CAFEIN^{TM} [7] for collaborative medical research. However, deploying strong formal guarantees like DP within operational clinical environment requires a foundational understanding of the model utility and explainability trade-off. This paper presents a prerequisite investigation, using a controlled benchmark to analyze the interplay between *sample-level* DP, model performance, and explainability, to guide future production-level implementation. Our main contributions are: *(i)* we construct a realistic FL benchmark with three homogeneous BraTS-derived clients and one real-world heterogeneous clinical client; *(ii)* we formally characterize and quantify an interaction we term the *heterogeneity amplifier effect*, to measure the disproportionate degradation of explanation fidelity on heterogeneous clients under DP; and *(iii)* we propose and evaluate Boundary-Interior Disentangled CAM (BID-CAM), a pragmatic, hybrid explanation method designed for DP-robustness, that provides structurally coherent explanations under privacy constraints.

2   Background

Federated Learning. FL is a distributed learning paradigm in which a set of clients $\mathcal{U}$ collaboratively train a shared global model θ under the orchestration of a central server [18]. One of the most common training algorithms is FedAvg [18], where in each communication round τ, clients perform local updates on their private datasets $\mathcal{D}_u$ and send their model parameters $\theta_{u,\tau}$ along with local dataset sizes $w_u = |\mathcal{D}_u|$ to the server. The server aggregates the models via weighted averaging:

$$\theta_{\tau+1} \leftarrow w_{\text{tot}} \sum_{u \in \mathcal{U}} w_u \theta_{u,\tau},$$

where $\frac{1}{w_{\text{tot}}} = \sum_{u \in \mathcal{U}} w_u$. In healthcare, FL is predominantly deployed in cross-silo settings [14], where a small cohort of hospitals collaboratively trains a shared model.

Differential Privacy. DP has emerged as a principled framework for providing provable, quantifiable privacy guarantees [11]. In DP, the privacy loss is controlled by two parameters: the privacy budget ε and δ, the probability of failure to meet the ε bound. Intuitively, smaller ε (and δ) imply stronger privacy. In FL, two privacy granularities are commonly used: *user-level DP*, which protects each client's entire dataset, and *sample-level DP*, which protects individual data points within each client's dataset. We focus exclusively on *sample-level DP*, since *user-level DP* typically requires noise to be calibrated to the total number of clients, making it impractical for cross-silo FL with few participants [14,17]. Formally, a randomized mechanism $\mathcal{M}$ satisfies (ε, δ)-DP if for any two adjacent datasets D and D' differing by one record, and for any measurable subset of outputs $\mathcal{S}$:

$$\Pr[\mathcal{M}(D) \in \mathcal{S}] \leq e^{\varepsilon} \Pr[\mathcal{M}(D') \in \mathcal{S}] + \delta.$$

DP-SGD [1] achieves sample-level DP by *(i)* clipping each *per-example* gradient to an ℓ_2-norm bound C, and *(ii)* adding Gaussian noise $\mathcal{N}(0, \sigma^2 C^2 \mathbf{I})$ to the aggregated clipped gradients. The noise multiplier σ and the clipping bound C, together with the total number of steps and the sampling strategy, determine the achieved (ε, δ) guarantee via the moments accountant or other privacy accounting methods [1,19].

Explainability. When applied to medical imaging, explainable AI (XAI) techniques aim to provide intuitions on model's decisions for a specific class c. This is achieved via saliency maps [29], a coarse localization of the regions that contributed the most to the model's predictions. The foundational method in this family is **Grad-CAM** [22], which generate heatmaps highlighting the regions of the input image I that influence mostly the model's output, via a weighted combination of the final convolutional feature maps, $A^k(I)$. When it is clear from the context, we omit the reference to the input I, and use A^k as a reference to the activation maps. The weights, α_c^k, are calculated by the global average pooling the gradients of the class score, y^c, with respect to the feature maps, $\alpha_c^k = \frac{1}{Z} \sum_i \sum_j \sum_l \frac{\partial y^c}{\partial A_{ijl}^k}$ where Z is the number of pixels in the feature map. The final explanation is a ReLU-activated weighted sum: $M_{\text{Grad-CAM}} = \text{ReLU}(\sum_k \alpha_c^k A^k)$. Although effective for classification, Grad-CAM's spatial averaging is too coarse for dense prediction tasks like semantic segmentation. To address this challenge, **Seg-Grad-CAM** [26] was developed to produce pixel-level explanations by avoiding spatial averaging and computing gradients in a spatially-aware manner. The method generates explanations as:

$$M_{\text{SGCAM}}(I) = \text{ReLU}\left(\sum_k \left(\frac{\partial S_{\text{seg}}(I)}{\partial A^k(I)} \odot A^k(I) \right) \right), \qquad S_{\text{seg}}(I) = \sum_s P_s(I)^2,$$

$$(1)$$

where $\odot$ denotes element-wise multiplication and S_{seg} is computed by adding the squared values of the model's predictions $P(I)$. Given its superior precision for dense predictions, Seg-Grad-CAM produces sharper, higher-fidelity explanations more suitable for segmentation tasks, thereby shaping the foundation of our explainability analysis.

3   The Compounding Cost of Privacy and Heterogeneity

While common saliency methods provide precise explanations for standard models, they suffer significant degradation when applied to DP-trained models (as shown in Table 1). The noise injected during DP-SGD perturb the gradients used by these saliency methods, leading to unstable and unfocused explanations. To address this fundamental limitation, we propose a pragmatic method, BID-CAM, which accounts for the noise characteristics of DP training by combining the strengths of different explanation approaches

BID-CAM. Observing that coarse explainability methods excel at identifying object cores while finer-grain methods are accurate in delineating boundaries. BID-CAM is a hybrid approach that applies different techniques to the spatial regions where each is most effective: a robust method for interior regions and a precise, noise-aware method for boundaries.

To obtain precise explanations along boundaries, we develop a DP-aware Seg-Grad-CAM (DPR-SGCAM) that recovers stable explanations by computing their expectation over the noise distribution used during DP training. The goal is to minimize random gradient perturbations to reveal the underlying signal. Moreover, unlike standard methods, our proposed method targets pre-activation logits where DP noise is effectively added during training:

$$M_{\text{DPR-SGCAM}}(I) = \mathbb{E}_{\mathcal{E} \sim \mathcal{N}(0,\sigma_{\text{cam}}^2 I)} \left[\text{ReLU} \left(\sum_k \left((\nabla_{A^k} S_{\text{logits}}(I) + \mathcal{E}_k) \odot A^k(I) \right) \right) \right] \tag{2}$$

where $S_{\text{logits}}(I) = \sum_s L_s(I)$ and the noise standard deviation is calibrated to the model's DP parameters: $\sigma_{\text{cam}} = C \cdot \sigma_{\text{train}}$. Integrating a non-linear function (ReLU) over a high-dimensional probability space makes the computation of Eq. 2 intractable, therefore we estimate $M_{\text{DPR-SGCAM}}(I)$ via Monte Carlo sampling using $N = 50$ samples. The second component of BID-CAM, spatial disentanglement, uses the robust $M_{\text{Grad-CAM}}$ for interior regions and $M_{\text{DPR-SGCAM}}$ for boundaries. We define disjoint spatial masks for interior points, $\text{M}_{\mathcal{I}} = P_B \ominus B$, and for boundary points, $\text{M}_\partial = P_B \setminus (P_B \ominus B)$, using a minimal morphological erosion ($\ominus$ with structure B) on the model's prediction $P_B = \mathbb{I}(P_{\text{pred}} > 0.5)$. The methods are then spatially combined to form the complete explanation: $M_{\text{BID-CAM}} = (M_{\text{DPR-SGCAM}} \odot \text{M}_\partial) + (M_{\text{Grad-CAM}} \odot \text{M}_{\mathcal{I}})$.

4   Experimental Setup

FL Setup. To assess the performance of our method, we design a cross-silo FL scenario with four clients for validation under realistic data heterogeneity conditions. We trained a 3D U-Net model with 2.7M parameters, implemented in Keras, using the FedAvg [18] algorithm for 200 communication rounds. For all experiments, each client used a batch size of 12 and the AdamW optimizer with a learning rate of 10^{-3}, running on a dedicated NVIDIA® A100 GPU with 40 GB of VRAM. We chose FedAvg because it is the most common aggregation algorithm in FL and serves as a foundational baseline to clearly establish the interplay between DP and heterogeneity.

DP Setup. We investigate various noise multipliers (σ) from the set {0.01, 0.05, 0.10, 0.15, 0.25, 0.50, 0.75, 1.00 , 1.25, 1.50, 3.00, 6.00}. The gradient clipping bound (C) was fixed across all experiments, set heuristically to the 90th percentile of per-sample gradient norms observed during initial training. The privacy budget (ε) was computed using Opacus [28] with the RDP accountant [19], a fixed batch size of 12, and $\delta = 10^{-5}$ (Table 1). The corresponding privacy budget for each client is reported in Appendix 2.

Homogeneous Clients. We partition the BraTS 2025 training dataset [4,10] for adult diffuse Pre- and Pos-treatment glioma segmentation across three clients which contains multi-modal MRI images, including T1, T1-gadolinium enhanced (T1Gd), T2, and T2-FLAIR. The PRE1 and PRE2 clients each contain 566 pre-treatment MRI scans, representing a near-IID condition of baseline. The POS client contains 727 MRI scans, introducing a significant *covariate shift* due to treatment-induced effects such as altered tissue architecture, different contrast enhancement patterns, edema, and the presence of resection cavities.

Heterogeneous Client. The Heterogeneous Client (HC) consists of 165 fully-anonymized multi-modal MRI scans from an European hospital, collected between 2021 and 2023. Examinations were performed on a 3.0 T Philips Achieva TX MRI system and include T2, FLAIR, and T1ce modalities. This client introduces significant domain shift compared to the glioma-focused BraTS dataset due to a wide range of pathologies, including tumors, strokes, multiple sclerosis, and white matter hyperintensities (WMH), and distinct scanner characteristics. Ground truth labels were provided by two experienced neuroradiologists via consensus using ITK-SNAP and confirmed with laboratory and biopsy data to ensure reliability.

Data Preprocessing and Harmonization. All datasets undergo standardized pre-processing including coordinate system alignment, image-level z-score normalization, resampling to isotropic 1mm^3 spacing, and padding to uniform dimensions of ($182 \times 220 \times 182$) voxels. When creating the BRATS clients, we retained only the first acquisition of any patient that appeared multiple times, preventing patient-level leakage across clients. Each client's dataset was subsequently split into training and test partitions with an $80 - 20$ ratio, enforced at the subject level. To harmonize different annotation schemas across clients, we convert all segmentation tasks to binary classification with pathological findings as Class 1 and healthy tissue as Class 0, enabling generalizable feature learning despite varying annotation protocols. Moreover, the heterogeneous client data does not contain T1 native modality. While methods exist for handling missing data IN FL [27], a formal investigation is outside the scope of this work. Consequently, we harmonize the client data by removing the T1w channel, ensuring the model receives a consistent set of three input MRI modalities (T1ce, T2, and FLAIR) from all clients.

Quantitative Metrics for Explainability. To objectively evaluate the quality of a generated explanation map M_{CAM} against a ground-truth lesion mask M_{GT}, we use the Focus metric used in different studies [2,16]. Evaluated as the fraction of the explanation energy that correctly falls within the ground-truth mask. A higher score indicates better alignment with relevant features. To measure the impact of DP on explanation fidelity, we first define the *Focus Drop* (Δ_{Focus}) as the percentage decrease in the Focus score for a DP-enabled model relative to its non-private baseline:

$$\Delta_{\mathrm{Focus}}(\%) = \frac{\mathrm{Focus_{non\text{-}DP}} - \mathrm{Focus_{DP}}}{\mathrm{Focus_{non\text{-}DP}}} \times 100\%$$

Table 1. Detrimental Impact of DP with Privacy budget ϵ and noise mulitplier σ on Model Performance (Dice) and Explainability (Focus), alongside the Heterogeneity Amplification ($\mathcal{A}$) effect. Colors are scaled column-wise to show trends within each metric

			Grad-CAM			Seg-GradCAM			BID-CAM		
ϵ	σ	Dice	HeF	$\overline{\mathrm{HoF}}$	$\mathcal{A}$	HeF	$\overline{\mathrm{HoF}}$	$\mathcal{A}$	HeF	$\overline{\mathrm{HoF}}$	$\mathcal{A}$
∞	0.00	0.887	0.196	0.824	1.00	0.191	0.125	1.00	0.717	0.941	1.00
$<10^6$	0.01	0.899	0.102	0.614	1.44×	0.343	0.443	1.97×	0.692	0.963	1.06×
$<10^4$	0.05	0.895	0.098	0.546	1.32×	0.296	0.447	2.31×	0.629	0.958	1.16×
$<10^3$	0.10	0.880	0.046	0.317	1.64×	0.326	0.526	2.47×	0.634	0.956	1.15×
$<10^3$	0.15	0.873	0.051	0.360	1.69×	0.216	0.490	3.47×	0.577	0.953	1.26×
224.50	0.25	0.856	0.053	0.362	1.63×	0.214	0.449	3.21×	0.560	0.944	1.28×
38.25	0.50	0.829	0.047	0.339	1.73×	0.143	0.440	4.71×	0.442	0.924	1.59×
14.43	0.75	0.815	0.046	0.324	1.67×	0.089	0.353	6.04×	0.380	0.903	1.81×
7.88	1.00	0.802	0.029	0.204	1.69×	0.130	0.483	5.69×	0.363	0.899	1.88×
5.25	1.25	0.789	0.025	0.158	1.53×	0.146	0.531	5.57×	0.370	0.902	1.86×
3.91	1.50	0.781	0.021	0.161	1.81×	0.135	0.510	5.79×	0.336	0.887	2.01×
1.55	3.00	0.690	0.011	0.095	1.94×	0.118	0.550	6.83×	0.291	0.797	2.06×
0.69	6.00	0.631	0.010	0.069	1.64×	0.136	0.541	5.83×	0.277	0.708	1.92×

Performance: Low — High Disparity ($\mathcal{A}$): Low — High

A higher Δ_{Focus} indicates a more severe degradation in explainability. Hence, to formally quantify the extent to which DP disproportionately harms explainability on the heterogeneous client, we define the *Amplification Factor* ($\mathcal{A}$). This factor measures how much greater the Focus Drop is on the heterogeneous client (Client 1) compared to the average drop across the homogeneous clients ($\mathcal{C}_{\mathrm{hom}} = \{\mathrm{Client}\ 2, 3, 4\}$):

$$\mathcal{A} = \frac{\Delta_{\mathrm{Focus}}(\mathrm{Client}\ 1)}{\frac{1}{|\mathcal{C}_{\mathrm{hom}}|} \sum_{i \in \mathcal{C}_{\mathrm{hom}}} \Delta_{\mathrm{Focus}}(\mathrm{Client}\ i)}$$

5 Experimental Results

Our experimental results, presented in Table 1, quantitatively demonstrate the challenges of ensuring privacy in realistic federated scenarios. These challenges include: the degradation of model utility and explainability, and the amplification of this cost by statistical data heterogeneity.

Impact of DP on Performance and Baseline Explainability. As the DP noise multiplier (σ) increases from 0.00 to 6.00, there is a clear and expected degradation in model utility, with the Dice score falling from 0.887 to 0.631. Critically, the explainability degradation is even more pronounced for both baseline saliency methods. On the heterogeneous client, Grad-CAM's Focus degrades from 0.196 to 0.010, and while Seg-GradCAM starts from a similar point, its Focus also degrades under high privacy. Moreover, the heterogeneity amplifier effect is severe for both baselines. While Grad-CAM's amplification remains high, the effect is even more extreme for Seg-GradCAM, where the amplification factor ($\mathcal{A}$) reached as high as $6.83\times$ and is $5.83\times$ at $\sigma = 6.00$, demonstrating that a method's initial precision is not strongly linked to its robustness.

Robustness to DP and Heterogeneity. Conversely, BID-CAM demonstrates improved robustness when evaluated on the heterogeneous client. In the non-private setting, it achieves a peak focus score of 0.717. Although its performance decreases as the noise level increases, its rate of degradation is slower than that of the baseline techniques. This robustness persists across all levels of privacy; under high noise ($\sigma = 6.00$), its score of 0.277 still substantially exceeds the high-noise scores of Grad-CAM (0.010) and Seg-GradCAM (0.136). The advantage of this hybrid design is particularly clear in the low-noise regime ($\sigma < 0.50$), where the high-quality prediction mask allows BID-CAM's spatial disentanglement to substantially outperform the baseline methods.

6 Conclusion

In this work, we investigate the impact of differential privacy, data heterogeneity, and model explainability within federated medical image segmentation. Our results quantitatively characterize a heterogeneity amplifier effect, where the noise added to protect client privacy disproportionately degrades the explanation fidelity on clients with unique data. This degradation makes standard saliency methods ineffective, posing a significant challenge to future federated learning collaborations. We introduce BID-CAM, a pragmatic hybrid method that demonstrates improved robustness against the degradation effect compared to baseline saliency methods. A practical step toward enabling individual and heterogeneous clients to generate more reliable local explanations for a private global model, contributing to the advancement of private and explainable AI in medicine.

Our future work will primarily focus on better understanding the interplay between differential privacy, data heterogeneity, and explainability, and on developing more robust explainability methods. A key priority is to investigate the "heterogeneity amplifier" effect across different levels and types of heterogeneity, as well as evaluating how the amplification manifests with more advanced, heterogeneity-robust aggregation schemes like FedProx or Scaffold. We also acknowledge the need to continually improve explainability methods robust against DP model degradation. While performant, our approach relies on the prediction mask, which can degrade in high-DP regimes. The model uncertainty can help in distinguishing high-confidence interior regions from uncertain boundaries, hence dropping the reliance on the predicted segmentation. The core principle of denoising gradients could be further applied beyond GradCAM to newer saliency techniques. Finally, the clinical relevance of our findings must move beyond computational metrics like Focus to formal user studies with clinicians to assess whether the prediction explanations are useful in diagnostic workflows.

A   Appendix

See Figs. 2, 3, 4 and 5

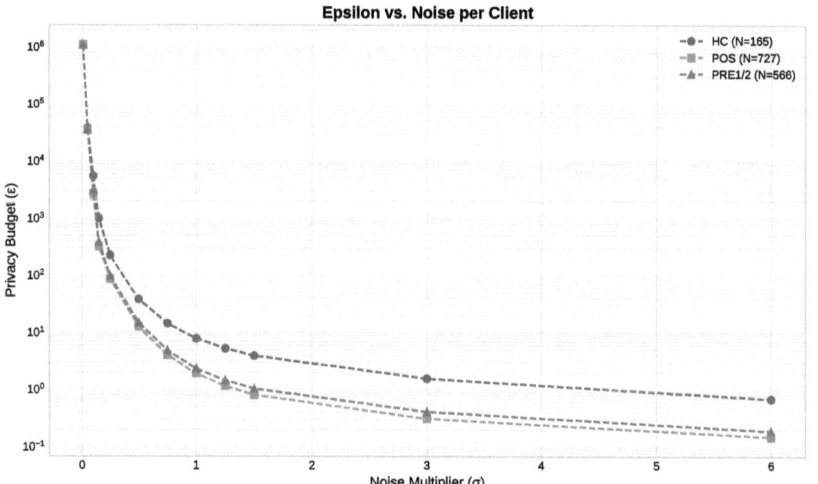

Fig. 2. Privacy level (ϵ) as a function of the noise multiplier (σ) for three dataset sizes (132, 452, 580) with 200 training rounds.

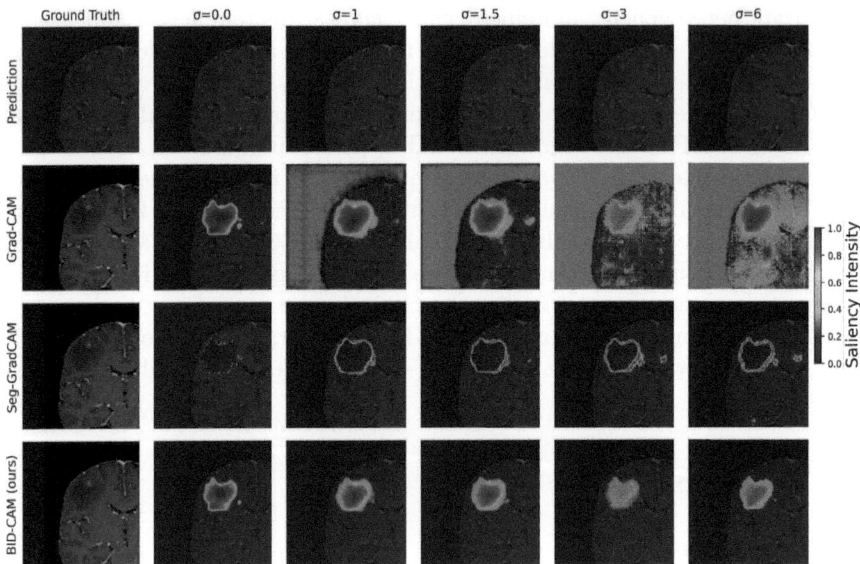

Fig. 3. Qualitative analysis of explanation methods on a sample from client 1 (real hospital).

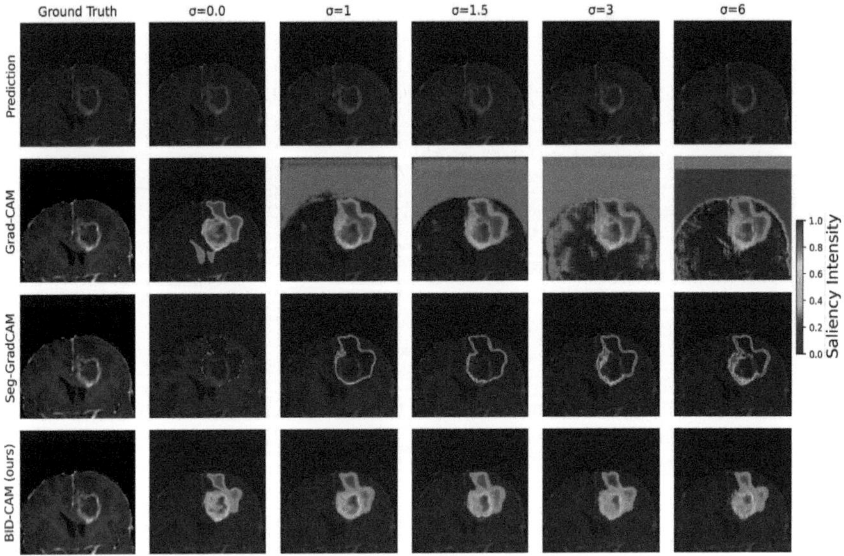

Fig. 4. Qualitative analysis of explanation methods on a sample from client 3 (PRE-BraTS 2025).

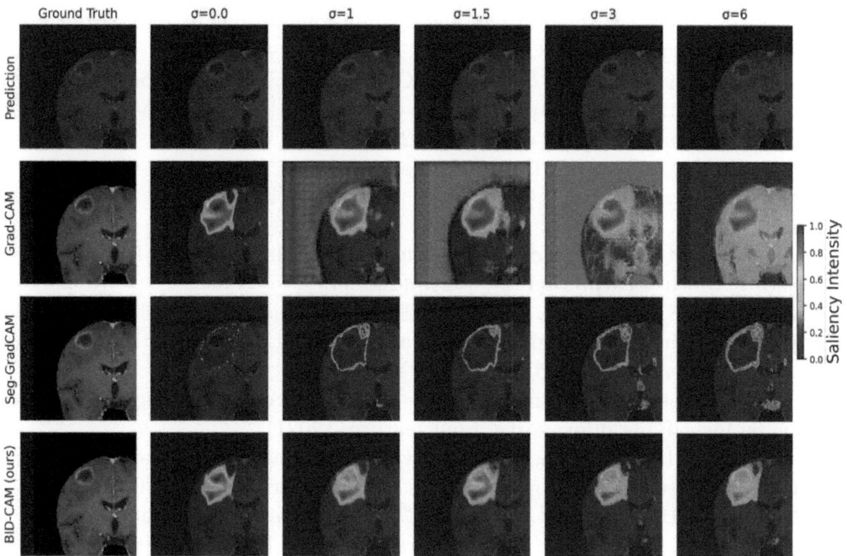

Fig. 5. Qualitative analysis of explanation methods on a sample from client 4 (POS-BraTS 2025).

References

1. Abadi, M., et al.: Deep learning with differential privacy. In: Proceedings of the 2016 ACM SIGSAC Conference on Computer and Communications Security, pp. 308–318 (2016)
2. Arias-Duart, A., Parés, F., Garcia-Gasulla, D., Gimenez-Abalos, V.: Focus! rating XAI methods and finding biases (2022)
3. Bagdasaryan, E., Shmatikov, V.: Differential privacy has disparate impact on model accuracy. CoRR, abs/1905.12101 (2019)
4. Baid, U., et al.: The RSNA-ASNR-MICCAI brats 2021 benchmark on brain tumor segmentation and radiogenomic classification (2021)
5. Bonawitz, K., et al.: Practical secure aggregation for privacy-preserving machine learning. In: Proceedings of the 2017 ACM SIGSAC Conference on Computer and Communications Security, pp. 1175–1191 (2017)
6. Borys, K., et al.: Explainable AI in medical imaging: an overview for clinical practitioners – saliency-based XAI approaches. Eur. J. Radiol. **162**, 110787 (2023)
7. CAFEIN. https://cafein.web.cern.ch (2024)
8. Camajori Tedeschini, B., et al.: Decentralized federated learning for healthcare networks: a case study on tumor segmentation. IEEE Access **10**, 8693–8708 (2022)
9. Agneya, A.D., Shekar, M.S., Bharadwaj, A., Vineeth, N., Neelima, M.L.: Deep learning in medical image analysis: a survey. In: 2024 International Conference on Innovation and Novelty in Engineering and Technology (INNOVA), vol. I, pp. 1–5 (2024)
10. de Verdier, M.C., et al.: The 2024 brain tumor segmentation (brats) challenge: glioma segmentation on post-treatment MRI (2024)

11. Dwork, C., Roth, A., et al.: The algorithmic foundations of differential privacy. Found. Trends® Theoret. Comput. Sci. **9**(3–4), 211–407 (2014)
12. Ezzeddine, F., Akel, R., Sbeity, I., Giordano, S., Langheinrich, M., Ayoub, O.: On the interplay of explainability, privacy and predictive performance with explanation-assisted model extraction (2025)
13. Holzinger, A., Langs, G., Denk, H., Zatloukal, K., Müller, H.: Causability and explainability of artificial intelligence in medicine. Wiley Interdisc. Rev. Data Min. Knowl. Discov. **9**(4), e1312 (2019)
14. Kairouz, P., et al.: Advances and open problems in federated learning. Found. Trends® Mach. Learn. **14**(1–2), 1–210 (2021)
15. Karimireddy, S.P., Kale, S., Mohri, M., Reddi, S., Stich, S., Suresh, A.T.: Scaffold: stochastic controlled averaging for federated learning. In: International Conference on Machine Learning, pp. 5132–5143. PMLR (2020)
16. Khakzar, A., et al.: Explaining COVID-19 and thoracic pathology model predictions by identifying informative input features (2021)
17. Li, T., Yu, Y., Liu, T., Chen, B.: User-level differentially private federated learning: Challenges, methods, and opportunities. arXiv preprint arXiv:2203.11600 (2022)
18. McMahan, H.B., Moore, E., Ramage, D., Hampson, S.: Communication-efficient learning of deep networks from decentralized data. In: Proceedings of AISTATS (2017)
19. Mironov, I.: Rényi differential privacy. In: 2017 IEEE 30th Computer Security Foundations Symposium (CSF), pp. 263–275. IEEE (2017)
20. Rieke, N., et al.: The future of digital health with federated learning. NPJ Dig. Med. **3**(1), 1–7 (2020)
21. Santos, D.R., et al.: A federated learning platform as a service for advancing stroke management in european clinical centers. In: 2024 IEEE International Conference on E-health Networking, Application & Services (HealthCom), pp. 1–7. IEEE (2024)
22. Selvaraju, R.R., Cogswell, M., Das, A., Vedantam, R., Parikh, D., Batra, D.: Grad-cam: visual explanations from deep networks via gradient-based localization. Int. J. Comput. Vision **128**, 336–359 (2020)
23. Stathopoulos, I., et al.: Evaluating brain tumor detection with deep learning convolutional neural networks across multiple MRI modalities. J. Imaging **10**(12) (2024)
24. Taiello, R., et al.: Enhancing privacy in federated learning: secure aggregation for real-world healthcare applications. In: International Conference on Medical Image Computing and Computer-Assisted Intervention, pp. 204–214. Springer (2024)
25. Tramèr, F., Boneh, D.: Differentially private learning needs better features (or much more data). CoRR, abs/2011.11660 (2020)
26. Vinogradova, K., Dibrov, A., Myers, G.: Towards interpretable semantic segmentation via gradient-weighted class activation mapping (student abstract). In: Proceedings of the AAAI Conference on Artificial Intelligence **34**, 13943–13944 (2020)
27. Wu, R., Wang, H., Chen, H.-T., Carneiro, G.: Deep multimodal learning with missing modality: a survey (2024)
28. Yousefpour, A., et al.: Opacus: user-friendly differential privacy library in pytorch. arXiv preprint arXiv:2109.12298 (2021)
29. Zhou, B., Khosla, A., Lapedriza, A., Oliva, A., Torralba, A.: Learning deep features for discriminative localization. In: Proceedings of the IEEE Conference on Computer Vision and Pattern Recognition, pp. 2921–2929 (2016)
30. Zhu, L., Liu, Z., Han, S.: Deep leakage from gradients. In: Advances in Neural Information Processing Systems, vol. 32 (2019)

Federated Reprogramming Knowledge Distillation for Medical Image Classification

Afsaneh Mahanipour$^{(\boxtimes)}$, Abdullah-Al-Zubaer Imran, and Hana Khamfroush

Department of Computer Science, University of Kentucky, Lexington, KY, USA
`{ama654,aimran}@uky.edu, khamfroush@cs.uky.edu`

Abstract. The rapid development of medical foundation models has shown great promise for various healthcare applications. However, fine-tuning these models for downstream tasks remains challenging due to privacy concerns that limit centralized data collection from diverse sources. Federated learning (FL) offers a privacy-preserving solution by enabling multiple clients to collaboratively train a global model without sharing their local data. Despite its advantages, FL must balance model performance with communication and computation costs. Existing approaches often use parameter-efficient fine-tuning (PEFT) techniques to reduce communication overhead by transmitting fewer parameters. However, these methods require clients to host large foundation models, which is impractical for clients with limited memory. Meanwhile, conventional knowledge distillation (KD) methods fall short in FL due to misalignment between pre-trained foundation models and specific downstream tasks. To overcome these limitations, we propose Federated Reprogramming Knowledge Distillation (FedRD), a method that uses lightweight student models in clients and a medical foundation model on the server. A reprogramming module aligns the foundation model's feature space with the downstream task, enabling student models to mimic this representation collaboratively. FedRD significantly reduces memory and computation requirements while maintaining high accuracy. Experiments on three medical imaging datasets under non-IID data distributions demonstrate that FedRD outperforms federated KD and PEFT methods, offering an effective trade-off between accuracy, communication, and computational efficiency.

Keywords: Federated Learning · Foundation Models · Knowledge Distillation · Medical Imaging

1 Introduction

Large-scale pre-trained foundation models are rapidly being developed for a wide range of downstream tasks [1,3,16,28]. However, developing medical foundation models remains challenging due to the limited availability of labeled data [26]. In many cases, publicly available datasets have already been used, making it

© The Author(s), under exclusive license to Springer Nature Switzerland AG 2026
G. Zamzmi et al. (Eds.): MICCAI 2025, LNCS 16135, pp. 143–152, 2026.
https://doi.org/10.1007/978-3-032-05663-4_14

necessary to rely on private or protected data to improve model generalization. Unfortunately, individual healthcare institutions often lack enough data for specific tasks, and combining data across centers is generally not feasible. This challenge is primarily due to strict data privacy regulations, such as the EU's GDPR, Singapore's PDPA, and Chinas cybersecurity laws, which prohibit sharing raw patient data for centralized model fine-tuning [5].

This problem can be addressed by Federated Learning (FL), a decentralized machine learning approach that enables clinics with varying resources and heterogeneous data to collaboratively train a global model without sharing raw data [13,14]. However, integrating FL with large foundation models is often impractical due to the substantial computational and communication overhead involved in optimizing and transmitting billions of parameters between clients and the server [22]. To mitigate this challenge, recent studies have adopted parameter-efficient fine-tuning (PEFT) methods, such as adapters [6,12,23] and Low-Rank Adaptation (LoRA) [8], which allow fine-tuning and exchanging only a small subset of model parameters. While these methods significantly reduce training and communication costs, they do not resolve memory and storage constraints, as the full foundation model still needs to reside on each client device.

Another approach is knowledge distillation (KD) [7,11], a model compression and enhancement technique that transfers knowledge from a foundation model to a smaller model, treating the foundation model as the teacher and the smaller model as the student. However, the effectiveness of KD may be limited by a lack of alignment between the pre-trained foundation model and the student model, particularly when the foundation models pre-training data is inconsistent with the specific downstream task. Model reprogramming is one method that can mitigate this problem [24,27].

In this work, we introduce the first federated reprogramming knowledge distillation framework, designed to enable the use of medical foundation models for downstream tasks in a distributed setting. In our approach, a frozen foundation model is hosted on the server, while lightweight student models are deployed on clients. Unlike federated PEFT methods, our framework does not require a foundation model on each client, eliminating the memory and design complexity associated with adapting large models to resource-constrained devices. To improve task relevance, a reprogramming module is incorporated on the server to align the foundation model's feature space with the target downstream task. These reprogrammed features are then used to guide the training of student models, allowing clients to learn more effective decision boundaries through distillation. Our key contributions are summarized as follows:

1. We propose the first federated reprogramming knowledge distillation (FedRD) method to adapt medical foundation models for downstream tasks in distributed environments. FedRD enables the training of lightweight student models on clients by transferring reprogrammed knowledge in a more communication- and computation-efficient manner.
2. We conduct extensive experiments on three datasets from different downstream tasks. The results show that our approach achieves a better balance

between model accuracy, communication overhead, and computational cost compared to existing federated PEFT and KD methods.

2   Federated Reprogramming Knowledge Distillation

2.1   Problem Statement

We consider a two-tier federated learning architecture. The first tier comprises M clients, denoted as $\{C_1, C_2, ..., C_m, ..., C_M\}$, where each client C_m holds a local dataset $\mathcal{U}_m = \{X, Y\} = \{(x_i, y_i)\}_{i=1}^{N_m}$, consisting of N_m data instances. The number of instances may vary across clients, reflecting a non-uniform data distribution. The second tier consists of a central server, denoted as s, which coordinates the training process. To preserve the federated nature of the system, M must be at least two, as a single client would reduce the setup to a centralized scenario. A pre-trained medical foundation model, denoted by F_t, resides on the server and acts as the teacher model. In parallel, a lightweight student model, denoted by F_s^{global}, is initialized and maintained on the server. At each communication round, this student model is broadcast to all clients, where it is referred to locally as F_s^{local}. The goal is to transfer knowledge from the foundation model to the student models in a way that maintains high performance while reducing communication and computation costs across the system.

2.2   Proposed Method

In this section, we introduce our proposed method, federated reprogramming knowledge distillation (FedRD). The goal is to collaboratively train lightweight student models on clients by leveraging the knowledge of a pre-trained teacher foundation model, without deploying the large foundation model on resource-constrained clients. This design choice addresses the practical limitations of memory, computation, and communication on the client side. FedRD utilizes a model reprogramming strategy on the server to adapt the foundation model to the specific downstream task, ensuring that the extracted features are both consistent and task-relevant before knowledge distillation occurs. Rather than retraining the entire foundation model, model reprogramming [24,27] enables efficient cross-domain adaptation by introducing lightweight trainable components including input transformation layers and an output mapping layer. This significantly reduces the computational overhead while taking advantage of the foundation models rich representational power.

Before initiating server-client communication, the pre-trained teacher foundation model is deployed on the server. At the start of the training process (round $r = 1$), the server initializes a randomly configured lightweight student model, referred to as the global student model, and distributes it to all clients, denoted as θ_m^r. Each client then performs local training to optimize its local student model by minimizing the following loss function L_m^r:

$$L_m^r(\theta_m^r) = \frac{1}{N_m} \sum_{i=1}^{N_m} \mathcal{L}(\theta_m^r(x_i), y_i) \tag{1}$$

where $\mathcal{L}$ denotes the training loss function, such as cross-entropy for standard classification tasks, and x_i and y_i represent the local input data and corresponding labels. After completing local training, each client sends its updated student model to the server. The server then aggregates these local models using a weighted average to update the global student model:

$$\theta_m^{r+1} = \frac{\sum_{m=1}^{M} N_m \theta_m^r}{\sum_{m=1}^{M} N_m} \tag{2}$$

On the server side, to leverage the pre-trained teacher foundation model, a trainable reprogramming module is employed as shown in Fig. 1(b). This module consists of standard residual blocks $\phi(.)$ as input transformation layers and a fully connected (FC) layer $g(.)$ as the output mapping layer. A publicly available dataset related to the downstream task is then used to jointly train both the reprogramming module and the global student model through a co-training mechanism. This setup ensures that the reprogrammed features extracted from the foundation model can be effectively mimicked by the student models features, allowing the student to learn decision boundaries that closely resemble those of the teacher model.

To further enhance feature alignment and enable robust knowledge distillation, Centered Kernel Alignment (CKA) [9] is used to measure the similarity between the reprogrammed features of the foundation model and those extracted by the student model. The overall training loss is thus formulated as follows:

$$\mathcal{L}_{train} = \mathcal{L}_{CE}(y, z_s) + \alpha \mathcal{L}_{CE}(y, z_t) + \beta(\mathcal{L}_{KL}(z_t, z_s) + \mathcal{L}_{CKA}(f_t, f_s)) \tag{3}$$

where $z_t = g(\phi(F_t(x)))$ and $z_s = g(F_s(x))$ represent the output logits of the teacher foundation model and the global student model, respectively. The functions $\phi(.)$ and $F_t(.)$ denote the input reprogramming module and the frozen teacher model, while $F_s(.)$ is the student model and $g(.)$ is the shared FC classifier. The hyperparameters α and β control the contributions of different loss components. In addition to the standard cross-entropy (CE) loss, the Kullback-Leibler (KL) divergence is used as a logits-based knowledge distillation loss. Furthermore, the CKA-based feature alignment loss ($\mathcal{L}_{CKA}$) is computed as follows:

$$\mathcal{L}_{CKA}(f_t, f_s) = -\frac{HSIC(P, Q)}{\sqrt{HSIC(P, P).HSIC(Q, Q)}} \tag{4}$$

where f_t and f_s denote the reprogrammed features extracted from the foundation model and the features extracted from the student model, respectively. The pairwise feature similarity matrices are defined as $P = f_t f_t^\top$ and $Q = f_s f_s^\top$. To measure the similarity between these feature representations, we compute the HSIC Criterion as:

$$HSIC(P,Q) = \frac{P'.Q'}{(n-1)^2} \tag{5}$$

where $P' = HPH$, $Q' = HQH$, and $H = I_n - \frac{1}{n}\mathbf{1}\mathbf{1}^\top$ is the centering matrix, with n representing the batch size.

After updating the global student model on the server, it is redistributed to all clients for the next training round as shown in Fig. 1(a).

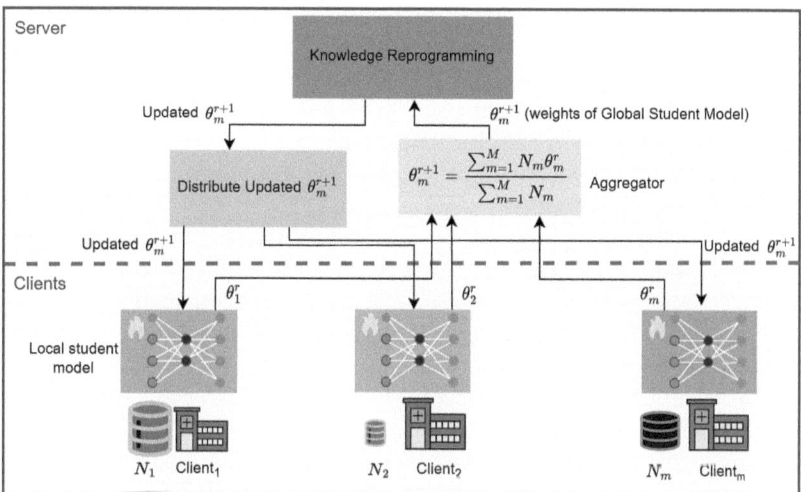

(a) Overview of the proposed FedRD framework.

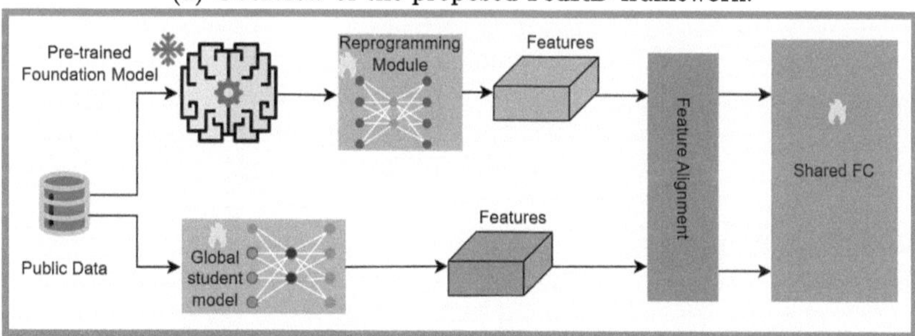

(b) Server-side Knowledge Reprogramming block.

Fig. 1. Illustration of the proposed FedRD framework. (a) shows the overall structure of the method, and (b) details the server-side Knowledge Reprogramming block

Table 1. Characteristics of downstream datasets for different tasks

Dataset	Task	Modality	Classes	Data Size
ISIC2018 [21]	Melanoma	RGB	7	11527
COVID [17,25]	COVID-19	CT	2	13716
BTC [19]	Brain tumor	MRI	4	3264

3   Experiments

Datasets: The proposed method is evaluated on three publicly available medical image datasets, each representing a different downstream task: Melanoma [21], COVID-19 (including two datasets from [17,25]), and Brain Tumor [19]. Detailed information about each dataset is provided in Table 1. For datasets without official train-test splits, we used an 80-20 division for training and testing data.
Teacher Foundation Models and Lightweight Student Models: To evaluate the proposed method, we employ two medical foundation models with distinct training approaches: PMC-CLIP [10] and LVM-Med [15]. PMC-CLIP is trained using contrastive learning on 1.6 million image-caption pairs and utilizes a ResNet-50 architecture as its visual encoder. In contrast, LVM-Med is developed through self-supervised learning on 1.3 million medical images and is based on the ViT-B (Vision Transformer Base) architecture. In all experiments, the parameters of both foundation models are kept frozen. Additionally, ResNet-18, ShuffleNet, and MobileNet are used as lightweight student models on the client side.
Implementation Settings: We conduct experiments in a simulated federated learning environment with three clients, selected through trial and error. Each client holds a non-IID partition of the dataset. Model training is performed using the AdamW optimizer with a learning rate of $5e-3$. The loss function includes two hyperparameters, α and β, which are both initialized to 1 and linearly decreased throughout the training process. Each experiment runs for 50 training rounds, and the results are reported as the average classification accuracy over three independent runs. All experiments are conducted using PyTorch 2.5.1 and Tesla V100-SXM2-32GB GPU.
Results and Analysis: For comparison, we select several widely used KD methods: Hint [18], VID [2], SemCKD [4], and Crd [20], and adapt them from centralized training to the federated learning setting. Additionally, we include a centralized reprogramming distillation (Cntr-RD) [27] baseline to provide a more comprehensive evaluation. Table 2 summarizes the accuracy performance of all methods across different datasets, teacher foundation models, and student models. In addition, Fig. 2 provides a comparison between the proposed method and other KD approaches on the COVID and ISIC datasets, using PMC-CLIP as the teacher model and ResNet-18 as the student model, evaluated in terms of F1 score. The results demonstrate that our proposed method consistently outperforms the federated KD baselines. This improvement highlights the benefit of aligning the feature space of the foundation model with the downstream task,

which enhances the quality of knowledge transfer compared to direct federated distillation approaches. As a result, our method achieves superior performance without incurring additional computation or communication costs.

Table 3 compares our proposed method with PEFT approaches, specifically Adapter [12] and LoRA [8], which we adapt from centralized to federated settings. In these PEFT methods, each client is required to host a full foundation model, resulting in high memory consumption, as reflected in the parameter size column. In contrast, our method significantly reduces both computational and memory requirements, as shown by the lower GPU utilization and smaller parameter size. Here, PMC-CLIP is used as the foundation model in all three methods, while ResNet-18 serves as the student model in our proposed method. Additionally, it achieves higher accuracy while maintaining a reasonable communication cost. Overall, the results demonstrate that our reprogramming-based knowledge distillation method offers a better trade-off between performance, computation/communication efficiency, and training time in federated learning environments.

Table 2. Comparison of the proposed method with state-of-the-art knowledge distillation methods in terms of accuracy

Dataset	Student	Teacher	Cntr- RD	Hint	VID	SemCKD	Crd	Ours
COVID	ResNet18	PMC-CLIP	0.9526	0.9215	0.9165	0.9319	0.9372	**0.9587**
		LVM-Med	**0.9552**	0.9345	0.9142	0.9449	0.8969	0.9484
	ShuffleNet	PMC-CLIP	0.7774	0.8242	0.8450	0.8382	0.8423	**0.8529**
		LVM-Med	0.7786	0.8546	0.8757	0.8619	0.8624	**0.8851**
	MobileNet	PMC-CLIP	0.9011	0.8958	0.8715	0.8669	0.9050	**0.9685**
		LVM-Med	0.8730	0.9176	0.9137	0.8883	0.8875	**0.9674**
ISIC	ResNet18	PMC-CLIP	0.7156	0.6994	0.6687	0.6797	0.6878	**0.7169**
		LVM-Med	0.7235	0.6943	0.6753	0.6891	0.6931	**0.7282**
	ShuffleNet	PMC-CLIP	0.6779	0.6736	0.6545	0.6604	0.6534	**0.7030**
		LVM-Med	0.6376	0.6839	0.6563	0.6697	0.6481	**0.7037**
	MobileNet	PMC-CLIP	0.6693	0.6658	0.6473	0.6666	0.6515	**0.6971**
		LVM-Med	0.6647	0.6684	0.6632	0.6521	0.6554	**0.6825**
BTC	ResNet18	PMC-CLIP	0.2944	0.2919	0.2855	0.2944	0.2923	**0.2970**
		LVM-Med	0.2969	0.2893	0.2718	0.2867	0.2784	**0.2995**
	ShuffleNet	PMC-CLIP	0.2741	0.2779	0.2858	0.2792	0.2804	**0.2978**
		LVM-Med	0.2791	0.2843	0.2868	0.2893	0.2886	**0.2944**
	MobileNet	PMC-CLIP	0.2740	0.2817	0.2861	0.2859	0.2833	**0.2998**
		LVM-Med	0.2706	0.2766	0.2953	0.2937	0.2867	**0.2969**

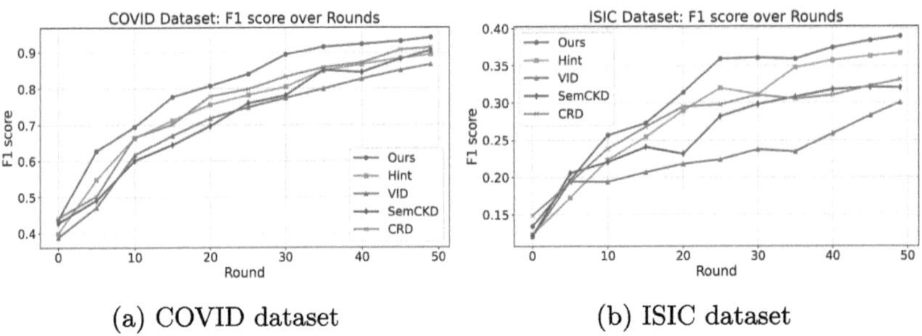

(a) COVID dataset   (b) ISIC dataset

Fig. 2. Comparison of the proposed method with KD methods using PMC-CLIP and ResNet18 in terms of F1 score

Table 3. Comparison of the proposed method with PEFT methods in terms of parameter size, communication cost, GPU utilization, and training time

			PMC-CLIP			
Dataset	Method	Acc.	Param Size (MB)	Comm. (MB/round)	GPU Util. (MB)	Time(s)
	Adapter	0.7773	1297.42	48.06	100	279.69
COVID	LoRA	0.6175	581.46	0.76	57.71	83.13
	Ours	0.9587	42.67	256.29	70.79	156
	Adapter	0.1466	337.50	27.04	90.41	44.37
ISIC	LoRA	0.0324	581.46	0.76	86.1	64
	Ours	0.7169	42.68	256.35	42.8	200.79
	Adapter	0.1878	1297.42	48.06	93.24	47.49
BTC	LoRA	0.2435	581.46	0.76	87.48	13.43
	Ours	0.2970	42.67	256.32	59.18	46.80

4   Conclusion

In this work, we propose Federated Reprogramming Knowledge Distillation (FedRD), a novel approach that differs from existing federated parameter-efficient fine-tuning (PEFT) and knowledge distillation (KD) methods. Instead of requiring each client to host a full foundation model, FedRD collaboratively trains a reprogramming module alongside lightweight student models to adapt a pre-trained medical foundation model for downstream image classification tasks in a federated setting. We conduct extensive experiments across three diverse medical imaging datasets using two medical foundation models and three lightweight student architectures. The results show that FedRD achieves a strong balance between model performance, communication efficiency, and computational cost, outperforming existing federated PEFT and KD baselines.

Acknowledgement. This work is funded by career grant provided by the National Science Foundation (NSF) under the grant number 2340075.

Disclosure of Interests. The authors have no competing interests to declare that are relevant to the content of this article.

References

1. Abukadah, H., Fereidouni, M., Siddique, A.: Mapping natural language intents to user interfaces through vision-language models. In: 2024 IEEE 18th International Conference on Semantic Computing (ICSC), pp. 237–244. IEEE (2024)
2. Ahn, S., Hu, S.X., Damianou, A., Lawrence, N.D., Dai, Z.: Variational information distillation for knowledge transfer. In: Proceedings of the IEEE/CVF Conference on Computer Vision and Pattern Recognition, pp. 9163–9171 (2019)
3. Bommasani, R., et al.: On the opportunities and risks of foundation models. arXiv preprint arXiv:2108.07258 (2021)
4. Chen, D., et al.: Cross-layer distillation with semantic calibration. In: Proceedings of the AAAI Conference on Artificial Intelligence, vol. 35, pp. 7028–7036 (2021)
5. Chen, H., Zhang, Y., Krompass, D., Gu, J., Tresp, V.: FedDAT: an approach for foundation model finetuning in multi-modal heterogeneous federated learning. In: Proceedings of the AAAI Conference on Artificial Intelligence, vol. 38, pp. 11285–11293 (2024)
6. He, X., Li, C., Zhang, P., Yang, J., Wang, X.E.: Parameter-efficient model adaptation for vision transformers. In: Proceedings of the AAAI Conference on Artificial Intelligence, vol. 37, pp. 817–825 (2023)
7. Hinton, G., Vinyals, O., Dean, J.: Distilling the knowledge in a neural network. arXiv preprint arXiv:1503.02531 (2015)
8. Hu, E.J., et al.: LoRA: low-rank adaptation of large language models. ICLR **1**(2), 3 (2022)
9. Kornblith, S., Norouzi, M., Lee, H., Hinton, G.: Similarity of neural network representations revisited. In: International Conference on Machine Learning, pp. 3519–3529. PMLR (2019)
10. Lin, W., et al.: PMC-CLIP: contrastive language-image pre-training using biomedical documents. In: International Conference on Medical Image Computing and Computer-Assisted Intervention, pp. 525–536. Springer (2023)
11. Liu, X., Li, L., Li, C., Yao, A.: NORM: knowledge distillation via n-to-one representation matching. arXiv preprint arXiv:2305.13803 (2023)
12. Lu, W., Hu, X., Wang, J., Xie, X.: FedCLIP: fast generalization and personalization for clip in federated learning. arXiv preprint arXiv:2302.13485 (2023)
13. Mahanipour, A., Khamfroush, H.: Embedded federated feature selection with dynamic sparse training: balancing accuracy-cost tradeoffs. arXiv preprint arXiv:2504.05245 (2025)
14. McMahan, B., Moore, E., Ramage, D., Hampson, S., y Arcas, B.A.: Communication-efficient learning of deep networks from decentralized data. In: Artificial Intelligence and Statistics, pp. 1273–1282. PMLR (2017)
15. MH Nguyen, D., et al.: LVM-Med: learning large-scale self-supervised vision models for medical imaging via second-order graph matching. Adv. Neural Inf. Process. Syst. **36**, 27922–27950 (2023)
16. Munia, N., Imran, A.A.Z.: Prompting medical vision-language models to mitigate diagnosis bias by generating realistic dermoscopic images. In: 2025 IEEE 22nd International Symposium on Biomedical Imaging (ISBI), pp. 1–4. IEEE (2025)

17. Rahimzadeh, M., Attar, A., Sakhaei, S.M.: A fully automated deep learning-based network for detecting covid-19 from a new and large lung CT scan dataset. Biomed. Signal Process. Control, 102588 (2021). https://doi.org/10.1016/j.bspc.2021.102588, https://www.sciencedirect.com/science/article/pii/S1746809421001853

18. Romero, A., Ballas, N., Kahou, S.E., Chassang, A., Gatta, C., Bengio, Y.: FitNets: hints for thin deep nets. arXiv preprint arXiv:1412.6550 (2014)

19. Saleh, A., Sukaik, R., Abu-Naser, S.S.: Brain tumor classification using deep learning. In: 2020 International Conference on Assistive and Rehabilitation Technologies (iCareTech), pp. 131–136. IEEE (2020)

20. Tian, Y., Krishnan, D., Isola, P.: Contrastive representation distillation. arXiv preprint arXiv:1910.10699 (2019)

21. Tschandl, P., Rosendahl, C., Kittler, H.: The ham10000 dataset, a large collection of multi-source dermatoscopic images of common pigmented skin lesions. Sci. Data $5(1)$, 1–9 (2018)

22. Wu, Y., Desrosiers, C., Chaddad, A.: FACMIC: federated adaptative clip model for medical image classification. In: International Conference on Medical Image Computing and Computer-Assisted Intervention, pp. 531–541. Springer (2024)

23. Xin, Y., et al.: Parameter-efficient fine-tuning for pre-trained vision models: a survey. arXiv preprint arXiv:2402.02242 (2024)

24. Xu, S., et al.: Towards efficient task-driven model reprogramming with foundation models. arXiv preprint arXiv:2304.02263 (2023)

25. Yang, X., He, X., Zhao, J., Zhang, Y., Zhang, S., Xie, P.: COVID-CT-dataset: a CT scan dataset about COVID-19. arXiv preprint arXiv:2003.13865 (2020)

26. Zhang, S., Metaxas, D.: On the challenges and perspectives of foundation models for medical image analysis. Med. Image Anal. **91**, 102996 (2024)

27. Zhou, Y., Du, S., Li, H., Yao, J., Zhang, Y., Wang, Y.: Reprogramming distillation for medical foundation models. In: International Conference on Medical Image Computing and Computer-Assisted Intervention, pp. 533–543. Springer (2024)

28. Zhou, Y., Zhao, Z., Li, H., Du, S., Yao, J., Zhang, Y., Wang, Y.: Exploring training on heterogeneous data with mixture of low-rank adapters. arXiv preprint arXiv:2406.09679 (2024)

FedSlowdown: Efficiency Attacks Against Federated Learning of Adaptive Neural Networks

Ayomide Akinsanya[(✉)] and Tegan Brennan

Stevens Institute of Technology, Hoboken, NJ 07030, USA
`{aakinsan,tbrenna5}@stevens.edu`

Abstract. The increasing computational and energy demands of deep neural networks (DNNs) have sparked significant interest in input-adaptive multi-exit architectures, known as Adaptive Neural Networks (AdNNs). AdNNs can significantly reduce inference time and energy usage by dynamically scaling the depth of computation, helping enable real-time medical image analysis and computer-aided diagnosis on resource-constrained devices and low latency medical applications. This is critical for portable ultrasound scanners and mobile diagnostic tools that operate in remote settings such as rural clinics, disaster-relief zones, or developing countries where access to healthcare is severely limited due to financial, infrastructural, and personnel constraints. Medical imaging data is often highly sensitive, necessitating strict privacy protections to comply with healthcare regulations (e.g., HIPAA, GDPR). Federated learning (FL) offers a privacy-preserving solution for training medical deep learning models across decentralized clinical sites without sharing raw patient data. While this makes training AdNNs in a FL environment a natural fit for medical data, we show that AdNNs trained under federated learning are vulnerable to efficiency attacks. Specifically, we introduce `FedSlowdown`, an attack that allows one or more participating clients to maliciously degrade the computational efficiency of the global AdNN model. This increases inference time and device energy usage, making real-time medical image analysis slower. We evaluate `FedSlowdown` across four AdNN architectures and two medical imaging datasets (HAM10000, Fed-ISIC). Our results show that `FedSlowdown` can reduce AdNN efficiency by up to 90–100%, with 1.5–5× longer inference times on devices deployed in constrained environments.

Keywords: Federated Learning · Adaptive Neural Networks · Efficiency Attacks

1 Introduction

DNNs have advanced computer aided diagnosis (CAD) and medical image analysis, achieving high accuracy in tasks such as cancer detection [32] and retinal screening [26]. However, these gains come with high computational costs [21],

G. Zamzmi et al. (Eds.): MICCAI 2025, LNCS 16135, pp. 153–163, 2026.
https://doi.org/10.1007/978-3-032-05663-4_15

making deployment difficult on resource constrained devices such as portable ultrasound scanners or low-power mobile devices installed in rural hospitals and clinics where latency and energy efficiency are critical.

AdNNs address the high computational costs of traditional DNNs by using early-exit classifiers to reduce inference time and energy use while maintaining accuracy [20,28] and thus help enable such deployments. However training AdNNs for CAD and medical image analysis remains challenging due to limited labeled data and strict privacy regulations (e.g., GDPR [2], HIPAA [1]) that restricts centralized data sharing. FL [24] enables collaborative model training without sharing raw data, preserving privacy across clinical sites.

While FL has been studied under accuracy-focused attacks [7,9,11,14,33], the efficiency properties of AdNNs introduce a new threat. A compromised participant in FL can degrade the efficiency of the global AdNN without reducing its accuracy. Such attacks increase inference time and energy use, undermining the core benefits of AdNNs in CAD systems, especially on battery powered devices.

In this paper, we investigate federated learning of AdNNs for CAD and medical image analysis under adversarial conditions that aim to degrade the efficiency of the global AdNN. Specifically, we ask:

> *Can a participant in FL poison the global AdNN in a way that severely degrades its efficiency (leading to increased inference times on edge devices used for CAD and medical image analysis) while preserving its accuracy?*

In answering this question, we make the following contributions:

- We introduce `FedSlowdown`, the first efficiency-targeting model poisoning attack on AdNNs trained in a FL environment for CAD and medical image analysis applications.
- We evaluate `FedSlowdown` across four AdNN architectures and two medical datasets (HAM10000, Fed-ISIC) under realistic adversarial conditions.
- We demonstrate the real-world impact of `FedSlowdown` on mobile diagnostic devices in constrained clinical settings.
- We assess possible defenses that can help mitigate `FedSlowdown` and discuss their limitations.

2   Background

2.1   Adaptive Neural Networks

AdNNs have been widely studied as a solution to the high computational demands of DNNs [18,20,28,34]. A common AdNN design, illustrated in Fig. 1, includes early-exit mechanisms or cascaded model selection strategies that enable dynamic inference. Early-exit networks insert intermediate classifiers along the backbone model, allowing "easy" inputs to exit early if a confidence threshold is met, reducing computation and energy use [13,18,20,28]. Alternatively, model cascades process inputs sequentially through a series of models with increasing complexity, stopping once sufficient confidence is reached [22,23,27,34]. Both approaches allow AdNNs to adapt resource usage to input difficulty, achieving efficient inference without compromising accuracy.

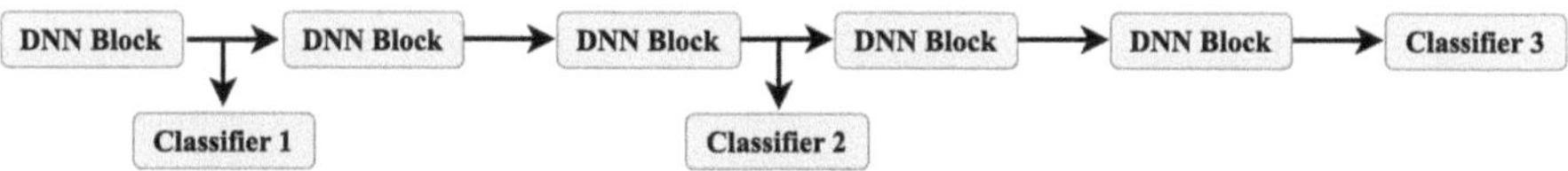

Fig. 1. An Illustration of the working mechanism of an AdNN

Given an AdNN $\mathcal{M}$ with K intermediate classifiers, the output of the k-th classifier is given as $\mathcal{M}_k(x) = \hat{y}$. Here, $\mathcal{M}_k$ represents the layers from the input to the k-th classifier. The overall loss is computed as:

$$\ell_{AdNN} = \sum_{k=1}^{K} L(\mathcal{M}_k(x), y) \tag{1}$$

where L is the loss at each classifier. The model is optimized using standard training algorithms.

3 Threat Model

We focus on AdNNs trained via FL, where the resulting global model is deployed to edge devices (e.g. portable scanners or clinical smartphones) that participated in training. We assume the adversary compromises one or more participants, allowing them to submit malicious updates to the central server (see Fig. 5b).

Adversary's Capabilities: Since FL grants participants full control over their data and training, the adversary controls their local training data, training procedures and hyperparameters. They can alter model weights before submission and adapt their strategy across multiple rounds. The adversary cannot control the aggregation server or the data or training of other benign participants.

Adversary's Objective: The adversary's goal is to degrade the efficiency of a global AdNN while preserving its diagnostic accuracy. By disrupting early exits, the adversary can force the model to compute like a traditional DNN, increasing inference time and energy use, hindering timely diagnosis on resource-constrained medical devices.

4 FedSlowdown

Problem Formulation: We structure `FedSlowdown` into two main parts: first, efficiency degradation training on compromised participants during local training, and second, malicious model update scaling so that this degradation persists after aggregation with benign updates.

4.1   Efficiency Degradation Training

Our proposed efficiency degradation (ED) training disables the AdNN's intermediate classifiers by excluding their loss during backpropagation. This restricts gradient updates to the path between the final classifier and the first layer, leaving intermediate classifiers untrained. As a result, the AdNN behaves like a standard DNN, losing its ability to make early predictions as inputs must traverse the full network, increasing inference latency and computational cost, and nullifying the AdNN's efficiency benefits. Our ED training results in the modification of Eq. 1 into Eq. 2 given below:

$$\ell_{adnn} = L(\mathcal{M}_{exit_k}(x), y) \tag{2}$$

where k is the final classifier.

4.2   Selective Weight Scaling

A simple attempt to degrade AdNN efficiency using only ED training fails because the server's aggregation nullifies most malicious updates. Prior work [7, 11] on model poisoning address this by scaling the entire update. In contrast, we refine this approach: `FedSlowdown` selectively scales only the untrained intermediate classifier weights—those responsible for early exits—thereby preserving the ED effect while avoiding unnecessary perturbation of the well-trained backbone layers.

Scaling Malicious Updates. For a FL environment with r rounds, where a subset of m participants are selected from n and a global learning rate η, the new global AdNN model $\mathcal{M}_k^{r+1}$ is obtained by Eq. 3:

$$\mathcal{M}_k^{r+1} = \mathcal{M}_k^r + \frac{\eta}{n} \sum_{i=1}^{m} (\mathcal{M}_{k,i}^{r+1} - \mathcal{M}_k^r) \tag{3}$$

As the global AdNN model converges, the difference between the global model and each participants local updates diminishes ($\sum_{i=1}^{m-1}(\mathcal{M}_{k,i}^{r+1} - \mathcal{M}_k^r) \approx 0$). Hence our adversary can solve for the malicious AdNN model H they need to submit on every round according to:

$$\frac{n}{\eta}H - (\frac{n}{\eta} - 1)\mathcal{M}_k^r - \sum_{i=1}^{m-1}(\mathcal{M}_{k,i}^{r+1} - \mathcal{M}_k^r) \approx \frac{n}{\eta}(H - \mathcal{M}_k^r) + \mathcal{M}_k^r \tag{4}$$

Equation 4 shows that the adversary can scale the weights of the untrained intermediate classifiers of their local malicious model H to ensure the ED survives aggregation. This selective weight scaling, combined with ED training, forms the core of our `FedSlowdown` attack, executed in every training round.

5   Experimental Evaluation

Datasets & AdNN Architectures: We evaluate `FedSlowdown` on two medical image datasets, HAM10000 [31] (IID) and Fed-ISIC2019 [30] (non-IID), using four AdNN architectures: Branchy-AlexNet [28], SDNet [20], MSDNet [19], and RANet [34].

Metrics. We evaluate `FedSlowdown` using two metrics: (i) the average inference time per sample and (ii) Early-Exit Capability (EEC) score [17]. EEC ranges from 0 to 1, where 1 means most samples exit at early classifiers (high efficiency) and 0 means most require the final classifier (low efficiency). It is obtained by calculating the area under the EEC curve. Lower EEC typically corresponds to higher latency.

Federated Learning Setup. We use the Flower FL framework [8] which leverages the FedAvg [24] aggregation scheme and run the FL procedure for 100 rounds with 10 participants for HAM10000 and 6 participants for Fed-ISIC2019 (as the data was collected from six hospitals). All the code for our experiments can be found here [5].

Comparison Baselines. We compare `FedSlowdown` against NOATTACK, which represents a benign FL setting, and ATTACKNOSCALE, a naive efficiency attack similar to [12,16,17] without any form of weight scaling.

5.1   Experimental Results

From our results in Table 1 and Fig. 2, we see that our FEDSLOWDOWN attack achieves significant efficiency degradation. This degradation in terms of EEC scores ranges from $\approx 4\times$ (for the MSDNet architecture trained on the HAM10000 dataset) to a remarkable over $35.5\times$ (for RANet trained on either dataset). The resulting changes in latency range from $2\times$ to $5\times$.

Table 1. The effectiveness of FedSlowdown on four different AdNN Architectures on the HAM10000 & Fed-ISIC2019 Datasets

Architecture	Attack Type	HAM10000 (IID)					Fed-ISIC2019 (non-IID)				
		Acc (%)	EECS	Δ_{EECS}	Time (ms)	Δ_{Time}	Acc (%)	EECS	Δ_{EECS}	Time (ms)	Δ_{Time}
B-AlexNet	NOATTACK	79.93	0.68	NA	5.14	NA	55.8	0.80	NA	1.13	NA
	ATTACKNOSCALE	79.98	0.66	-1.03×	5.84	-1.14×	56.60	0.81	+1.01×	1.08	+1.05×
	FEDSLOWDOWN	81.98	0.12	-5.67×	9.79	-1.90×	58.17	0.12	-6.67×	2.57	-2.27×
VGG-SDN	NOATTACK	85.92	0.74	NA	7.39	NA	58.02	0.86	NA	1.69	NA
	ATTACKNOSCALE	86.52	0.72	-1.02×	8.54	-1.16×	58.49	0.85	-1.01×	1.98	-1.17×
	FEDSLOWDOWN	87.15	0.05	-14.8×	19.89	-2.69×	58.90	0.05	-17.2×	7.49	-4.43×
MSDNet	NOATTACK	84.77	0.71	NA	6.23	NA	54.98	0.79	NA	2.19	NA
	ATTACKNOSCALE	84.92	0.70	-1.01×	6.51	-1.04×	55.1	0.79	1.00×	2.13	+1.03×
	FEDSLOWDOWN	85.32	0.16	-4.44×	14.58	-2.34×	56.54	0.16	-4.94×	5.15	-2.35×
RANet	NOATTACK	87.52	0.71	NA	8.75	NA	57.73	0.78	NA	2.34	NA
	ATTACKNOSCALE	88.07	0.71	1.00×	8.69	+1.01×	57.55	0.76	-1.03×	2.68	-1.15×
	FEDSLOWDOWN	89.17	0.02	-35.5×	41.48	-4.74×	58.73	0.02	-39.0×	12.36	-5.28×

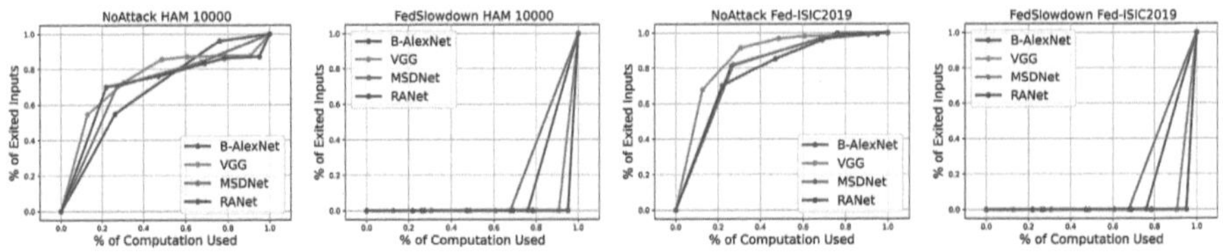

Fig. 2. EEC Curves for AdNNs on HAM10000 and Fed-ISIC2019

Moreover, the significance of the ***weight scaling*** technique is highlighted by the fact that the ATTACKNOSCALE attack fails to achieve any significant efficiency degradation in most cases, demonstrating the crucial role of weight scaling in achieving effective efficiency attacks in a federated learning environment.

6   Real-World Implications of `FedSlowdown`

To show the practical impact of `FedSlowdown`, we simulate a federated skin cancer pre-screening setup using the Flower FL framework with ten clients (simulating 10 hospitals) jointly training an AdNN for early-stage diagnosis on local patient data. One hospital is compromised by an adversary, aiming to degrade model efficiency without hurting accuracy. After training, all hospitals deploy the model on typical mobile devices. Testing on a Samsung Galaxy S9+ with 2,000 skin cancer images (from the HAM10000 dataset), we show that `FedSlowdown` greatly increases power consumption and drains the device battery faster (Fig. 3), demonstrating its real-world consequences for edge-based medical diagnostics.

7   Possible Defenses

Weight scaling raises two questions: (1) Does `FedSlowdown` succeed under defenses like weight clipping, DP noise, or anomaly detection? (2) Can adversarial updates be detected and filtered before aggregation?

Weight Clipping and DP Noise. Our experiments show that defense mechanisms such as clipping and DP noise addition [15] limit the influence of malicious model updates but don't fully cancel out their effects. We perform experiments using Branchy-AlexNet trained on the HAM10000 dataset where the central server incorporates both weight clipping and DP noise addition using various clipping thresholds and noise levels to explore whether such a technique is successful in mitigating `FedSlowdown`. Our results in Fig. 4b show that even with a strict clipping-bound of 5 and 0.01 std of noise, `FedSlowdown` still achieves an efficiency degradation of 55% (0.68 to 0.31). This is in contrast to a 500% degradation (0.68 to 0.12) without any defense. However, we also observe an accuracy drop of 10%. Stricter clipping thresholds or higher noise values result in a more drastic drop in the accuracy (see Fig. 4), making them less practical for medical deployments.

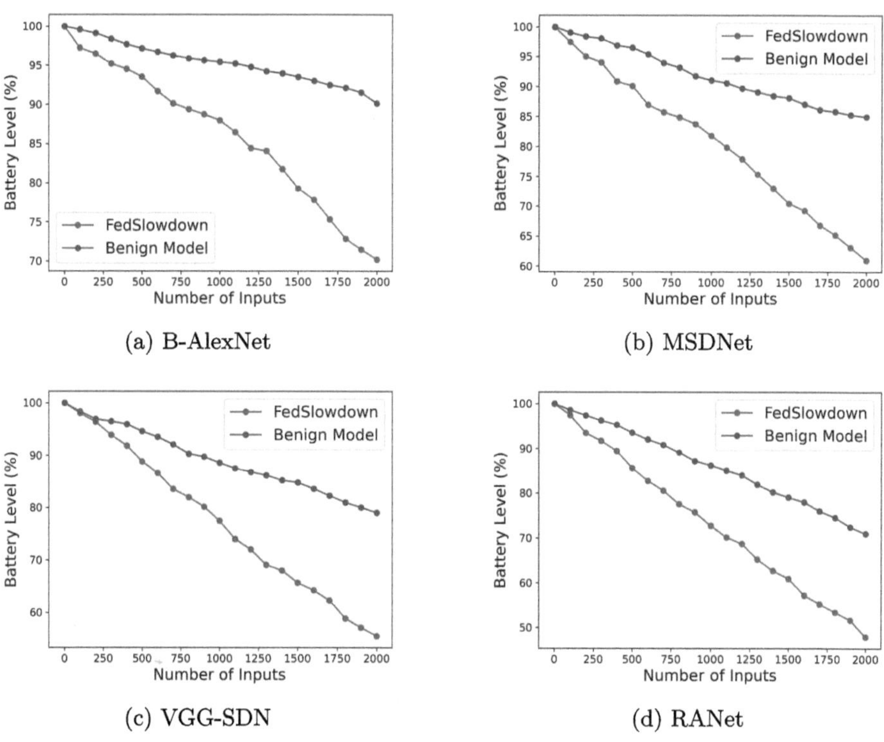

(a) B-AlexNet

(b) MSDNet

(c) VGG-SDN

(d) RANet

Fig. 3. Mobile Device Battery Depletion: `FedSlowdown` vs. No Attack

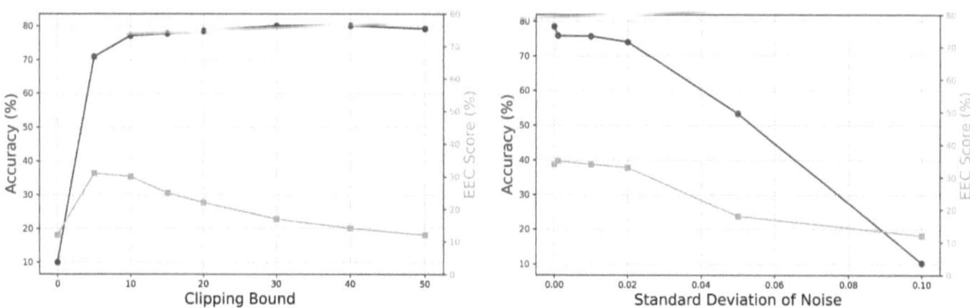

(a) Impact of clipping with noise $\sigma = 0.01$ (b) Impact of noise with clipping bound $= 5$

Fig. 4. Impact of weight clipping and Gaussian noise

Anomaly Detection: Anomaly detection techniques like clustering updates by norm or cosine similarity could help filter malicious updates. However, we argue that this is challenging as FL by design prioritizes participant privacy through secure aggregation [10], which prevents the aggregator from inspecting individual updates, and prior work [25] has shown how raw model updates can leak sensitive participant data. Moreover, in FL, participant data is usually diverse due to

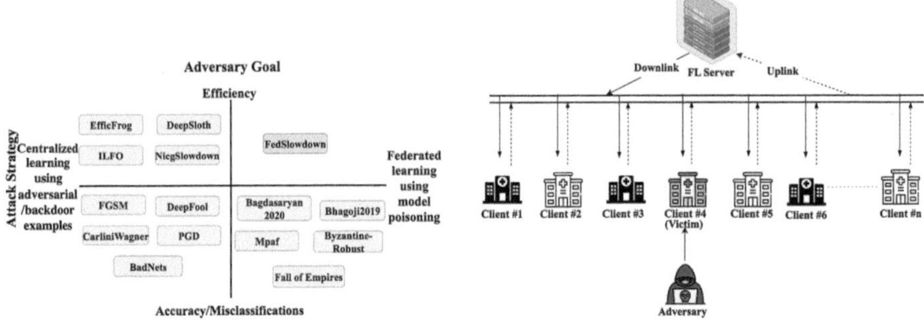

(a) <code>FedSlowdown</code> vs. Related Work   (b) <code>FedSlowdown</code> Threat Model

Fig. 5. Comparison of `FedSlowdown` with Related Work and its Threat Model

variations in devices and image quality, so the aggregator must tolerate local models that diverge from the global consensus.

8   Related Work

Model Poisoning in Federated Learning Environments: Our work is related to prior model poisoning attacks in FL such as `Bagdasaryan2020` [7], `Bhagoji2019` [9], `Mpaf` [11], `Byzantine-Robust` [14], and `Fall of Empires` [33], which use weight scaling to degrade model accuracy or inject backdoors. In contrast, we focus on using model poisoning to degrade efficiency rather than accuracy, and specifically target AdNNs, unlike prior work which focuses on standard DNNs.

Efficiency Attacks on AdNNs: Prior works have demonstrated the vulnerability of AdNNs to efficiency attacks. DeepSloth [17] introduces adversarial inputs that slow down inference. Haque *et al.* [16] craft energy-surging inputs to exhaust computational resources. Chen *et al.* [12] repurpose backdoor triggers for stealthy efficiency attacks. Our work differs from these in three key aspects:

1. **Target Environment—Federated Learning:** To the best of our knowledge, no prior work has studied the vulnerability of AdNNs to efficiency attacks during FL, especially in the context of CAD and medical image analysis. Existing works [12, 16, 17] focus only on centralized settings. As organizations [4, 6], increasingly adopt FL to meet privacy requirements, understanding how these attacks manifest in decentralized environments is essential. Our work helps developers of AdNNs [3, 29, 34] assess these risks.

2. **Attack Goal—Maximize Efficiency Degradation:** Prior works focus on efficiency degradation using only adversarial [16, 17] or backdoor [12] inputs. Our attack degrades efficiency across the entire input space, making it more widely applicable, especially when input control is limited like in many CAD and medical image analysis applications.

3. **Inference-Time Input Modification:** Our attack does not require modifying inputs at inference time, unlike previous methods. This makes `FedSlowdown` more practical for real-world deployment scenarios.

Figure 5a illustrates the differences between our `FedSlowdown` and these other attacks discussed above.

9   Conclusion

In this paper, we present `FedSlowdown`, an attack that degrades the efficiency of AdNNs trained with FL for CAD and medical image analysis. Our experiments show that `FedSlowdown` greatly increases an AdNN's latency without reducing its accuracy, even against defenses like weight clipping and DP noise. These findings highlight the risks of FL for AdNNs and can help developers design more robust training protocols protect against these kinds of attacks.

Acknowledgement. This material is based upon work supported by the National Science Foundation under Grant No. 2348432.

Disclosure of Interests. The authors have no competing interests to declare that are relevant to the content of this article.

References

1. Health insurance portability and accountability act of 1996 (HIPAA). https:// www.hhs.gov/hipaa/for-professionals/privacy/laws-regulations/index.html (1996), public Law 104-191, 110 Stat. 1936
2. Regulation (eu) 2016/679 of the European parliament and of the council of 27 April 2016. https://eur-lex.europa.eu/eli/reg/2016/679/oj (2016), official Journal of the European Union, L 119/1
3. BlockDrop: Dynamic Inference Paths in Residual Networks. https://research. ibm.com/publications/blockdrop-dynamic-inference-paths-in-residual-networks (2018)
4. Explore advancements in Machine Learning. https://machinelearning.apple.com/ research?page=1&domain=Privacy (2025)
5. Fedslowdown. https://github.com/akinsanyaayomide/FedSlowdownDeCaF.git (2025)
6. NVIDIA FLARE. https://developer.nvidia.com/flare (2025)
7. Bagdasaryan, E., Veit, A., Hua, Y., Estrin, D., Shmatikov, V.: How to backdoor federated learning. In: International Conference on Artificial Intelligence and Statistics, pp. 2938–2948. PMLR (2020)
8. Beutel, D.J., et al.: Flower: a friendly federated learning research framework. arXiv preprint arXiv:2007.14390 (2020)
9. Bhagoji, A.N., Chakraborty, S., Mittal, P., Calo, S.: Analyzing federated learning through an adversarial lens. In: International Conference on Machine Learning, pp. 634–643. PMLR (2019)

10. Bonawitz, K., et al.: Towards federated learning at scale: system design. Proc. Mach. Learn. Syst. **1**, 374–388 (2019)
11. Cao, X., Gong, N.Z.: MPAF: model poisoning attacks to federated learning based on fake clients. In: Proceedings of the IEEE/CVF Conference on Computer Vision and Pattern Recognition, pp. 3396–3404 (2022)
12. Chen, S., Chen, H., Haque, M., Liu, C., Yang, W.: The dark side of dynamic routing neural networks: towards efficiency backdoor injection. In: Proceedings of the IEEE/CVF Conference on Computer Vision and Pattern Recognition, pp. 24585–24594 (2023)
13. Fang, B., Zeng, X., Zhang, F., Xu, H., Zhang, M.: FlexDNN: input-adaptive on-device deep learning for efficient mobile vision. In: 2020 IEEE/ACM Symposium on Edge Computing (SEC), pp. 84–95. IEEE (2020)
14. Fang, M., Cao, X., Jia, J., Gong, N.: Local model poisoning attacks to {Byzantine-Robust} federated learning. In: 29th USENIX Security Symposium (USENIX Security 20), pp. 1605–1622 (2020)
15. Geyer, R.C., Klein, T., Nabi, M.: Differentially private federated learning: a client level perspective. arXiv preprint arXiv:1712.07557 (2017)
16. Haque, M., Chauhan, A., Liu, C., Yang, W.: ILFO: adversarial attack on adaptive neural networks. In: Proceedings of the IEEE/CVF Conference on Computer Vision and Pattern Recognition, pp. 14264–14273 (2020)
17. Hong, S., Kaya, Y., Modoranu, I.V., Dumitraş, T.: A panda? No, it's a sloth: slowdown attacks on adaptive multi-exit neural network inference. arXiv preprint arXiv:2010.02432 (2020)
18. Huang, G., Chen, D., Li, T., Wu, F., van der Maaten, L., Weinberger, K.Q.: Multi-scale dense networks for resource efficient image classification (2018)
19. Huang, G., Chen, D., Li, T., Wu, F., Van Der Maaten, L., Weinberger, K.Q.: Multi-scale dense networks for resource efficient image classification. arXiv preprint arXiv:1703.09844 (2017)
20. Kaya, Y., Hong, S., Dumitras, T.: Shallow-Deep Networks: understanding and mitigating network overthinking. In: International Conference on Machine Learning, pp. 3301–3310. PMLR (2019)
21. Kim, Y.D., Park, E., Yoo, S., Choi, T., Yang, L., Shin, D.: Compression of deep convolutional neural networks for fast and low power mobile applications. arXiv preprint arXiv:1511.06530 (2015)
22. Kouris, A., Venieris, S.I., Bouganis, C.S.: A throughput-latency co-optimised cascade of convolutional neural network classifiers. In: 2020 Design, Automation & Test in Europe Conference & Exhibition (DATE), pp. 1656–1661. IEEE (2020)
23. Lee, R., Venieris, S.I., Dudziak, L., Bhattacharya, S., Lane, N.D.: MobiSR: efficient on-device super-resolution through heterogeneous mobile processors. In: The 25th Annual International Conference on Mobile Computing and Networking, pp. 1–16 (2019)
24. McMahan, B., Moore, E., Ramage, D., Hampson, S., y Arcas, B.A.: Communication-efficient learning of deep networks from decentralized data. In: Artificial Intelligence and Statistics, pp. 1273–1282. PMLR (2017)
25. Melis, L., Song, C., De Cristofaro, E., Shmatikov, V.: Exploiting unintended feature leakage in collaborative learning. In: 2019 IEEE Symposium on Security and Privacy (SP), pp. 691–706. IEEE (2019)
26. Pratt, H., Coenen, F., Broadbent, D.M., Harding, S.P., Zheng, Y.: Convolutional neural networks for diabetic retinopathy. Procedia Comput. Sci. **90**, 200–205 (2016)

27. Taylor, B., Marco, V.S., Wolff, W., Elkhatib, Y., Wang, Z.: Adaptive deep learning model selection on embedded systems. ACM SIGPLAN Notices **53**(6), 31–43 (2018)
28. Teerapittayanon, S., McDanel, B., Kung, H.T.: BranchyNet: fast inference via early exiting from deep neural networks. In: 2016 23rd International Conference on Pattern Recognition (ICPR), pp. 2464–2469. IEEE (2016)
29. Teerapittayanon, S., McDanel, B., Kung, H.T.: Distributed deep neural networks over the cloud, the edge and end devices. In: 2017 IEEE 37th International Conference on Distributed Computing Systems (ICDCS), pp. 328–339. IEEE (2017)
30. Ogier du Terrail, J., et al.: Flamby: datasets and benchmarks for cross-silo federated learning in realistic healthcare settings. In: Advances in Neural Information Processing Systems, vol. 35, pp. 5315–5334 (2022)
31. Tschandl, P., Rosendahl, C., Kittler, H.: The ham10000 dataset, a large collection of multi-source dermatoscopic images of common pigmented skin lesions. Sci. Data **5**(1), 1–9 (2018)
32. Wu, N., et al.: Deep neural networks improve radiologists' performance in breast cancer screening. IEEE Trans. Med. Imaging **39**(4), 1184–1194 (2019)
33. Xie, C., Koyejo, O., Gupta, I.: Fall of empires: breaking byzantine-tolerant SGD by inner product manipulation. In: Uncertainty in Artificial Intelligence, pp. 261–270. PMLR (2020)
34. Yang, L., Han, Y., Chen, X., Song, S., Dai, J., Huang, G.: Resolution adaptive networks for efficient inference. In: Proceedings of the IEEE/CVF Conference on Computer Vision and Pattern Recognition, pp. 2369–2378 (2020)

Author Index

If you have any concerns about our products,
you can contact us on
ProductSafety@springernature.com

In case Publisher is established outside the EU,
the EU authorized representative is:
**Springer Nature Customer Service Center GmbH
Europaplatz 3, 69115 Heidelberg, Germany**

Printed by Libri Plureos GmbH
in Hamburg, Germany